# SECURING YOUR ASSETS

## A Physician's Guide to Financial Planning

### Linda G. Ginsberg, B.S., J.D.

**PRACTICE MANAGEMENT INFORMATION CORPORATION**
4727 Wilshire Blvd.
Los Angeles, CA 90010
800-MED-SHOP

Library of Congress Cataloging-in-Publication Data
Ginsberg, Linda G.
  Securing your assets : a physician's guide to financial planning
Linda G. Ginsberg.
    p.   cm.
  Includes index.
  ISBN 1–878487–21–3
  1. Physicians—Finance, Personal.   I. Title.
R728.5G47   1990
610'.681—dc20                                        90–6148
                                                     CIP

This publication is designed to provide accurate and authoritative information in regard to the subject matter covered. It is sold with the understanding that the publisher is not engaged in rendering legal, accounting, or other professional service. If legal·advice or other expert assistance is required, the services of a competent professional person should be sought.

*From the Declaration of Principles jointly adopted by a Committee of the American Bar Association and a Committee of Publishers and Associations.*

Practice Management Information Corporation
4727 Wilshire Blvd., Ste. 300
Los Angeles, CA 90010


Printed in the United States of America

10 9 8 7 6 5 4 3 2

*To my wonderful children—Leslie, Marc, and Tracy—who have been understanding, patient, and loving while their mother developed a vocation. To Herb O'Keefe, C.P.A., who has been a good friend and consultant for many years. And in memory of my departed husband, Dr. Murray T. Ginsberg, who taught me how to make lemonade out of life's lemons.*

# ABOUT THE AUTHOR

As an attorney, author, national lecturer, and president of American Practice Appraisers, Inc., Linda G. Ginsberg has directed her energies and attention toward helping others develop programs that will help them pass along their financial legacies as they have directed.

She is a member of the American Bar Association as well as of the Indiana and Indianapolis Bar associations and an associate member of the Southern and Northern District Courts of Indiana. She is a member of the Institute of Business Appraisers, the National Health Lawyers, Practice Valuation Study Club, and a life member of Hadassah. She is past-president of the auxiliary of the Georgia Dental Association and has obtained her private pilot's license.

Through magazines, newspapers, and speaking engagements all over the country, Linda Ginsberg has told the story of her personal tragedy—of her periodontist husband's death from cancer at the age of 34 and the economic disaster that followed. She possesses the experience, knowledge, and courage to frankly discuss this personal tragedy.

After her husband died, Ginsberg attended law school and worked part-time for publishing companies and attorneys, giving seminars all over the country and doing freelance writing.

She has been honored by the First Church of Latter Day Saints, the American Dental Association, Jacksonville University, Savannah Business and Professional Women, and International Authors and Writers.

The author can be reached at 125 East 45th Street, Savannah, Georgia 31405.

# CONTENTS

# LIST OF CHARTS

The following charts, presented throughout the book, are reproducible forms and sample letters that can be used as guidelines in drawing up your personal financial planning program. The text contains discussions and illustrations helpful in completing these charts. It is recommended that in any comprehensive financial planning program, the advice of competent professionals should also be obtained. The most important step, however, is to secure your assets by compiling and analyzing the facts about your financial situation, using these charts as guidelines.

# INTRODUCTION

I have learned the subject matter in this book first-hand. I was the wife of a periodontist until my husband, at age 34, succumbed to cancer, thinking he had provided future care for me and for our three children. He never knew the economic disaster that followed.

During the course of your life, you, too, will undoubtedly face numerous choices and decisions about what is best for you and your family's financial situation, just as I have. This book is designed to clarify your present situation by showing you how to collect and assess all relevant personal and financial data such as your assets, your liabilities, wills, trusts, insurance policies, and the like and then help you decide where you want to go by identifying your financial strategy and personal goals and objectives. It will help you draw up a written financial plan, the length and complexity of which will depend on your personal financial situation. This book exposes the hidden rules, regulations, and red tape that can jeopardize your family's financial survival overnight just as they did mine.

My first recommendation is to periodically review and revise your financial survival plan. This is essential in order to keep abreast of changes in your personal and economic condition. While you may accomplish this task without assistance, you will find the glossary, forms, and other useful reference material beneficial.

However, any financial plan is helpful only if the recommendations are put into action. And, the decisions that you make to implement, modify, or reject any of the recommendations presented here remain your sole responsibility.

Doctor, this information will be helpful to you at one time or another, and it is structured so that you can easily find the information you need. For example, all charts are placed conveniently at the end of each chapter, and, when appropriate, the material is documented so that you can research the subject further.

It is my hope that this book will help you develop a plan that will pass along your financial legacies as you have directed.

# 1

# THE IMPORTANCE OF FINANCIAL PLANNING: A CASE STUDY

What does a 34-year-old dentist, with a wife and three children,
do when he learns he has two months left to live?

It is always difficult to accept a loved one's death, but especially so when that death is at an early age. I do not believe that anyone who has not experienced the death of a spouse can fully understand the emotions that are involved.

We all know that we will die someday. But we also know that life goes on, and the better we prepare for it, the easier we can make the adjustment. Thus, when my husband Murray was diagnosed with terminal cancer, he set out to teach me how to be a widow.

We began with a review of our assets. Murray explained our financial holdings—what banks to pay property mortgages to, how to keep each piece of property in a separate account with separate records, who carried the different types of insurance, and how to figure the annual cost of living expenses.

If Murray had not been ill, we probably would not have read the will that he had made six years earlier. We were both astounded at some of

1

the outdated things contained in it. Since our attorney was out of the office and we knew the situation was critical, we contacted Fred Clark, an old friend and an attorney, and asked him to draw up a new will for Murray.

Since I had taken care of normal monthly household expenses, I was used to keeping records of when insurance premiums were due and how much was to be paid. However, the only property mortgage that I took care of was the one on our home. Murray attended to the rest of the property, and he now explained the other holdings in great detail.

He showed me office bookkeeping, how to work the pegboard system at the office, how to write payroll checks, how to balance daily sheets and transfer that data into the office ledger, how to meet payroll taxes, and the other basic business skills necessary for running his professional corporation as well as our personal lives. Above everything else, Murray wanted me to understand my responsibilities as family financier and to be able to meet them effectively.

Whenever Murray explained a function, he would ask me to explain it to him in return. He would watch me as I filled out the proper forms, wrote checks, or recorded certain data in the ledgers. I also took notes on everything that Murray told me so that I would be able to refer to them later, in his absence, for reassurance.

Murray explained that I would need our marriage license, all of the birth certificates of the members of the immediate family, and his military discharge papers to take to the Social Security office to file them. He told me that I was entitled to a small Veterans Administration benefit since he had served in the navy during the Viet Nam war; a burial benefit might also be available.

I was informed about notifying the insurance companies to request the proper forms, each of which would have to be filled out and returned with a death certificate. Murray told me that all of this information, although painful to discuss at that time, would help me when I most needed it—at a time when grief, hurt, anger, and all the other emotions of bereavement would be at their most intense. He did not want me to feel overwhelmed by stress and helplessness, not knowing in which direction to turn. We discussed everything but how to sell his professional practice. When I asked Murray what to do about that, he said he wasn't really sure, and I would have to rely on our advisors.

Murray died thinking that he had fully provided for all our material needs. He never knew of the economic disaster that followed.

After Murray's funeral, I was immediately thrown into the problems of settling the estate. After all our careful planning and long discussions, I thought that making arrangements for the family's financial welfare would be relatively swift and painless.

Being comfortable with our newly acquired attorney, Fred Clark, I asked him to handle our affairs. When we discussed the sale of my husband's practice, Fred was honest in telling me that he had never handled the sale of a professional practice but, as he put it, "Let's see if we can work things out."

Before Murray had learned of his illness, another periodontist had contacted him expressing the desire to join him in the practice. Dr. A, as I'll call him, was informed about Murray's condition as we knew it and I even made long-distance telephone calls to keep him posted as to Murray's progress. Contracts were drawn up by our former attorney between Dr. A and Murray, and Dr. A began work in the office on the very day that Murray left for testing at the Mayo Clinic in September, 1976.

When we returned from the Mayo Clinic, Murray contacted a second periodontist who was then in military service, but who was interested in private practice. Murray suggested that he also join the practice following his discharge the following January. A second contract had been drawn up, again by our former attorney, which Dr. B, as I'll call him, and Murray signed in September. And so Murray was satisfied that his active practice would be covered no matter what happened to him.

When Murray died in November, Dr. A was already at work in the office, therefore, he seemed to be the logical one to approach about buying it. The first meeting with my accountant (a C.P.A.) and my new attorney, Fred Clark, ended abruptly when the accountant told me that the total value of the practice was $5,000 for "goodwill," plus the book value of the equipment. However, Dr. A was using the same C.P.A. as I.

Murray had been netting over $200,000 a year when he died and was establishing a national reputation for his work and his lectures. I just could not believe that the practice could be worth so little. The C.P.A. assured me that the way in which the contract had been written for Murray's newly acquired associate was so ambiguous that I should jump at this first offer. "After all," he said, "when a doctor dies, his practice is not worth anything."

I began doing some research on my own. I called in a noted management consultant, Martin (Bud) Schulman of Dental Corporation of America from Washington, D.C., and also studied reports from the Internal Revenue Service as well as other books on evaluating a dental practice when there is a deceased professional. I read a good many books pertaining to dental management, goodwill, and related topics.

I discovered that, when a doctor purchases a practice, he is buying something more than equipment and supplies. He purchases goodwill, also, the value of which includes the rights to patients' records, x-rays, recall cards, the assurance that he will not have the usual problems of an empty appointment book, that he will have auxiliary personnel readily available and trained, and that he will have the office in a particular location, in operating condition. I wrote about all my findings to Dr. A.

By way of reply, Dr. A said that he was leaving the practice. My attorney sent him a letter asking if he would like to pay the corporation for the newly installed equipment that he had purchased. He never answered. He just walked out, leaving me with an $18,000 90-day note on his equipment that was cosigned on behalf of the dental corporation. Not long after, I heard that Dr. A had opened another office two blocks away. After all (as he is reported to have said) why pay $5,000 for Murray's practice when he already had half of the patients for nothing.

I suppose I can understand Dr. A's wanting to get a bargain on Murray's practice. What surprised me was the reaction of many other dentists in the area, Murray's so-called "good friends." They urged me to accept the offer, to virtually give the practice away. They said they were concerned about the patients.

So was I. But the patients could easily find another periodontist. My problem was greater: how could I protect the financial welfare of my family without getting a fair price for the practice that my husband had worked so hard to build. Dr. A left the office in January, 1977, leaving me with an 90-day, unsecured demand note in the amount of $18,000 for equipment that he had purchased and now didn't want.

Dr. B joined the practice that very month, January, 1977, after his military discharge. He said that he had agreed only to work for the practice, not to buy it, and I was free to find another doctor. He promised to keep the practice going. Lucky for me, I thought, since the practice would continue without a break. That is when I visited the office for the first time after Murray's death, and that is when I got my next big shock!

I had taken a business management course and, with Murray's help, learned how to handle the books as well as run the front desk and appoint patients. I quickly found that the office was operating at a loss under Dr. A. He had not even been covering overhead expenses, and yet he had kept two full-time office staffs because he liked them and could not decide whom to let go. So he kept them all—paying them out of my account. Murray had turned over the office books to him, giving him full authority to sign checks and order supplies, thinking he would manage affairs as efficiently as Murray, himself, had done.

Murray had left $17,000 in the office account when he died in November, and now, in January there was a minus $10,000. I will never know how one doctor managed to spend $27,000 in just a couple of months.

Dr. A was now out of the office and Dr. B was in residence. There was no time to brood over past disasters. I discharged both the secretary and the home-care assistant and took over the front desk myself. Again Dr. B said to me, "Find a buyer. I'm willing to work for someone else, but I don't think I want to buy a practice until I find out if I like the community."

I wondered about the possibility of legal complications. While Murray was alive, I did not involve myself in his business decisions. I knew when he was buying or selling an asset, or when he was bringing in an associate, but I never asked about the terms. I trusted his decisions. Given this tradition, I never thought to read the contracts drawn up for the two associates brought in during Murray's illness. Murray had the papers drawn up by our former attorney and they were signed. We had assumed that things were done properly.

On this assumption, I sought and found a buyer. A periodontist, Dr. C, came down from Kansas City to look at the practice. He liked it and agreed to my price. He hired an attorney and a C.P.A. Then he called to say, "Linda, if you can get Dr. B to renegotiate his contract I will buy the practice."

That was the first time that I had actually considered the terms of the contract. Much to my surprise, this document stated that, in August of his first year, only eight months from the time he had come into the practice, Dr. B would own one-third of Murray's practice. It went on to state that, in January, one year from his beginning in the office, Dr. B would own 50 percent of the practice, and the remaining 50 percent of the stock in Murray's corporation could be sold to Dr. A, the associate who had just left. If Murray had lived, would he own any share of his own corporation?

Incredibly, neither contract contained provisions for buying out Murray's share in the event of his death, even though the former lawyer, who drafted the agreement, and both Drs. A and B had full knowledge of his terminal illness. My management consultant, Bud Shulman, said he could find no way out of the legal bind that my former attorney had gotten me into. His sympathy was such that he refused to charge a fee for his services.

I asked Dr. B if he would be willing to renegotiate the terms of his contract. He refused. "Murray's lawyer drafted the agreement, and I didn't even know what it said," he replied.

He was on firm legal ground, and I found out early that money speaks louder than sympathy, friendship, or any other emotional bond. Under the circumstances, Dr. C withdrew his offer to buy the practice.

Even though Dr. B was not interested in renegotiating the contract, neither was he interested in staying with the practice. The office was much too large and too expensive for a single practitioner, and, since Dr. A now had half of the patients, Dr. B could not bring in another periodontist. He gave me a date on which he would leave.

At that time, I gave him the patient charts on those cases he had begun or had completed treating. He did buy a substantial amount of office furniture and Murray's used dental equipment, but not quite enough to pay off the $18,000 note at the bank that Dr. A had left behind. I did appreciate that. He also had his assistant help me when he began clearing out the office, pulling current x-rays out of the patients' charts so that they could be sent back to their general dentist or so that he could take care of them. Since letters had been written to the general dentist on all patients who had any type of periodontal procedure, I did not feel it necessary to send or give back charts.

Nonetheless, the remaining professional equipment was still a problem. I called several supply companies, asking them to either buy back the equipment or please help me sell it. I phoned and wrote dental schools, and contacted a local hospital. Most of this equipment was the newly installed equipment purchased by Dr. A, the first associate, less than a year before. But no one was interested, and, since I would not take $5,000 for goodwill of a practice grossing over $200,000 a year, the word was out that Linda Ginsberg was "difficult" to deal with.

Again, I started looking for the most financially sound method of getting rid of the equipment. My new C.P.A., Herb O'Keefe, helped me to realize that I needed an outlet that would serve me as well as the recipient. Dr. Barry Simmons, a close friend and founder of Dental Health International (D.H.I), provided me with that outlet. I donated the equipment to D.H.I., and it was sent by Dr. Simmons to Banso Baptist Hospital in an underdeveloped nation, Cameroon, in western Africa. A permanent clinic, which would serve approximately 15,000 people was set up in Murray's name, thanks to the dedication of Dr. Simmons, who spent several months each year helping to bring dentistry to less developed countries throughout the world. In addition, I was able to use the donation as a tax write-off, since the recipient was a nonprofit organization, and I will have the satisfaction of knowing that it will be put to a much-needed use.

As you can see from this history, Murray's practice is now dismantled. I received not a penny for the goodwill or other assets—only a charitable deduction for my contribution of the equipment. I rented Murray's office to two physicians, and the estate provided for us for awhile.

Legally, there was nothing I could do to prevent any of this from happening, because of our former lawyer's ruinous agreements with Drs. A and B. But the practice was not the only part of the estate that had been mismanaged by our "advisors."

Murray had partners in several other sideline business ventures, and I was quite surprised one day to find out that I was being sued by one of these partner/tenants because he thought he was paying too high a rent for two years with no lease agreement. Why, I wondered, if he didn't like it, hadn't he said something to Murray at the time? Why did he wait until after Murray's death to bring suit?

Again, Murray had relied on the friendship of a former attorney, and had not checked to see that things were properly done. I finally agreed to buy this partner out, only to find that, before we could complete the transaction, the title had to be cleared. There was a lien on the property from before Murray had purchased the property, thinking that all was in order.

Thanks to the advice of a friend, I was not only the beneficiary, but also the owner of Murray's insurance policies. This, I hoped, would help keep it out of the taxable estate. But why hadn't our own attorney given us that advice? And why were we not told that Murray could have given me an amount equal to the annual exclusion each year and to each of our children as a gift, tax-free, which would have kept that portion out of his estate, and which I could have used to pay premiums as they came due.

Murray and I tried to plan for an untimely death even before we knew he was ill. He was really not at fault for the many errors made in the preparation of his estate. Like so many other professionals, he thought that the details should be left to qualified specialists—his attorney and accountant. Also, cancer and other terminal illnesses do not give their victims time to make clear, conscientious decisions or the opportunity to double check on the execution of their wishes.

We both, however, should have thought further into our future when he started practicing. Even at such an early age as 34, we should have been prepared for the unthinkable disaster that befell us. But it was difficult to admit that it might happen to us. "Death is a reality of others," we believed. And when Murray became unable to check our legal and financial status, I should not have felt intimidated to do so. I know that now. So while Murray's practice will not remain intact, his memory will. Selling him short would have hurt me more than it helped me. Had we taken a few precautions, I would never have been forced to break up the practice, and Murray's plans for our well-being would have been executed as he wished.

My story has not been a happy one. Perhaps it even shocks you. Frankly, I hope so. I hope it shocks you into making ironclad provisions with your partners, your colleagues, your supply houses, and your local society for the disposition of your practice in the event of your own untimely death, and into determining your long-term goals for you and your family.

# 2

# CALCULATING YOUR NET WORTH: YOUR FINANCIAL PLANNING GUIDE

Doctor, before you can determine your objectives and develop strategies to meet these objectives, you must organize and compile a list of everything you own and everything you owe.

## WHAT IS FINANCIAL SURVIVAL?

Knowing where to start is essential in planning for your family's financial survival. What is financial survival? It is deliberate planning, such simple things as keeping clear and complete records; knowing where things are and whom to contact; putting your assets and financial affairs in order to minimize loss through expenses and taxes and to maximize the benefit to yourself and your family; knowing where your records are located and letting someone else know so that, if something were to happen to you, your assets would not be lost!

Once upon a time, these meant planning for death. It doesn't anymore. Financial survival does not have to compromise your own needs and desires while you live. To the contrary, your plan may point out financial advantages that you can enjoy now, as well as in years to come.

The term *estate planning* does not begin to cover the scope of what must be done. I am talking about the economic survival of all the family members, with or without the major breadwinner. And all of the family members must share in the process and become a part of it.

Estate planning connotes the head of the family's sitting down with a battery of lawyers, bankers, accountants, and financial advisors to draw up a bunch of legal documents. Financial survival demands much more than that. For example, it demands that the spouse know every aspect of the other's practice, to know what must be done if he/she becomes incapacitated, or to sell it for top dollar if he/she should die. It means such a seemingly simple thing as keeping clear and complete records of your bills, so that either family member can pick up the payments if the other cannot.

As for how wealthy you have to be to benefit from this, I would say that the less money there is, the more important it becomes. Anyone who owns a home, a practice, a savings account, life insurance, or just a well-stuffed piggy bank is a property owner. If you value your property and the well-being of other members of your family, you should make plans to protect them and secure your assets.

Just what is involved in this planning? Your tools for the job are knowing what your assets are (starting with your net worth), your will, life insurance, gifts, trust, and practice arrangements. All of these factors rest upon one another like a handful of steel balls in a fishbowl. If you move one of them, all the others will be affected. That is why you must study and review all aspects of what you own and what you owe. Any family financial plan begins with an assessment of where you stand now, today. So let us take a good hard look at your current finances and determine your "net worth."

## WHAT DOES "NET WORTH" MEAN?

Simply put, net worth means all of your assets, less all of your debts (i.e., your debts subtracted from your assets). The difference between your assets and your debts is your net worth. It is the best single guide to your economic growth and maturity in this one-way trip through life.

Is there some model plan to follow? No. Everyone has different kinds and amounts of assets. More important, their desires and objectives are different, and the laws relating to inheritance and gift taxes, wills, and other estate matters vary from state to state.

These problems cannot be solved by any formula. In most cases, there are not any perfect alternatives in trying to find the one that offers the biggest tax savings with the greatest benefits—consistent, of course, with your objectives.

For the same reason that you ask a trained physician or dentist to examine your body or teeth, you need a trained professional to help in your planning. The work is too complex and important to be left to an amateur. A plan of even moderate complexity cuts across many fields: law, accounting, banking, life insurance, investments. Even if you are knowledgeable about any one of these fields, you would still need the advice and expertise of other specialists. You, of course, can help by providing the necessary information and making your wishes known. One way of doing this is by compiling information (such as shown by the examples) about your assets on the charts included at the end of each chapter.

As helpful as outside consultants may be, they can never substitute for your own personal involvement. It is not their money at stake—it's yours! No one will ever protect your interests as well as you yourself will.

The ten most common mistakes doctors make in planning for their family's financial survival are the following:

1. Each family member's not understanding the economic role of the other and not being able to step into the other's role if need be.
2. Failure to make a will or update it periodically.
3. Leaving fixed benefits in trust to beneficiaries, without giving them flexibility to meet changing conditions.
4. Not providing for enough spot cash to meet final expenses at death so valuable assets don't have to be unloaded at "fire sale" prices.
5. Not planning for the disposition of your professional practice at death, not having it appraised, and not reviewing buy-sell agreements.
6. Not reviewing and arranging your life insurance so that the proceeds form a cohesive plan with your other sources of income.
7. Not taking advantage of ways of reducing taxes.
8. Not planning for retirement—what you want to do, when you want to do it, and how much money it will require.
9. Depending too much on Social Security and other benefits to solve your planning problems for you.
10. Not keeping a list of what you own and what you owe.

Not keeping a list of what you own and what you owe is a mistake. It is the cause and the potential cure for all the other planning ills.

Maybe the following case will illustrate the point even better: A wealthy couple was traveling on their yacht from Nassau to Miami. The yacht was fully equipped with all types of expensive safety and computerized equipment. However, the husband had not taught the wife anything about using this equipment. Without warning, the husband had a massive coronary and died. The wife was totally unprepared. Her husband had not taken the time to explain to her where things were—not even how to use the radio. She was in a panic and tried screaming for help, waving her arms back and forth. After four days of grief and misery, the Coast Guard finally rescued her.

Could this happen to you under a different setting? If a crisis, such as death, should occur, would you be as unprepared as the wife in the boat, unable to use the signaling equipment? Unable to know whom to contact or where to go for advice?

Many people work hard all their lives to accumulate some property, yet fail to give themselves and their families the greatest benefit from that property. That is why you should do something about it NOW! Taking a firm grip on your finances is an urgent necessity.

Secure your financial future today. Tomorrow may be too late! Do you want to spend the rest of your life working for the government—or for your family? With proper planning and accurate information presented in plain English, you can help ensure your family's financial survival.

If you sit down and calculate your own net worth, you will find the results interesting. The forms in this chapter are my modified versions of the Estate Tax Form 706 (see Figure 2–1 at the end of the chapter; also see Appendix A) and, by completing them, you can calculate your net worth. They will save you time and money when you least expect it, and may need it most. They will provide a review of your financial growth, a vivid graph of your long-range goals, and a plan for achieving them. If anything should ever happen to you, your survivors will know where your assets and liabilities are, and your assets will not be lost to the state in which they are located. You won't have to pay $50, $75, $100 or more, for someone else to do the research that you are capable of doing now, while there is no crisis in your life. Charts 1–11 (Figures 2–2 to 2–12) at the end of the chapter are worksheets that can be photocopied and used for your personal recordkeeping.

Before we begin, you should know that there are states whose laws are slightly different from the rest. Those states are called *community property states*.

## COMMUNITY PROPERTY STATES

If you are living in one of the community property states, you will encounter special estate problems. There are eight states called community property states: Arizona, California, Idaho, Louisiana, Nevada, New Mexico, Texas, and Washington, plus Wisconsin, which has adopted the Uniform Marital Property Act.

In these states, property ownership does not depend upon title (as is the case under common law) but upon classification as community property or separate property. Separate property is property brought into the marriage or acquired by gift or inheritance. Community property is property acquired during marriage, other than by gift, devise, or descent.

Separate property, if commingled with property acquired or held as community property, is presumed to be community property, unless it can be proved otherwise. Commingling often occurs in bank accounts when community and separate funds are haphazardly deposited and withdrawn.

Written documentation is one way to prove which property is *community* and which is *separate*. Separate accounts and records are another means of preserving property status.

Several states are considering adopting the Uniform Marital Property Act,[1] which is a community property law. This Act creates a new system of property rights applicable to property owned by spouses during marriage. It takes into consideration the laws from various community property states (Arizona, California, Idaho, Louisiana, Nevada, Texas, Washington) and the Commonwealth of Puerto Rico. The Act sees a marriage as being a partnership to which each spouse makes a different but equally important contribution. Each spouse has a vested ownership right to all property acquired by either one of them during the marriage. This is called marital property. Property brought into the marriage or acquired by gift or inheritance is individual property; however, income from any of it becomes marital property, making all income of both spouses marital property. Since spouses may contract with all property matters, choosing not to have the Act apply in whole or in part, or having it apply to all or part of their property before they come subject to its terms, they may sign a written property agreement.

If you move to and from a community property state, special planning is required. You should identify and classify the property as of the date you move. This may be accomplished by a memorandum or a signed marital property agreement that would classify assets. A prenuptial agreement could be used to identify separate property brought to the marriage and establish separate rights in future income or appreciation that would otherwise be treated as community property. And, the use of a postnuptial agreement may be used to partition community property or to clarify or change the ownership rights of you or your spouse.

You have the power to dispose by will your separate property and one-half of the community property. If you were to die without a will, your one-half share of community property would go to your spouse (in most

---

[1] The Uniform Marital Property Act was adopted by the National Conference of Commissioners on Uniform State Laws on July 28, 1983. It was enacted April 4, 1984, by Wisconsin, effective January 1, 1986; 1983 Wisconsin Act 186.

states) or be split between your spouse and your children (in the other states). Only that part owned by you is included in your estate for tax purposes.

When you are filling out the work sheets, if you live in community property states do not fill out the chart entitled "Jointly Owned," as your community property should be listed on all the other charts. Remember, salaries and assets acquired during marriage are considered to be owned equally by you and your spouse. Use the chart entitled "Separately Owned Property" to include any property that is separate and not commingled.

## HOW TO CALCULATE YOUR NET WORTH

### Real Estate

List all real estate that you own or have contracted to purchase, indicating the owner or owners (there is a separate chart for things jointly owned). Include the date purchased, the price, the current value, and any rental amounts due on any of the property. Attach appraisals if you have them. In making a record of your real estate holdings, the location of your property should be described as completely as is practical, including both its common and legal descriptions (Table 2–1). For example, the common description should be followed by the legal description, as shown here:

> 125 East 45th Street, Savannah, Georgia 31405. Deed book #3-A, Folio (page) # 35: Bohand Ward, Subdivision E, Lots 1 and 2 (residential property).

**Table 2–1.** Example: Real estate chart.

For jointly owned property, use Chart 3 (Figure 2–4). In community property states, use Chart 8 (Figure 2–9) for separately owned property.

| Owner (H/W) & # of item | Description | Purchase Price/Date | Value/Date |
|---|---|---|---|
| Example: | | | |
| 1. Home and lot: 125 East 45th Street Savannah, Ga. 31405; Bohand Ward, Subdivision E, Lots 1 & 2; Deed Book #3-A, Folio 35. Value based on appraisal. In wife's name alone | | $150,000 9/71 | $300,000 1/90 |
| 2. Office and lot: 5212 Paulsen Street Savannah, Ga. 31405; Bohand Ward, Block V, Lots 13—16 (2250 sq. ft.). Value based on appraisal. In husband's name. | | $175,000 | $350,000 |
| 3. Rent due on item 2 for year: ($1500 × 12 = $18,000) | | | |

The legal description may be obtained from the deed itself, the financial institution that holds the mortgage on your property, or your property tax records.

Classify the property as to "type" such as: residential, commercial, or the like. Include acreage, by parcel, and the following categories of land use: (1) cultivatable and current crop status (e.g., "planted in corn;" "lying fallow"); (2) pasture; (3) standing saw timber (hardwood, pine, etc.). You may want to list a farm or ranch on the "Specially Valued Property" chart (Figure 2–3).

Information for any existing mortgage on any of your real estate, including the amount and terms of payments, should be put down on the "Liabilities" chart (Figure 2–11).

## Specially Valued Property

List any farm, ranch, or large amounts of business real estate that you own on Chart 2 (Figure 2–3) just as you have done on the other charts.

Generally, all property in your estate is included for federal estate tax purposes at its fair market value (determined by appraisers with expert knowledge) at its highest and best use or at the value of the retail or sales price if the property was sold in a market to the public. However, there are special rules that help to lessen the tax impact on estates holding considerable amounts of farm or business real estate when certain requirements of the I.R.S. are met. According to I.R.C., Sec. 2032A:

> 1) At least 50% of the adjusted value[2] of the gross estate must consist of the adjusted value of real or personal property that was being used as a farm or in a closely held business and that was acquired from, or passed from, the decedent to a qualified heir of the decedent.
>
> 2) At least 25% of the adjusted value of the gross estate must consist of the adjusted value of qualified farm or closely held business real property.

In addition, Section 2032A can be used only if you (or a family member) are "actively involved" in the operation of the farm, ranch, or business, it has been used as such for five of the eight years prior to death, and is left to a qualified heir (family member).

The benefits under this section will be lost unless the land operation continues to meet this rigid test for ten years following your death. This

---

[2] Adjusted value is the value of property determined without regard to its special-use value. The value is reduced for unpaid mortgages on the property or any indebtedness against the property, if the full value of the decedent's interest in the property (not reduced by such indebtedness) is included in the value of the gross estate.

creates a potential tax liability for the recapture tax should the property be sold or transformed into something other than the farm, ranch, or business.

Be sure to get good legal and accounting advice when electing this provision. Each person who receives an interest in the specially valued property must be listed with the I.R.S. and each is required to sign an agreement to be legally bound by the terms set forth in the Internal Revenue Code, Section 2032A. (See also Revenue Ruling 88-89, 1988-42 I.R.B. 4; Revenue Ruling 89-30, 1989-9 I.R.B. 31; and Revenue Ruling 89-22, 1989-8 I.R.B. 5.)

## Stocks and Bonds

On Chart 3 (Figure 2–4) write down all stocks, bonds, and money market funds that you own. (See Table 2–2 for an example.) List buy-sell or business agreements. Attach appraisals and any documents that restrict or in any way affect the sale of stock of your practice or any other business in which you have an interest. List cooperative apartments in which the basic attribute of your interest in ownership is stock.

List stocks alphabetically as the first item, then list the bonds alphabetically. List worthless securities last. Interest accural or dividends due should follow each item along with the month in which such interest (or dividends) are paid.

All items should be listed at their current market value on the valuation date you have chosen. The *Wall Street Journal* or your broker can give you a current market value, if you don't already have it. For estate tax purposes, these items are included at their fair market value on the date of death. The fair market value for publicly held stocks and bonds is the mean (midpoint) between the highest and lowest quoted selling prices on the date of death or within a reasonable period after the date of death if there are no available selling prices on the date of death.

### Stocks

Information on the stocks you own should include the number of shares, the price per share, the issue, whether common or preferred, the CUSPID[3] number, par value where needed, as well as the original cost and the date of purchase. For reference, list the broker with whom you do business and the company's address and telephone number for each. Then, if a question should ever arise, the information will be at your finger tips and you will know whom to contact.

### Money Market Funds

Money market funds are mutual stock funds that invest in highly liquid money market instruments that pay daily dividends and, in many

---

[3] CUSPID (Committee on Uniform Security Identification Procedure) is a nine-digit number that is assigned to all stocks and bonds traded on major exchanges and to many unlisted securities. It is printed on the face of the stock certificate.

**Table 2–2.** Example: Stocks and bonds chart.

For jointly owned property, use Chart 3 (Figure 2–4). In community property states, use Chart 8 (Figure 2–9) for separately owned property.

| Item number | Ownership and description (Face value and number of shares) | Interest or dividends paid/Date | Value |
|---|---|---|---|
| Example: 1. (1 bond) | Athens Clark County Pollution Revenue Authority at 7%. Matures 4/1/2020. Bond #LNG 125. H's name. | $231.00 Jan./July | $5,000 |
| 2. (25 shares) | McCaw Cellular 75 shares common stock CUSPID # XXXXXXX Purchased 10/89. In W's name. | $2.00 per share payable in Jan. | $2,550 |
| 3. (800 shares) | Minitronics Corp., common. Last known address: 1 Wildwood Ave. Monega, Penn. Incorp. Delaware, 1976. Stock worthless & returned no value. See attached letter dated 1/20/85, from Richard Smith, former President and Treas. of issuing company. | none | none |

Note: Items (1) (2) and (3) were purchased from John Smith at Brokerage Inc., 222 Main Street, Anywhere, USA. Mr. Smith can be reached at (phone number).

cases, offer free check redemption services. List these also. All checks that clear through this fund are maintained in a single account, not in the customer's name, but under the name of the money fund, and the checks are probably "lost" among the thousands written by thousands of shareholders (if you keep withdrawals under $2,000).

### Bonds

If you own U.S. Savings bonds or tax-exempt bonds, list them. Savings bonds are included in your estate (at date of death) by either the redemption value of the bond or the bond's par value. For net worth purposes, list their value as of the valuation date you have chosen. Describe any bonds you own as to quantity or denomination, name of obligor, date of maturity, interest rate, and interest due date.

Registered or bearer municipal bonds are income tax free. Almost all bonds sold before July, 1983, were bearer bonds. They were owned anonymously and interest and principal were paid to whomever holds them. All municipal bonds since 1983 are registered, and computerized ownership records are kept. Even though municipal bonds are income tax free, they are not tax free for estate and inheritance tax purposes. Describe them as to the amount of the coupon (or amount received) and in what month, the name of the obligor, the date on which the bond matures, the face value, and the interest rate.

### Flower Bonds

Flower bonds are marketable U.S. Treasury bonds that can be redeemed by an executor at par value plus accrued interest to pay federal estate taxes. Include these bonds at their par value, even if their market value is less than par. If the market value is greater than par, they should be included between the highest and lowest quoted selling prices.

### Mutual Funds

Mutual funds are shares in an open-end investment company. The fair market value of shares in mutual funds is either the redemption price (bid price) quoted by the company for the date of death or the last public redemption price quoted by the company for the first day before the date of death for which there is a quotation.

### Buy-Sell Agreements

Buy-sell agreements pertaining to your practice should be attached if you have a professional (closely held) corporation. Other documents and financial data for the prior five years may be required to be submitted with your return. Attach any documents you use to value the shares including balance sheets, profit and loss statements for each of the five years preceding the date of death, and appraisals. See I.R.C. Sec. 2031 and Revenue Ruling 77-287, 1977-2 C.B.319.

## Retirement Benefits, Notes, and Cash Owed You

On Chart 4 (Figure 2–5), list mortgages, promissory notes, or cash that is owed to you. (Follow the example in Table 2–3.) Write down retirement plan information, any land you have contracted to sell, and cash you have in banks, savings and loan associations, and other types of financial institutions.

### Retirement Benefits

Putting a value on your retirement plan—Keogh, I.R.A., pension or profit-sharing plan—may not be an easy task. The plan actuary or trustee could help determine its value. List the type of plan, its face value, the trustee, vested employees, beneficiaries, and any other information that would identify the plan.

Retirement benefits are earned over an extended period of time that might include married and unmarried periods in your life. In most community property states, retirement benefits are apportioned based on the respective time periods.

### Cash

List the name and address of each bank or financial institution; the amount in each account; the account (or serial) number; and the type of

**Table 2–3.** Example: Notes, cash, retirement plans chart (include: savings and checking accounts, C.D.s).

For jointly owned property, use Chart 4 (Figure 2–5). In community property states, use Chart 8 (Figure 2–9) for separately owned property.

| Item number/ Name | Description (account #, where located) | Value |
|---|---|---|
| Example: | | |
| 1. In W's Name: | First Union Bank Saving Account 1 Main Street Anywhere, USA Account Number 125-1230 Contact person: Mr. Hawkins, Vice President | $30,000 |
| 2. H financed: | Promissory Note of Richard Doe. Unpaid balance as of 12/31/90 $4,000; dated 1/5/76; interest at 6.5% a year. | $10,000 |
| 3. H's Name: | Bond and mortgage for $20,000, dated 9/1/80 to T.S. Smith, address: 16 Wilmington Road, Southpoint, N.Y., due 9/1/85, interest payable at 12% per yr. quarterly on 9/1, 12/1, 3/1, and 6/1. Unpaid principal as of date | $13,000 |

account (whether checking, savings, time deposit, etc.), as well as who is listed on the signature card.

Everyone has some cash put away, so put down something. If you don't, it's a red flag for the I.R.S. to investigate when the time comes. There is a law that requires banks to photocopy any transaction over $100, but since it would cost too much to sort checks, most banks microfilm all of them. Your bank records belong to the bank (not to you). They are the property of the bank. A fact for you to remember is that your financial dealings reveal "you." Your financial transactions are revealed through your checkbook: your religious beliefs, your political views, your associations, your other activities. It reveals **YOU!** The I.R.S. has examined financial transactions when they have done a full scale audit or suspected fraud, and, after all, your checkbook is a financial picture of "you."

### Contract to Sell Land

If you are the party to a contract to sell land, list the name of the purchaser, the date of the contract, a description of the property (similar to that under the real estate section), the sale price, the initial payment, the amounts of installment payments, the interest rate, and unpaid balance of principal.

### Mortgages and Promissory Notes

If anyone owes you money be sure to list the face value and unpaid balance, the date of the promissory note or mortgage, the date of maturity, name of person to whom you lent the money, the property secured (if any), the interest rate, and the number of installment payments due. Attach supporting documentation when available.

## Life Insurance

List full details pertaining to insurance on your life on Chart 5 (Figure 2–6). Table 2–4 shows you how. Any policy on your life of which another person is the owner should also be listed with full details. Include all types of life insurance that you have: whole life, term, universal, or any others.

Describe the insurance as completely as possible, including the name of the national insurance company, the policy number, the face value of the policy, the beneficiary, the premium amount and the month due, and the local agent's name and address. After all, someone should know whom to contact if the need should arise.

Your cash value only from any whole life policies is included in your net worth; however, the face value of all types of life insurance is included in your estate for tax purposes under Section 2042 of the Internal Revenue Code if you purchased the insurance and either your estate or another beneficiary receives it.

If you have any "incidents of ownership" at all in the policy, it will be included in your estate for tax purposes. Incidents of ownership in a

**Table 2–4.** Example: Life insurance chart.

For jointly owned property, use Chart 5 (Figure 2–6). In community property states, use Chart 8 (Figure 2–9) for separately owned property.

| Type | Name and address of company Policy number and beneficiary | Face value | Cash value | Premium due/ month |
|------|-----------------------------------------------------------|------------|------------|--------------------|
| Example: | | | | |
| 1. Term | ABC Mutual<br>2 Main Street<br>Anywhere, USA<br>Policy # 234-78910<br>Spouse is beneficiary<br>Agent: John Michael<br>234 Bay Street<br>Hometown, Ga. | $20,000 | –0– | $150.00<br>Premium<br>paid<br>annually<br>in<br>February |
| 2. Term | Equality Life Insurance Co.,<br>Group policy No. 6431; Employee<br>Cert. No.1027; Beneficiary: spouse,<br>Owner: spouse (so will be excluded<br>from gross estate of insured spouse)<br>as of June 15, 1970. Letter from in-<br>surer and copy of transfer of own-<br>ership. | $50,000 | | $250.00<br>annually<br>due in<br>January |

policy include (1) any rights you may have to its economic benefits; (2) the power to change the beneficiary; (3) the power to surrender or cancel the policy; (4) the power to assign the policy or revoke an assignment; (5) the power to pledge the policy for a loan; (6) the power to obtain from the insurer a loan against the surrender value of the policy; and (7) any reversionary interest of more than 5% of the value of the policy (such as if you were to direct to whom the proceeds should be paid if the primary beneficiary should die before you).

Upon death of the insured, the estate executor must obtain Form 712 from the insurance company for *each* policy and attach it to the estate tax return, as required by the I.R.S. Form 712 verifies the amount (proceeds) that was sent by the insurance company and to whom the money was sent. The I.R.S. may also require evidence showing the source of premium payments for a policy on your life that was owned by or transferred to another person. They may even require evidence that the other person paid the premiums from his or her own funds, as well as information on how the transfer of life insurance was handled for gift tax purposes.

Some states, like California and Washington, apportion life insurance proceeds according all premiums paid. In Wisconsin, the proceeds are community property if the insured is listed as owner; but the proceeds are separate property if someone else is listed as the owner of your policy.

## Other Insurance

Other insurance should include such policies as major medical, homeowners, auto, boat, disability, and the like. Doctor, include your malpractice insurance, overhead and accounts receivable insurance, and the other types bought personally or through your practice. See Chart 6 (Figure 2–7). These are not part of your estate or your net worth, but they are an important part of keeping up with what you have. If you have a group medical plan, could your spouse continue the policy if something were to happen to you? This may be something that you should look into.

## Jointly Owned Property

If you do not own property in a community property state, fill out Chart 7 (Figure 2–8), using the example in Table 2–5. If you do own property in a community property state, fill out Chart 8, "Separately Owned Property" (Figure 2–9).

**Table 2–5.** Example: Jointly owned property chart.

Those in community property states do not use this chart. You use Chart 8 (Figure 2–9) for separately owned property.

List name and address of each joint owner

| Name | Address, City, State, Zip | % of Ownership |
|---|---|---|
| 1. H.J. Harvey, | 3 Main Street, Phoenix, Ariz. | 50% owner |
| 2. Spouse | | |
| 3. | | |
| 4. | | |

| Owner from above | Description (including purchase price and date) | Full value | % of Ownership and value |
|---|---|---|---|
| 1. Condominium, 29 Bay Island, #1-A Daytona Beach, Fla. (Lot 9, Square 15, Palms Subdivision); Two bedroom apartment on first floor. Value based on sale to unrelated third party on 10/18/85. See copy of closed statement attached. | | $75,000 | 50–50 |
| 2. First National Bank of Georgia 6 Main Street, Atlanta, Ga. checking account #234–479 | | $10,000 | |

Joint property with right of survivorship is often used in common law states to pass property from one person to another without the need for probate. This form of ownership isn't used in community property states, except in Wisconsin, which permits community property to be held with right of survivorship if the words *survivorship marital property* are used in the document of title. Washington and Texas allow marital agreements creating a right of survivorship in community property between spouses.

### Joint Property

List all property that is held jointly with right of survivorship, tenants by the entirety, or as tenants in common. Joint ownership should include all property of whatever type, whether real estate, personal property, bank accounts, and the like, in which you hold an interest either with your spouse or with another—even property acquired by gift or inheritance as a joint tenant.

In property held jointly with right of survivorship or as tenants by the entirety, the key element is "survivorship." When one owner dies, the other automatically becomes the sole owner of the property. If you co-own property without the property being subject to the key element of "survivorship," you hold title to property as "tenants in common" with another and your will controls what happens to your share of the property.

On the chart (Table 2–5), describe any jointly owned property just as you have done for the other charts.

For each, put down the name and address of persons owning an interest with you along with the full value of the jointly owned property. In the "Percentage" column, enter the percentage of the total value of the property in which you have an interest.

### Separately Owned Property

Those who live in community property states should list all property that is "separately owned" as opposed to "community" property.

List property acquired before marriage with your own separate funds, or property acquired by inheritance or gift to you alone and kept separately (not commingled with community property) just as you listed your assets on the previous charts.

Income from separate property is separate property, except in Idaho, Louisiana, Texas, and Wisconsin where it is community property.

If property is encumbered with a mortgage and subsequently paid with community funds, the interest is proportionate as to part individual and part community property.

When one spouse dies, one half of the community property belongs to the decedent and the other half belongs to the surviving spouse. The decedent's estate would be made up of one-half of the community property and his separate property. When this happens, the community character of the property is terminated.

## Miscellaneous Property

### *Personal Items*

On Chart 9 (Figure 2–10), list all of the things you own personally that are not listed on any other chart, such as silverware, jewelry, furs, cars, antiques, coin collections, practice assets, boat, and the like. (Follow the example in Table 2–6.) Include rights or interest you may have in any one of the following: household goods and personal effects, royalties, lease-holds, reversionary or remainder interests, farm products and growing crops. If you maintain a safe deposit box, list the box number, where it is located, and who has access to it.

**Table 2–6.** Example: Miscellaneous property.

For jointly owned property, use Chart 9 (Figure 2–10). In community property states, use Chart 8 (Figure 2–9) for separately owned property.

(Include your business interest here if not elsewhere.)

| Item Owner | | Description | Date acquired/ How acquired | Current value |
|---|---|---|---|---|
| 1. H | One | 1969 Cutlass Olds 4-door, value based on local dealer sales prices of similar cars. | 1/70 | $3,200 |
| 2. W | One | 1987 Buick, 2-door, value based on local dealer sales prices of similar cars. | 6/87 | $5,000 |
| 3. H | One | Renkin Sports Motor Boat. 1970 Model, fiberglass, 15 ft., 155 H.P. stern drive. Value based on third-party sale from Alfred Marine. See sales con-tract attached. | 8/85 | $2,000 |
| 5. H | | Household goods and personal effects. Value based on ap-praisal. See attached. | | $50,000 |

(Other items may include the following: plane, silverware, jewelry, furs, coin/stamp collection, art work, antiques, and the like.)

| | | | | |
|---|---|---|---|---|
| 6. H | | Solo dental practice, value based on appraisal attached. | | $200,000 |

7. Safe Deposit Box # 21. Location: First Union Bank, 1 Main Street, Anywhere, USA

Signatures required on Box: H and W

### Professional Practice

Doctor, if you own an interest in a sole proprietorship, partnership, or unincorporated business, attach a statement of its worth on a set valuation date and attach a statement of assets and liabilities for the five years prior to the valuation date. Attach an appraisal if you have one. Even though it may be difficult to place a value on your practice, it must be done if you want an accurate picture of your net worth, and it will have to be done eventually for estate tax purposes. The tangible assets of your practice would include the value of the equipment, furniture, supplies (average for the prior two months), and accounts receivable.

The net value of your practice should be determined on the basis of all relevant factors (see Revenue Ruling 59-60 for guidelines) including (1) all the assets of your practice, (2) the earning capacity of your practice, and (3) applicable factors used in determining the value of your interest. Special attention should be given to the value of goodwill when you have a surviving partner and have not determined, in advance, how the respective interests should be valued. Include balance sheets, profit and loss statements, and any other financial data you may have for the five years prior to the date of death.

### Vehicles

For a boat, plane, or other vehicle, use the price that you would receive if your used vehicle were sold directly to a buyer (not a dealer). A bank leasing department, a dealer, or *Kelley's Blue Book* may have helpful information.

### Articles with Artistic or Intrinsic Value

List those articles that you own with an artistic or intrinsic value such as jewelry, furs, silverware, coin or stamp collection, oriental rugs, books, statuary, vases, or the like. If any one item is valued at more than $3,000 or any collection of similar articles is valued at over $10,000, an appraisal should be attached to this chart.

Take color photographs of any art work or other antiques that are of value. A list of guidelines and pertinent factors to use in art valuation issues have been formalized in Rev. Proc. 66-49, 1966-1 C.B. 48. This Revenue Procedure will serve as a checklist for the type of information you will need in order for an opinion of value to be formed.

### Household Items

Listing household goods is really what financial experts have called a "guesstimate" of what's inside. The government presumes the husband paid for these items unless you have other evidence to the contrary.

Evidence of ownership must be proved. Unlike criminal law cases where you are innocent until proven guilty, you might say that in the area of tax law, you are guilty until you prove otherwise. Evidence of ownership

**Table 2–7.** Example: Liabilities.

| Creditor (Name/Address) | Description Terms | Property Secured | Unpaid Balance |
|---|---|---|---|
| Example: | | | |
| 1. Fla. National Bank<br>1 Main Street<br>Anywhere, FL | $60,000 (5-year note)<br>Installment payments<br>$500.00 monthly<br>10% interest | Unsecured | $18,000 |
| 2. Center Bank<br>2 Center Rd.<br>Atlanta, GA | Mortgage on real<br>property listed on<br>Chart 1, Item 1, in<br>the face amount of<br>$35,000 dated 5/1/72,<br>payable monthly<br>over 15 years at 9%<br>interest. | | $15,200 |

may be proved by looking to see who is the insured or under whose social security number the item is listed. Both your insurance and your social security number are records and sources of evidence of ownership.

## Liabilities

List all of your liabilities (mortgages, loans, deed-to-secure debts) on Chart 10 (Figure 2–11), even if it is painful (see Table 2–7). Do you have any outstanding loans against your life insurance, stocks, cars, or office equipment? Whatever you owe is a liability. This liability diminishes your net worth. If you had to liquidate all of your assets and pay all of your debts, what would be left over?

Attach any copies of loan applications and financial statements filed in connection with any item on this chart. The lender will furnish you with copies. State the name of the financial institution and address, your account number, the amount of the original loan, the rate of interest at which the money was borrowed, the term (the number of payments and how much you pay monthly), and any other information available to you. Be sure to indicate which property is secured by each note. You may want to put down the loan balance and date to get an idea of where you stand.

## RECAPITULATION: YOUR NET WORTH

On Chart 11 (Figure 2–12), record and add the figures from charts 1 through 9. Now subtract from that figure the total of the figures on Chart 10. What is left is your net worth.

Your net worth is the best guide you will have to your economic growth and maturity. Besides, you can now put your mind at ease knowing your assets won't be lost if something should happen to either you or your spouse and you can begin planning your long-range goals since you now know what you own and what you owe.

Make copies of these forms as you need them. It would be wise for you to update them at least annually.

Remember, keeping your affairs in order is a matter of caring, of love, and of just plain common sense.

Figure 2-1. I.R.S. Form 706.

| Form **706** | **United States Estate (and Generation-Skipping Transfer)** | | | OMB No. 1545-0015 |
|---|---|---|---|---|
| (Rev. October 1988) Department of the Treasury Internal Revenue Service | **Tax Return** Estate of a citizen or resident of the United States (see separate instructions). To be filed for decedents dying after October 22, 1986, and before January 1, 1990. For Paperwork Reduction Act Notice, see page 1 of the instructions. | | | Expires 8-30-91 |

**Part 1.—Decedent and Executor**

| 1a Decedent's first name and middle initial (and maiden name, if any) | 1b Decedent's last name | | 2 Decedent's social security no. |
|---|---|---|---|
| 3a Domicile at time of death | 3b Year domicile established | 4 Date of birth | 5 Date of death |
| 6a Name of executor (see instructions) | 6b Executor's address (number and street including apartment number or rural route; city, town, or post office; state; and ZIP code) | | |
| 6c Executor's social security number (see instructions) | | | |
| 7a Name and location of court where will was probated or estate administered | | | 7b Case number |
| 8 If decedent died testate, check here ▶ ☐ and attach a certified copy of the will. | | 9 If Form 4768 is attached, check here ▶ ☐ | |
| 10 If Schedule R-1 is attached, check here ▶ ☐ | See page 2 for representative's authorization. | | |

| | | |
|---|---:|---|
| 1 Total gross estate (from Part 5, Recapitulation, page 3, item 10). . . . . . . . | | 1 |
| 2 Total allowable deductions (from Part 5, Recapitulation, page 3, item 25) . . . . . | | 2 |
| 3 Taxable estate (subtract line 2 from line 1) . . . . . . . . . . . . . | | 3 |
| 4 Adjusted taxable gifts (total taxable gifts (within the meaning of section 2503) made by the decedent after December 31, 1976, other than gifts that are includible in decedent's gross estate (section 2001(b))). . | | 4 |
| 5 Add lines 3 and 4 . . . . . . . . . . . . . . . . . . . | | 5 |
| 6 Tentative tax on the amount on line 5 from Table A in the instructions . . . . . . | | 6 |
| Note: *If decedent died before January 1, 1988, skip lines 7a–c and enter the amount from line 6 on line 8.* | | |
| 7a If line 5 exceeds $10,000,000, enter the lesser of line 5 or $21,040,000. If line 5 is $10,000,000 or less, skip lines 7a and 7b and enter zero on line 7c | 7a | |
| b Subtract $10,000,000 from line 7a . . . . . . . . . . . . | 7b | |
| c Enter 5% (.05) of line 7b . . . . . . . . . . . . . . . . | | 7c |
| 8 Total tentative tax (add lines 6 and 7c) . . . . . . . . . . . . . . | | 8 |

**Part 2.—Tax Computation**

| | | | |
|---|---|---|---|
| 9 | Total gift tax payable with respect to gifts made by the decedent after December 31, 1976. Include gift taxes paid by the decedent's spouse for split gifts (section 2513) only if the decedent was the donor of these gifts and they are includible in the decedent's gross estate (see instructions) | | 9 |
| 10 | Gross estate tax (subtract line 9 from line 8) | | 10 ▨ |
| 11 | Unified credit against estate tax from Table B in the instructions. | 11 | |
| 12 | Adjustment to unified credit. (This adjustment may not exceed $6,000. See instructions.) | 12 | |
| 13 | Allowable unified credit (subtract line 12 from line 11) | | 13 |
| 14 | Subtract line 13 from line 10 (but do not enter less than zero) | | 14 |
| 15 | Credit for state death taxes. Do not enter more than line 14. Compute credit by using amount on line 3 less $60,000. See Table C in the instructions and **attach credit evidence** (see instructions) | | 15 |
| 16 | Subtract line 15 from line 14 | | 16 ▨ |
| 17 | Credit for Federal gift taxes on pre-1977 gifts (section 2012)(attach computation) | 17 | |
| 18 | Credit for foreign death taxes (from Schedule(s) P). (Attach Form(s) 706CE) | 18 | |
| 19 | Credit for tax on prior transfers (from Schedule Q) | 19 | |
| 20 | Total (add lines 17, 18, and 19) | | 20 |
| 21 | Net estate tax (subtract line 20 from line 16) | | 21 |
| 22 | Generation-skipping transfer taxes (from Schedule R, Part 2, line 12) | | 22 |
| 23 | Section 4980A increased estate tax (attach Schedule S (Form 706)) (see instructions) | | 23 |
| 24 | Total transfer taxes (add lines 21, 22, and 23) | | 24 ▨ |
| 25 | Prior payments. Explain in an attached statement | 25 | |
| 26 | United States Treasury bonds redeemed in payment of estate tax | 26 | |
| 27 | Total (add lines 25 and 26) | | 27 |
| 28 | Balance due (subtract line 27 from line 24) | | 28 |

Under penalties of perjury, I declare that I have examined this return, including accompanying schedules and statements, and to the best of my knowledge and belief, it is true, correct, and complete. Declaration of preparer other than the executor is based on all information of which preparer has any knowledge.

_____        _____
Signature(s) of executor(s)           Date

_____     _____     _____
Signature of preparer other than executor     Address (and ZIP code)     Date

**Figure 2–2.** CHART 1: Real Estate. (For jointly owned property, use Chart 7. In community property states, use Chart 8 for separately owned property.)

| Item no. | Description | Purchase price | Date purchased | Value to date | % of $ furnished |
|---|---|---|---|---|---|
| | | | | | |
| | | | | | |
| | | | | | |
| | | | | | |
| | | | | | |
| | | | | | |
| | | | | | |
| | | | | | |
| | | | | | |
| | | | | | |
| | | | | | |
| | | | | | |
| | | | | | |
| | Total $ _____ | | | Total $ _____ | |

**Figure 2–3.** CHART 2: Special Valuation (2032A).

1) Qualified Use (check one)  _____ Farm used for farming or
_____ Business other than farming

2) Real property used in a qualified use, passing to qualified heirs, and to be specially valued on this Form.

| A<br>Chart and item<br>number | B<br>Full value | C<br>Value based on<br>qualified use |
|---|---|---|
| | | |

3) Persons holding interests (list family members who will be inheriting an interest in this property).

| | Name | Address | Relationship<br>to owner |
|---|---|---|---|
| A. | | | |
| B. | | | |
| C. | | | |
| D. | | | |

Copyright © 1991 by Practice Management Information Corp.

**Figure 2–4.** CHART 3: Stocks and Bonds. (In community property states use this chart for property during marriage that is community rather than separate.)

| Type and serial no. | Ownership | Broker | Date acquired | Original value | Face amount |
|---|---|---|---|---|---|
| | | | | | |
| | | | | | |
| | | | | | |
| | | | | | |
| | | | | | |
| | | | | | |
| | | | | | |
| | | | | | |
| | | | | | |
| | | | | | |
| | | | | | |
| | | | | | |
| | | | | | |

**Figure 2-5.** CHART 4: Mortgages, Notes, Cash, Pensions, and Profit-Sharing Plans. (For jointly owned property, use Chart 7. In community property states use this chart for property acquired during marriage that is community rather than separate.)

| Item no. | Description (Include checking and savings accounts) | Date | Value |
|---|---|---|---|
|  |  |  |  |
|  |  |  |  |
|  |  |  |  |
|  |  |  |  |
|  |  |  |  |
|  |  |  |  |
|  |  |  |  |
|  |  |  |  |
|  |  |  |  |
|  |  |  |  |
|  |  |  |  |
|  |  |  |  |
|  |  |  |  |
|  |  |  |  |

Total $ _____

**Figure 2–6.** CHART 5: Life Insurance.

| Type | Owner | Name of company and policy no. | Face value | Date due Premium no. Amount | Primary beneficiary | Secondary beneficiary | Cash value |
|------|-------|-------------------------------|-----------|----------------------------|---------------------|----------------------|-----------|
|      |       |                               |           |                            |                     |                      |           |
|      |       |                               |           |                            |                     |                      |           |
|      |       |                               |           |                            |                     |                      |           |
|      |       |                               |           |                            |                     |                      |           |
|      |       |                               |           |                            |                     |                      |           |
|      |       |                               |           |                            |                     |                      |           |
|      |       |                               |           |                            |                     |                      |           |
|      |       |                               |           |                            |                     |                      |           |
|      |       |                               |           |                            |                     |                      |           |
|      |       |                               |           |                            |                     |                      |           |
|      |       |                               |           |                            |                     |                      |           |

**Figure 2–7.** CHART 6: Other Insurance: (Major Medical, Homeowners, Auto). (This chart is strictly an organizational tool. It is not part of either your net worth or your estate.)

| Type | Name of company | Policy no. | Value | Premium | Date due | Coverage |
|------|-----------------|------------|-------|---------|----------|----------|
|      |                 |            |       |         |          |          |
|      |                 |            |       |         |          |          |
|      |                 |            |       |         |          |          |
|      |                 |            |       |         |          |          |
|      |                 |            |       |         |          |          |
|      |                 |            |       |         |          |          |
|      |                 |            |       |         |          |          |
|      |                 |            |       |         |          |          |
|      |                 |            |       |         |          |          |
|      |                 |            |       |         |          |          |
|      |                 |            |       |         |          |          |
|      |                 |            |       |         |          |          |
|      |                 |            |       |         |          |          |

**Figure 2–8.** CHART 7: Jointly Owned Property.

If you own property as a joint tenant with right of survivorship or as a tenant by the entirety, state the name and address of each co-tenant:

| Name | Address (number and street, city, state, zip) |
|---|---|
| A. | |
| B. | |
| C. | |

Give the full details for each property below:

| Item no. | Description and stock number (if available) | Original purchase price and date | Percent of contribution you furnished | Value |
|---|---|---|---|---|
| | | | | |
| | | | | |
| | | | | |

Total $ _____

Copyright © 1991 by Practice Management Information Corp.

**Figure 2–9.** CHART 8: Separately Owned Property. (Use this chart in community property states for separately acquired property.)

| Item no. | Description | Purchase price | Date purchased | Value to date |
|---|---|---|---|---|
| | | | | |
| | | | | |
| | | | | |
| | | | | |
| | | | | |
| | | | | |
| | | | | |
| | | | | |
| | | | | |
| | | | | |
| | | | | |
| | | | | |
| | | | | |

Total $ _____          Total $ _____

**Figure 2–10.** CHART 9: Miscellaneous Property. (In community property states use this chart for property during marriage that is community rather than separate.)

| Description | Purchase price | Date purchased | Original value | Current appraisal (value/date) |
|---|---|---|---|---|
| | | | | |
| | | | | |
| | | | | |
| | | | | |
| | | | | |
| | | | | |
| | | | | |
| | | | | |
| | | | | |
| | | | | |
| | | | | |
| | | | | |
| | | | | |
| | | | | |

**Figure 2–11.** CHART 10: Liabilities.

| Item no. | Description of mortgages and liens | Total no. of payments and percentage | Total loan | Interest per year | Amount left |
|---|---|---|---|---|---|
| | | | | | |
| | | | | | |
| | | | | | |
| | | | | | |
| | | | | | |
| | | | | | |
| | | | | | |
| | | | | | |
| | | | | | |
| | | | | | |
| | | | | | |
| | | | | | |

Total $ _____    $ _____

**Figure 2–12.** CHART 11: Recapitulation Sheet: Your Net Worth.

| Item No. | Gross estate—Assets | Value |
|---|---|---|
| | (add up the totals from the charts) | |
| 1. | Chart 1: Real Estate | $_____ |
| 2. | Chart 2: Special Valuation Property | $_____ |
| 3. | Chart 3: Stocks and Bonds | $_____ |
| 4. | Chart 4: Mortgages, Notes, Cash, Pensions, and Profit Sharing Plans | $_____ |
| 5. | Chart 5: Life Insurance | $_____ |
| 6. | Chart 6: Other Insurance | $_____ |
| 7. | Chart 7: Jointly Owned Property totals | $_____ |
| | or | |
| | Chart 8: Separately Owned Property (for those in community property states) | |
| 8. | Chart 9: Miscellaneous Property totals | $_____ |
| 9. | TOTAL ASSETS | $_____ |
| 10. | Chart 10: Liabilities (Subtract liabilities from assets) | −_____ |
| Assets minus liabilities = NET WORTH | | $_____ |

Copyright © 1991 by Practice Management Information Corp.

# 3

# INHERITANCE TAXES ON YOUR ESTATE

One of the most frustrating things about financial planning is knowing that a large portion of your estate could go to the government and not to your loved ones when you die. However, by understanding estate taxes, you can manage your savings and investments so as to minimize the taxes and pass along the absolute maximum possible to those loved ones who survive you.

In one of the first court cases pertaining to estate taxes, an uncle in Texas died leaving his property to his nephew. The nephew claimed that the inheritance tax imposed was a direct tax on the property received and therefore was unconstitutional. (*Fernadez* v *Wiener*, 1939). The I.R.S. won out.

When estate taxes first came into existence, there was a lot of conversation about this new tax. Some said it was legal, others said it was not. But they all agreed it was oppressive, a chore to report, and a burden to pay. It is no different today.

Estate taxes are inheritance taxes levied, not on the property that passes at death, but on the "privilege" of transferring that property when you die. The Supreme Court claims that this is not a direct tax on the property. It is an excise tax! But, how, you might ask, is the tax computed? It is computed on the value of that property!

The Supreme Court has gradually expanded its definition of an "excise" tax to include an indirect tax on intangibles—the privilege of buying, selling, receiving, using, and doing business, besides transferring property. Yes, even your license to practice is the privilege of being able to work.

Your estate calculations (Form 706) are filled out only once, and someone else must do it for you. How much is it likely to amount to? What can you do to reduce it? You have already taken the first big step toward answering these questions: you have calculated your net worth. It is typical that you should want to assure your family a comfortable life, with the hope that, if you are the first to die, your family will be adequately provided for.

Once you know the amount of your income for the year, you can probably guess within a thousand dollars how much your income tax will be. That's because Form 1040 is an old friend and you have to cope with it each and every year. But do you know how much your eventual estate taxes will be and what types of property your estate consists of?

## YOUR ESTATE

Your estate consists of four types of property: personal assets, business assets, life insurance, and retirement benefits.

1. Personal assets, which include cash on hand, bank accounts, real property (such as your home or office), and personal property (such as jewelry, stamp or coin collections, cars, boats, even silver you may have inherited).

2. Business assets, which include your interest in your practice and any other business venture in which you have an interest.

3. Life insurance that was personally purchased and owned by you, even though payable directly to a named beneficiary, is included in your estate for tax purposes (unless someone else is the owner of your life insurance policy).

4. Benefits such as pension and profit sharing plans, an individual retirement account (I.R.A.), Keogh, and even group insurance, if bought through your practice.

These are the types of property that you can draw on for financial resources during your life. They are the assets that are transferred to your beneficiaries at your death. Before your beneficiary can draw on these assets of your estate, there are certain expenses and taxes that must be paid. How are these taxes determined?

## CALCULATING YOUR TAXABLE ESTATE

Simply put, the steps you take to calculate your estate taxes are as follows: (1) determine your gross estate, (2) subtract the allowable deductions, (3) apply the appropriate tax rates, and (4) deduct any credits to which the estate is allowed or entitled. The result is your net estate tax due.

Your gross estate includes all property in which you have an interest including real property outside the United States.

To calculate your taxable estate add (see Chart 12, Figure 3–1, at the end of the chapter):

1. Charts 1 through 4 from Chapter 2 plus either Chart 7 or 8. From Chart 5, include the face value of life insurance policies that you own or that your estate is to receive (under the net worth section we included only the cash value). You may have heard that life insurance is not taxable income. That is true, but what you may not have heard is that it is taxable as a part of your estate when you die. (See I.R.C. Section 2042[1] and Section 2035.)

   Joint bank accounts (from Chart 7) are included in your taxable estate, either half or entirely (unless there is evidence to the contrary that you did not contribute entirely to the account). What about any other property that you may hold jointly? Your share, or percentage of interest owned, will be included in your estate for tax purposes.

   If you included Chart 8, now add in separately owned property. Chart 8 is only for community property states, as all other property should be listed on Charts 1 through 4. Four community property states (Arizona, Idaho, New Mexico, and Washington) require that both halves of your community property be included in the probate administration upon the death of either you or your spouse. In California and Nevada, only your one-half of the community property is subject to probate administration.

2. Add in any dower or curtesy interest. There are some states that recognize these old common law rights entitling a surviving spouse

---

[1] According to Section 2024, if an individual dies while the individual is insured with life insurance, which life insurance policy is payable to the individual's estate, then the decedent's gross estate includes, for estate tax purposes, the amount that is receivable by the estate under the terms of the life insurance policy even if the decedent does not have an incident of ownership in the life insurance policy at the individual's death.

Further, Section 2024 provides that if an individual dies while the individual is insured with life insurance, which life insurance policy is payable to a person other than the individual's estate, and if the individual has an "incident of ownership" in the life insurance policy, then the decedent's gross estate includes, for estate tax purposes, the amount which is receivable by the beneficiary of the life insurance policy under the terms of the life insurance policy.

to an interest for life in a decedent spouse's real estate, regardless of what the will says.

3. Add in the value of any custodial accounts for your children if you are named as custodian. If you are the named custodian and if you deposited money into the account, then that account will be included in your estate for tax purposes. It is hard to believe, isn't it, that the college education fund you set up years ago for your children could now be taxed in your estate. However, if your spouse is custodian and you fund the account, then it can be excluded from your taxable estate!

4. Add in any gifts or trusts you may have created with retained rights. Suppose you have signed over your home to your children with the stipulation that you have the right to live there for the rest of your life. Or, suppose you set up a grantor-retained income trust (see Chapter 5), and the title to the property is to be returned to you after a fixed period of time. Such revocable transfers and transfers with retained interests are part of your taxable estate according to I.R.C. Section 2036.[2]

5. Add in the value of any annuities you have purchased.

6. Add in any powers of appointment you may have in any trusts that have been created for your benefit. (I.R.C. Sec. 2041.)

7. Add in lottery winnings. Examine your state laws or you may find those winnings included in your estate for tax purposes as they were in *Estate of D'Amico* v *Department of Treasury*, 429 N.W.2d 659 (Mich. App. 1988), in which the court held that the inheritance tax is not a tax on property, but a tax on the right to transfer property.

## ESTIMATING YOUR ESTATE TAXES

Once you have added up your gross estate and entered it as the first item on Chart 13 (Figure 3–2), you may determine the amount of estate tax that is due at your death as follows:

1. Subtract the amount that is deductible for costs of administration, debts, taxes, and losses. (See I.R.C. Sections 2053 and 2054.)

---

[2] The general rule in Section 2036(a) is that the value of the gross estate shall include the value of all property to the extent of any interest therein of which the decedent has at any time made a transfer (except in case of a bona fide sale for an adequate and full consideration in money or money's worth), by trust or otherwise, under which he has retained for his life or for any period not ascertainable without reference to his death or for any period which does not in fact end before death:

(1) the possession or enjoyment of, or the right to the income from, the property, or

(2) the right, either alone or in conjunction with any person, to designate the persons who shall possess or enjoy the property or the income therefrom.

See also Notice 89-99, 1989-38, I.R.B.4 (August 31, 1989).

If you are living in or own property in one of the states listed as a community property state, you will encounter special estate problems. Your assets include part community property and part separate property. The computation for federal estate taxes in community property states is slightly different from the computation for those in the other states and is shown in Chart 14 (Figure 3–3).

2. Subtract the amount that qualifies for the charitable deduction. (See I.R.C. Section 2055.)

3. Subtract the amount that qualifies for the marital deduction. (See I.R.C. Section 2056.)

4. Subtract the amount that is deductible for sales to employee stock ownership plans (if this applies to you). (See I.R.C. Section 2057.)

The result shows your taxable estate. In other words, your taxable estate is the gross estate minus the deductions we have just listed above.

5. Next, add to your taxable estate any taxable gifts that you have made after December 31, 1976, for which you have filed a gift tax return. (See I.R.C. Section 2001(b).) This is done because there is one Unified Rate Schedule or tax table (Table 3–1) that applies to

**Table 3–1.** Rate and tax for estates of those dying in 1988 and later.

| If amount is: over (1) | but not over (2) | Tax on amount in col. (1) (3) | Tax rate on excess over amount in col. (1) (4) |
|---|---|---|---|
| $ 0 | $ 10,000 | $ 0 | 18 |
| 10,000 | 20,000 | 1,800 | 20 |
| 20,000 | 40,000 | 3,800 | 22 |
| 40,000 | 60,000 | 8,200 | 24 |
| 60,000 | 80,000 | 13,000 | 26 |
| 80,000 | 100,000 | 18,200 | 28 |
| 100,000 | 150,000 | 23,800 | 30 |
| 150,000 | 250,000 | 38,800 | 32 |
| 250,000 | 500,000 | 70,800 | 34 |
| 500,000 | 750,000 | 155,800 | 37 |
| 750,000 | 1,000,000 | 248,300 | 39 |
| 1,000,000 | 1,250,000 | 345,800 | 41 |
| 1,250,000 | 1,500,000 | 448,300 | 43 |
| 1,500,000 | 2,000,000 | 555,800 | 45 |
| 2,000,000 | 2,500,000 | 780,800 | 49 |
| 2,500,000 | 3,000,000 | 1,025,800 | 53 |
| 3,000,000 | - - - - - - - - | 1,290,800 | 55 |

NOTE: Deduct Unified Credit of $192,800.

both estate and gift taxes. The table (or schedule) is used to determine the tentative tax on the taxable estate (which includes the taxable gifts).

6. Determine the tax tentatively from the tax table (Unified Rate Schedule, Table 3–1) of your total taxable gifts and estate payable with respect to the sum of your taxable estate and adjusted taxable gifts.

7. Subtract the gift tax that you paid on the taxable gifts with respect to your gifts made after 1976.

8. Subtract the unified credit that is allowed. The amount of the unified credit allowed for estates of individuals dying in 1988 and later is $192,800.

The result is "Your Net Estate Tax" or your taxable estate (without taking into consideration any state or other credits to which you may be entitled). Other credits that may be deducted from your gross estate tax to determine your net estate tax are credit for state death taxes, credit for gift taxes, credit for tax on prior transfers, and credit for foreign death taxes. Sometimes a credit is allowed for any tax paid to more than one foreign country.

## NONRESIDENTS AND NONCITIZENS

For those who are neither a resident nor citizen of the United States: your gross estate is made up in the same manner as the gross estate of a U.S. citizen or resident, no matter where your property is located. But, only the part of the entire gross estate that is located in the United States is subject to the tax. There are special rules, a different tax rate, different credits for you, and the marital deduction may not be available to you, so be sure to consult an attorney. (See I.R.C. Sections 5032, 5033, and 2100 and the Technical and Miscellaneous Revenue Act of 1988—TAMRA'88).

## DEDUCTIONS FOR YOUR ESTATE

Your estate has demand "mortgages" to pay: Final and administrative expenses and other settlement costs are primary charges against your estate—the deductions from your estate—as well as casualty and theft losses incurred during estate administration and which are not reimbursed by insurance and unpaid mortgages, claims, and other indebtedness against the property. They are also the charges that must be paid before any distribution can be made to your beneficiaries. They are obligations—demand mortgages you might say—that will mature at some unknown future date—the date of your death.

Be sure to list the names and addresses of persons to whom such expenses will be payable and describe the nature of the expense. Don't forget, the following are the deductions you are allowed:

1. Final expenses, which include funeral and medical expenses of the last illness that were not reimbursed by insurance.
2. Administrative expenses, which include attorney and accountant fees, executor or administrator fees, court costs (probate) and filing fees, legal notices, appraisal fees, and other miscellaneous expenses involved in settling the estate.
3. Casualty and theft losses during administration or expenses incurred which were not reimbursed by insurance.
4. Unpaid mortgages and other charges of indebtedness against the property including any interest accrued to the date of death.

You pay property taxes, tangible and intangible taxes, state and federal income taxes all the time. The federal government claims that we are not taxed on the property itself when it comes to estate taxes. It is, however, an "excise" tax, which is a tax measured by the value of the property that is transferred. Why, when someone dies, must we pay taxes again on the same property that has had taxes paid on it all the time? Just for transferring it? The Internal Revenue Service seems to deprive us of money and put us through a nightmare of paperwork to keep track of the property and its value.

## Administrative Costs

Administrative costs are the "shrinkage" of your estate because they must be paid before your assets can be distributed to your beneficiaries. These expenses include any commissions you must pay the executor or administrator, fees of attorneys for the estate, and other miscellaneous expenses such as court costs, accountants' fees, appraisers' fees, and other expenses necessary for preserving and distributing the estate. They also include the cost of storing or maintaining property of the estate for a reasonable period of time before the property is distributed.

Administrative costs range from 4% to 6% of your gross estate. They will be payable in full, in cash, at the time you file the estate tax return. Keep track of them. Table 3–2 shows you how.

## Claims Against the Estate and Other Indebtedness

If there are any personal obligations and/or interest that has accrued on these obligations at the time of your death, they may be deducted as claims against your estate. These claims may include medical expenses from the last illness that were not reimbursed by insurance, property taxes,

**Table 3–2.** Example: Final and administrative expenses.

| ITEM | DESCRIPTION | $ AMOUNT |
|---|---|---|
| Example: | | |
| A. | FINAL EXPENSES | |
| 1. | Harbor Light Funeral Home in Atlanta, Ga. | $ 4,500 |
| 2. | Monument Works Co., Atlanta (headstone) | 1,050 |
| 3. | City tax on cemetery plot | 150 |
| 4. | Memorial Hospital (last illness charge) | 2,500 |
| B. | ADMINISTRATIVE EXPENSES | |
| 1. | Executor's commissions (see Table 6–2 in Chapter 6, page 105) | ? |
| 2. | Appraisers Inc., 200 East Point, Chamblee, Ga. | 1,500 |
| 3. | Seymour Accountant, CPA, 52 Front Street, Atlanta, Ga.—fee for preparation of final tax return | 500 |
| 4. | Attorney fees | 10,000 |
| 5. | Probate and other fees | 250 |
| 6. | Telephone, postage, and telegraph costs | 150 |
| 7. | Other miscellaneous administrative expenses | 400 |

unpaid income taxes on income you received while you were living, unpaid gift taxes, any self-employment taxes, and the payment of insurance proceeds to a former spouse. Any unpaid mortgages and other indebtedness against property that is included in your estate may also be deducted if you have not deducted it elsewhere.

### Casualty or Theft Losses

Deductions are allowed for losses you may have suffered that were not reimbursed during the settlement of your estate. They may be due to fire, flood, theft, or the like.

## WHEN ARE ESTATE TAXES DUE?

The executor or personal representative is responsible for filing a federal estate tax return (Form 706) nine months from the date of death. However, there is an alternate valuation date (six months after the date of death) if you sell any property in the estate before the nine months. You may decide to pay the federal estate tax in installments under I.R.C. Section 6166 and make a similar election to pay state death taxes in installments. Also see Rev. Rul. 86–38, 1986–1 C.B. 296. The return must be *delivered* to and *received* by the I.R.S. for it to be considered timely filed, not just mailed and postmarked as with your 1040 income tax return.

The address of your legal residence at the time of your death determines where the estate tax return must be filed.

## TAXABLE ESTATE VERSUS PROBATE ESTATE

Your taxes are determined by what the I.R.S. terms your "taxable" estate, not your "probate" estate. Your probate estate (for our purpose here) is defined as property that you leave your beneficiaries under your will. Your taxable estate may include property that is not part of your probate estate, but is included in your estate for tax purposes because of some type of "incident of ownership."

Incidents of ownership may be found in a trust, life insurance policy, or in transferred property. It includes the following:

1. any rights you may have to any economic benefits;
2. the power to change a beneficiary;
3. the power to surrender or cancel;
4. the power to assign the asset or revoke an assignment;
5. the power to pledge it for a loan; and
6. any reversionary interest.

People have made a great deal of money talking about how to avoid probate. This statement is misleading because your estate, especially if it contains any type of real estate, will be probated, with or without a will. The problem is not "how to avoid probate," but how to avoid (or minimize) taxes with which we should be most concerned as the example below shows.

First, let us discuss ways to avoid probate. One avoids probate through the use of joint bank accounts or joint property with rights of survivorship, certain types of trusts, and life insurance.

For example, you may have joint property with right of survivorship with another. This property may go to the other person by right of survivorship but your proportionate interest is included in your estate for tax purposes—even though it is not part of your probate estate.

The same is true for these other types of nonprobate property. You have avoided probate, but you have not avoided taxes.

To understand this a little better let us assume that wife (W) dies and is survived by husband (H) and Son. In W's estate are the following assets: $100,000 in a checking account; $600,000 in securities; $25,000 in a joint checking account with right of survivorship with H; $20,000 in a joint checking account with right of survivorship with Son; $30,000 in trust from which W received interest income during her life and at W's death the trust goes to Son; a $145,000 life insurance policy with H as beneficiary; and a $50,000 life insurance with Son as beneficiary.

W's accountant must now take her estate and determine which assets are to be included in her probate estate and which assets are to be included in her taxable estate. Some assets may be included in both her taxable and probate estates. Since H is W's husband, only half of the joint checking account will be included in W's taxable estate and it is not included at all in W's probate estate since it is with right of survivorship. However, the I.R.S. assumes W put all the funds in the joint checking account with Son (unless there is evidence to the contrary), therefore, the entire account will be included in her taxable estate even though it is not included at all in her probate estate as the money legally goes to Son by right of survivorship.

Take a look at the example below: W has avoided probate, but has W avoided taxes? The amount shown in her taxable estate is the amount on which her estate will be taxed for federal estate tax purposes before any adjustments or credits.

Probate Estate versus Taxable Estate
Assets in W's Estate

| Taxable Estate | | Probate Estate |
|---|---|---|
| $100,000 | Checking Account | $100,000 |
| $600,000 | Securities | $600,000 |
| $ 25,000 | Joint ck. with H | |
| $ 20,000 | Joint ck. with Son | |
| $ 30,000 | Trust for Son | |
| $145,000 | Life Insur. H is beneficiary | |
| $ 50,000 | Life Insur. Son is beneficiary | |
| $970,000 | Gross Estate | $700,000 |

## UNIFIED CREDIT (EXEMPTION EQUIVALENT)

Prior to the unification of estate and gift taxes, a gift tax was imposed on gifts made during your life and a separate estate tax was imposed on transfers of property at death. Each tax had a separate progressive rate schedule.

We no longer have separate estate and gift taxes. Congress replaced the separate exemptions with a single tax rate schedule (called a Unified Rate Schedule) with one unified credit that applies to both estate and gift taxes. This tax rate schedule is used to determine the tax on the taxable estate.

A unified credit of $192,800 is available to all taxpayers. It automatically offsets all gift tax and all estate tax upon the first $600,000 of taxable transfers that the taxpayer makes during his or her life and at death. See I.R.C. Sections 2010 and 2505.

The amount that can be passed free of transfer tax—because the unified credit is equivalent to an amount that is exempt from transfer tax—is sometimes known as the *credit shelter* or *exemption equivalent* amount.

The unified credit allows you to transfer more property tax-free to your spouse (when you transfer property that does not qualify for the marital deduction), to your children, or to whomever you want, than you could under the old laws. In other words, you can make the exemption equivalent (minus that portion of it that is represented by such things as the state taxes and administration costs that are not deducted for federal estate tax purposes but are consumed) available for enjoyment by one or more beneficiaries, without including in any person's transfer tax base any of that property that isn't left to that person.

Whether you should consider sheltering the exemption equivalent would depend on the amount of your and your spouse's combined transfers that are taxable for gift tax and estate tax purposes. Generally, you should shelter (rather than qualify for the marital deduction) such amount of your property as both (a) does not exceed your unused exemption equivalent and (b) would cause that spouse's taxable transfers to exceed his or her unused exemption equivalent if added to your spouse's property.

If, however, you died and your taxable estate for tax purposes were less than the exemption equivalent of $600,000, it does not matter whether you leave your property outright or otherwise, since no sheltering is necessary to eliminate estate tax and gift tax. For example:

Unified Credit Example

| | |
|---|---|
| Taxable estate valued at | $600,000 |
| Apply tax from table | $192,800 |
| Subtract unified credit | − 192,800 |
| Tentative tax due | –0– |

If, however, your taxable estate for tax purposes is over the exemption equivalent amount, you should consider some type of sheltering of the exemption equivalent in order to eliminate or reduce the gift tax and estate tax. For example: Assume that you have $650,000 and your spouse has nothing. Then only $50,000 of your exemption equivalent should be sheltered allowing an outright disposition of the $600,000.

Assume, however, that you died with a taxable estate of $120,000. Your estate tax would be $235,000 after application of a unified credit of $192,800. However, if you were to leave $600,000 to your surviving spouse (which would qualify for the marital deduction), your taxable estate would then be $600,000 and, after application of a unified credit of $192,800, your taxable estate would be zero. Naturally, these are simplified examples and you should consult your attorney and accountant for legal and financial advice in your planning.

## THE MARITAL DEDUCTION

The marital deduction is a deduction from the gross estate of the value of property that is included in your estate but is left to your surviving spouse under I.R.C. Section 2056.

To understand the marital deduction, you must first have a little understanding of the property laws in some of our states where Spanish and Napoleonic laws had an influence. These states (Arizona, California, Idaho, Louisiana, Nevada, New Mexico, Texas, and Washington, plus Wisconsin) are known as community property states, and the family property is automatically deemed to belong to both husband and wife equally. In all of the other states the English concept of property law is followed: ownership is attributed to the traditional head of the household, the husband.

The unlimited marital deduction brought major tax reform and eliminated many formerly significant distinctions between common law and community property states. It is unlimited because property that you leave your spouse goes to your spouse virtually tax free.

The marital deduction, which sounds like a bargain, might be a tax trap for the unwary. The marital deduction is actually a tax deferral provision and *not* a true deduction. What you have left your spouse will be taxed to your spouse's estate when he or she dies.

Property that is left to a surviving spouse must be made to qualify for the marital deduction, according to the I.R.S., and should be listed on Schedule M, Form 706. In order to qualify, the property—separate or community—must be left to the surviving spouse outright, with no strings attached.

Certain interests in property that you leave to your surviving spouse are referred to as *terminable interest.* This interest does not qualify for the marital deduction because it terminates or stops after the passage of time or upon the occurrence or nonoccurrence of some contingency. Examples are life estates, annuities, estates for terms of years, and patents.

A marital deduction would not necessarily be available for a life estate left to your surviving spouse, because the surviving spouse's interest terminates when he or she dies. However, you (or your executor) may elect the marital deduction for all or part of this interest if it meets the requirements of qualified terminable interest property (QTIP). (See I.R.C. Section 2056.) This election is made on the estate tax return. The term *qualified terminable interest property* (QTIP) refers to property that passes from the decedent in which the surviving spouse has a qualifying income interest for life. This will be discussed later in this chapter.

The idea behind the marital deduction is that the property passing to the surviving spouse is limited to property that will be taxable to his or her estate at death. And, when he or she dies, there will be no marital deduction to shelter the property for the children.

Social patterns in our society are and have changed, but the bulk of property in many families living in common law states is still legally regarded as belonging to the husband. Therefore, gifting to the other spouse is often necessary to make full use of the unified credit. This is not as much of a concern in community property states where most of the marital assets consist of community property.

If you want to leave your spouse with the maximum amount of property and the maximum control over that property, you should consider one of the following methods: (1) leave everything outright to your spouse, or (2) leave income "in trust" for your spouse giving him or her full powers (of appointment) to remove the trust principal either during life or at death (by will). A general power of appointment would enable the survivor to pay income from the trust to him or herself, to the estate, or to creditors.

## LIFE ESTATES

A life estate is an interest in property (generally real estate or interest income) that you leave to someone for his or her lifetime, and when that person, the beneficiary, dies, that property (known as the remainder interest) goes to another named beneficiary. For example: When Celeste V. Crawford died of cancer in 1984, her will said that her white Spitz dog, Teddy, could live in her home for the rest of his life allowing a named caretaker who had rented the basement apartment of her home since 1968 to stay there to look after the animal. When Teddy dies, this life estate would go to Mrs. Crawford's sisters and brothers. The remainder beneficiaries went to court seeking permission to sell the house and divide the proceeds. The Montgomery County Circuit judge ruled that they would have to wait until the dog's death.[4]

## DEDUCTIONS FOR CHARITABLE GIFTS

If your estate is large enough, you may wish to make a charitable gift. Charitable gifts are controlled by state and federal laws. Unlike the income tax provision, which prescribes a percentage limitation on the amount of donations you may make to a qualified charity, the federal estate tax places no limitation on the amount you may give away. However, if you are making a charitable gift, the gift must be either given outright, or, if you use a trust, the trust must conform to the requirements governing qualified charitable trusts, otherwise the estate tax charitable deduction will not be allowed. (See *Estate of Dyer*, Tax Ct. Memo 1990–51.)

Example: Sara Cassidy died leaving all but ten acres of her 235-acre farm in trust for the benefit of her son, Paul, during his lifetime. At Paul's

---

[4] Savannah *News-Press*. Jennifer Brandlon, "Well-Off Dog Escapes Date With Tattooer." Saturday, June 24, 1989. p. 10-A.

death, the farm was to be given to the Episcopal Theological Seminary in Kentucky, a qualified charity. The I.R.S. and the Tax Court denied Sara's estate an estate tax charitable deduction for the remainder interest in the farm because the bequest was not in the form required by the I.R.S. for a qualified charitable remainder trust, nor was it a gift outright to the charity. (Estate of *Cassidy* v. *Comm'r*, 49 T.C.M. 580, 1985).

A charitable remainder annuity trust is a trust from which a specified amount is paid at least annually to one or more persons who were living at the time the trust was created. At the death of the income beneficiary, the remainder interest must be held for the benefit of a qualified charitable organization or paid to it. Any other form of charitable remainder interest will not qualify for the charitable deduction.

Something that you may easily overlook if you are making a charitable gift in your will or trust is the name of the charitable institution itself. In most instances, you may have a particular national, state, or local charity in mind. The problem, however, is that many charities have very similar names and certain of these charities are interrelated. Therefore, in order to avoid confusion and ambiguity later, make sure you designate a charitable beneficiary by using a correct name. In this way, the charitable institution is clearly identified in your will or trust.

## YOUR SPOUSE'S ESTATE TAX

There may be no tax due when you die if you leave everything to your spouse; however, there is no longer any marital deduction for the surviving spouse's estate (assuming your spouse doesn't remarry or leaves the assets to others than the new spouse). The full amount of the estate is subject to tax: everything that was left when you died and everything that has been accumulated in the survivor's name alone. This is known as the "federal one-two punch"—a light jab followed by a haymaker. Because of it, more than one-fifth of everything a family has managed to accumulate over a working lifetime will go to the government, unless they do something about it.

What will the surviving spouse's estate tax be? Fill out Chart 15 (Figure 3–4) to find out.

## GIFTS AND TRANSFERS (TRUSTS)

If you make a gift, directly or through a trust, to another person, but you retain one of the three types of interests in the property, then the value of that property will be included in your estate for tax purposes according to I.R.C. Section 3026. The three types of retained interests are (1) the possession (or enjoyment) of the property transferred; (2) the right to the income from the property transferred; or (3) the right to designate the person who may possess (or enjoy) the property or income from the property. In other words, these gifts or transfers you have made will be subject to estate taxes because of the nature of the transfer. The Internal Revenue Service's underlying theory is that you may not have made a complete gift or transfer during your lifetime; that you have not divested yourself of all benefits or control over the property; and that until your death there is not complete or unrestricted enjoyment of the property. That is, there is evidence of an "incident of ownership."

In these instances, because you have retained a "string" on the property, the entire fair market value of the property will be included in your gross estate for tax purposes. For example: If you retain 50 percent of the net income from an irrevocable trust until you die, then 50 percent of the fair market value of the trust estate, at your death, will be included in your gross estate.

Another example might be that you have transferred 700 acres of farm land by gift to your son, but you continue to collect the income from the farm and continue to otherwise use the farm until you die. In this instance, the entire value of the farm land, at your death, would be included in your gross estate. But, if you did not collect the income and only lived on, say, one acre of the farm land, then only the value of that one acre would be included in your gross estate.

In summary, a federal tax is imposed on certain types of transfers—gifts and trusts—that you make. Either you, the person making the gift (the donor), must pay the tax, or the person receiving the gift (the donee) may have to pay the tax.

If you give a gift that is over the annual exclusion during a calendar year, you must file Form 709, United States Gift Tax Return, for that year. However, you don't have to file if the transfer is under the annual exclusion or if you make a transfer to your spouse (because of the unlimited marital deduction). Generally, Form 709 must be filed by April 15th of the year after the year you made the gift with the Internal Revenue Service serving the state in which you are a legal resident.

Have you made any gifts that are subject to gift taxes? If so, copies of deeds or gift tax returns related to the gifts, together with evidence of their ownership, should be attached to Chart 16, "Gifts and Trusts," as should copies of trust agreements. (See also Table 3–3.)

Any gifts you have made during your lifetime for which you had to file a gift tax return can reduce the amount or value of property that you can transfer at your death. This is because the estate and gift tax is calculated from the same table and taxed at the same rate. Gifts and estates are taxed under one progressive rate schedule that is called a "unified" tax table. You might say that your estate is your last gift.

**Table 3–3.** Example: Transfers during your life.

| Item no. | Description of gift | Date and value of gift |
|---|---|---|
| 1. | No taxable gifts made | –0– |
| 2. | Hayday Life Insurance Company Policy #2345CH; beneficiary, Janice Harvey; insurance transferred to Janice Harvey, daughter, on March 4, 1982; proceeds payable in one sum. Form 712 to be attached should death occur. | $50,000 |

## TESTAMENTARY TRUSTS

Estate planning for married persons has dramatically changed over the years. If you have competent reasons for not devising all of your estate to your surviving spouse, then the estate plan you may have incorporated is the familiar two trust plan: Trust A and Trust B.

Trust A gives the surviving spouse income for life. In Trust B, the surviving spouse gets interest income annually (or on a more frequent basis) along with the power to invade principal annually for the greater of $5,000 or 5 percent of the principal. At the death of the spouse, this trust is dissolved and the assets are distributed to the children. There is no tax savings upon the first spouse's death. The tax savings, if any, are deferred until the surviving spouse's subsequent death. (See Table 3–4.)

To examine the federal estate consequences of the marital deduction in community property and common law states, assume a Trust A/Trust B arrangement has been used in both places. The will of each spouse makes a gift either outright or into a marital deduction trust (Trust A) for the survivor with the remaining assets going to Trust B (the unified credit trust). Assume there are $1.6 million in assets in the community property state and the same amount of assets are held as separate property by the husband in the common law state.

Example in the community property state: Since the marital assets are community property, the tax due would be $153,000 no matter which spouse dies first. Suppose H (husband) died first. H's gross estate would equal $800,000 (one-half $1.6 million) minus a marital deduction of the property passing to Trust A ($200,000 in this instance). No tax would be due on the resulting taxable estate of $600,000 (passing to Trust B). As survivor, W's (wife) taxable estate of $1,000,000 ($800,000 plus $200,000 marital deduction) is subject to $153,000 federal estate tax (tentative estate tax of $345,800 minus the unified credit of $192,800 = $153,000 federal estate tax).

Example of property held in H's name alone in a common law state: The computations would differ, however, the result would be the same as

**Table 3–4.** Testamentary trusts.

| MARITAL TRUST "A" | FAMILY TRUST "B" |
| --- | --- |
| 1. All income paid to spouse. | 1. Income paid to spouse or others. |
| 2. Trustee may use principal for spouse's benefit. | 2. Trustee may use principal for spouse and greater of $5,000 or 5% of B's assets. |
| 3. Spouse would have at least one of the following powers:<br>a) to appoint all while living<br>b) to appoint all by will | 3. No taxable power for spouse.<br>a) no power to withdraw or appoint<br>b) right to income determined by trustee, NOT spouse |
| 4. Qualifies for marital deduction | 4. Does NOT qualify for marital deduction unless<br>a) general power of appointment or<br>b) QTIP election |
| 5. Taxed in surviving spouse's estate. | 5. Taxed to surviving spouse's estate to extent value exceeds unified credit. |
| 6. Not taxed in decendent's estate. | 6. Trust B taxed to other's not spouse's estate . . .<br>QTIP Trust—taxed to surviving spouse's estate. |

in the example above if H died first: $153,000 total tax due. H's gross estate of $1,600,000 minus $1,000,000 marital deduction (left to Trust A) equals a taxable estate of $600,000 (going to Trust B). No federal estate taxes would be due on H's death. But his wife's taxable estate of $1,000,000 would result in $153,000 federal estate taxes due at her later death. The results would be quite different if the wife were to die first (as the unified credit would remain unused by her or her estate) and H were to die later. H's taxable estate of $1,600,000 would owe federal estate taxes in the amount of $408,000 (tentative tax of $600,800 minus unified credit of $192,800 = $408,000). The solution would have been for H to make a lifetime gift of $600,000 to his wife. If he had done this, the tax would have been reduced to $153,000.

# QTIP TRUSTS

Qualified terminable interest property (QTIP) trust is a way for you to control the disposition of the principal of the marital deduction trust on the death of your surviving spouse. You will get a full marital deduction on the amount of property passing to the QTIP trust while the ultimate gift in trust goes to whomever you have selected. It is similar to a B Trust, except the surviving spouse has only a life interest in the property, and dissimilar to a B Trust in that it does qualify for the marital deduction.

Even though the surviving spouse must receive all the interest income for life, payable at least annually, it may not be something he or she is in favor of. Why? The right to use and enjoy the property "terminates" with death, and, the survivor cannot control who is to get the property even though it is taxed in the survivor's estate when he or she dies! Because of this, many states give a surviving spouse the right to elect against the decedent spouse's will. And, the surviving spouse could "disclaim" or "renounce" the share under the will. If the survivor makes a proper disclaimer (or renunciation) with respect to any interest in the property, then such an action is treated as though the interest were never transferred to him or her in the first place. Arguments in favor of QTIP are: It is for a second or childless marriage; it protects children from a previous or current marriage if the surviving spouse remarries; and it protects the surviving spouse who may be susceptible to pressures from others, such as a confused elderly person. QTIP is not for everyone.

## SUMMARY CHECKLIST FOR PREPARATION
## OF THE FEDERAL ESTATE TAX RETURN

| | *Attached* | *N/A* |
|---|---|---|
| 1. A certified copy of the will if decedent died testate. | _____ | ____ |
| 2. A certified copy of Letters Testamentary. | _____ | ____ |
| 3. A copy of the death certificate. | _____ | ____ |
| 4. Assist with inventory of safe deposit box; list of contents excluded from gross estate. | _____ | ____ |
| 5. See that an "Estate Checking" account is set up (All receipts and disbursements pertaining to the estate must go through this account). | _____ | ____ |
| 6. Obtain form 4768 if extension of time to file or pay has been granted. | _____ | ____ |
| 7. Notice of election where installment payment of estate tax on closely held business interest is elected; and copy of consent required if special lien is elected for payment of deferred tax. | _____ | ____ |

8. List of executors' social security numbers if there is more than one individual executor.  _____  ____

9. Notice of election and signed agreement where special use valuation is elected.  _____  ____

10. Additional notice of election where special treatment for qualified woodlands is elected.  _____  ____

11. Copies of federal gift tax returns (Forms 709 and 709-A).  _____  ____

12. Form 712 from life insurance company that lists beneficiaries and shows owner of policy.  _____  ____

13. Copies of any trusts not created by decedent but under which decedent had an interest.  _____  ____

    a. Statement regarding certain lifetime transfers.

    b. Powers of appointment instruments.

14. Copies of any trusts created by decedent.  _____  ____

15. Copy of written instrument of charitable transfer.  _____  ____

16. Certificate of payment of state inheritance taxes.  _____  ____

17. Copy of any buy-sell agreements, partnership agreements, or the like.  _____  ____

18. Real estate appraisals.  _____  ____

19. Practice appraisal.  _____  ____

20. List of property qualifying for marital deduction. (Claim a marital deduction for qualified terminable interest property also.)  _____  ____

**Figure 3–1.** CHART 12: Your Gross Estate.

| ITEM NO. | GROSS ESTATE | VALUE |
|---|---|---|
| 1. | Property from net worth section (Chapter 2) | |
| | Chart 1: Real estate (Figure 2–2) | $ _____ |
| | Chart 2: Special valuation property (Figure 2–3) | $ _____ |
| | Chart 3: Stocks and bonds (Figure 2–4) | $ _____ |
| | Chart 4: Retirement plans, notes, cash (Figure 2–5) | $ _____ |
| | Chart 5: Life insurance (face value) (Figure 2–6) | $ _____ |
| | Chart 6: Jointly owned property totals (Figure 2–7) | $ _____ |
| | or | |
| | Chart 7: Separately owned property (Figure 2–8) | |
| | (for those in community property states) | |
| | plus | |
| | Community property | $ _____ |
| | Chart 8: Miscellaneous property totals (Figure 2–9) | $ _____ |
| 2. | Dower or curtesy interest | $ _____ |
| 3. | Custodial gifts | $ _____ |
| 4. | Transfers with retained interest | $ _____ |
| | (Clifford trusts and revocable transfers) | |
| 5. | Annuities | $ _____ |
| 6. | Powers of appointment | $ _____ |
| 7. | Lottery winnings | $ _____ |
| | GROSS ESTATE | $ _____ |

Copyright © 1991 by Practice Management Information Corp.

**Figure 3–2.** CHART 13: Federal Estate Taxes.

| | |
|---|---|
| 1. Gross estate | $ _____ |
| Deductions: | |
| Final expenses as medical and funeral | $ _____ |
| Administrative expenses | $ _____ |
| | $ _____ |
| 2. Subtract total deductions from gross estate | − _____ |
| 3. Result: Adjusted Gross Estate (AGE) | $ _____ |
| 4. Total deductions: Marital _____ | |
| Charity bequests _____ | |
| 5. Sales to employee stock ownership plans | − _____ |
| 6. Subtract total deductions in item 4 from (AGE) | − _____ |
| 7. Result: Your taxable estate | $ _____ |
| 8. Add your taxable gifts made after 12/31/76 | + _____ |
| 9. Result: Total estate and gifts | $ _____ |
| 10. Apply tax from tax table to item 9 | $ _____ |
| 11. Deduct tax you paid on taxable gifts in item 8 | − _____ |
| 12. Deduct Unified Credit | − _____ |
| 13. Result: Your net estate tax | $ _____ |
| (without such credits as state taxes, etc.) | |

Copyright © 1991 by Practice Management Information Corp.

**Figure 3–3.** CHART 14: Gross Estate Adjusted for Community Property.

| | |
|---|---|
| 1. Gross Estate | $ _____ |
| 2. Less: a. Community Property interest | − _____ |
| b. Proportion of allowable expenses, | − _____ |
| etc. | |

$$\left( \frac{\text{sep. prop.}}{\text{gross estate}} \times \text{deductible expenses} \right)$$

| | |
|---|---|
| 3. Total reductions from line 2 (a) and (b) | − $ _____ |
| 4. Adjusted Gross Estate (line 1 minus line 2) | $ _____ |
| | _____ |

Copyright © 1991 by Practice Management Information Corp.

**Figure 3–4.** CHART 15: What Will the Surviving Spouse's Tax Be?

1. What is the value of property passing to your spouse under your will? _____
2. Life insurance proceeds owned by spouse: _____
3. QTIP (qualified terminable interest property): _____
4. The value of business interest owned by your spouse: _____
5. Estimate the value of property your spouse will receive through gift or inheritance from another: _____
6. Property in spouse's name (fair market value) _____

Total value of spouse's estate: $ _____

Tentative tax from table $ _____
Less unified credit  − _____
Net estate tax payable  $ _____

**Figure 3–5.** CHART 16: Transfers During Life (Gifts and Trusts).

| Item no. | Description | How distributed | Cost | Value | Owner | Trustee | Beneficiary |
|----------|-------------|-----------------|------|-------|-------|---------|-------------|
| | | | | | | | |
| | | | | | | | |
| | | | | | | | |
| | | | | | | | |
| | | | | | | | |
| | | | | | | | |
| | | | | | | | |
| | | | | | | | |
| | | | | | | | |
| | | | | | | | |
| | | | | | | | |

# 4

# JOINT OWNERSHIP: JOINT TROUBLE?

For most couples, marriage brings the concept of owning things together rather than owning things individually. One doctor summed up the situation—and the problem—very nicely when he said confidently: "My wife and I own everything jointly, because it bypasses probate. If I should die first, my wife will be spared all the hassle, publicity, and expense connected with it."

What the doctor said is true—depending, of course, upon the *type* of joint ownership he has. But like most people, he considers "avoiding probate" reason enough, without weighing the other issues involved. And, it may be that avoiding taxes is what we should be most concerned with.

Joint ownership, however, has been and still is the prevailing way in which married couples hold title to their real estate and other types of assets. But many people who hold joint titles are totally unaware of the potential pitfalls. If you and your spouse, or you and someone else, own or are planning to purchase property jointly, be sure you understand the disadvantages as well as the advantages of such a purchase, including the type of ownership involved in the state where the property is located and the legality of living together (if you aren't married).

## TYPES OF JOINT OWNERSHIP

Joint ownership is a common term of owning property with another person. The *type* of joint ownership, however, may affect the title and the tax

**Table 4–1.** Examples of joint ownership.

---

**(1) JOINT TENANCY WITH RIGHT OF SURVIVORSHIP**
A and B own property jointly.
A dies.
B now owns the property.

**(2) JOINT TENANCY BY THE ENTIRETY**
Husband and Wife own property jointly.
Husband dies.
Wife now owns property.

**(3) JOINT TENANCY IN COMMON**
A, B, and C own property jointly.
A dies.
B, C, and A's heirs own property.

**(4) COMMUNITY PROPERTY**
Husband and Wife own property 50/50 each.
Husband dies.
Wife owns one-half. Husband's half is distributed by will or state law.

---

consequences produced by each. A sale may be lost because of the inability to convey or transfer a good title, not to mention the fact that reopening an estate to process a half or a fractional interest, as well as amending tax returns, can be costly.

The key element of survivorship is in two types of ownership: (1) joint ownership with right of survivorship and (2) joint ownership by the entirety, which means that, when one owner dies, the other automatically, by right of survivorship, becomes the sole owner of the property. "Tenancy by the entirety" is not recognized by a majority of states, and ownership in this type of property is by right of survivorship but is restricted to married couples (husbands and wives), whereas, "joint ownership with right of survivorship" may be used by singles as well as married couples. (See Table 4–1.)

One dangerous misconception of joint ownership is that it is often seen as a substitute for a will. Joint ownership does guarantee that the surviving owner will become sole owner when his or her joint owner dies (if it is with the right of survivorship). And with such advantages beginning to line up, no wonder couples want to own things jointly.

## DANGERS FOR SURVIVORS

Besides benefits, there are dangers lurking in joint titles: Two or more people can co-own property without the property being subject to the key element of "survivorship." That is, if you hold title to property as "tenants in common," there is no right of survivorship, and your will controls what happens to your share of the property.

If you don't leave a will, the disposition of your property will be by the intestate laws of your state. That is, your share of the property will be divided up according to the state's scheme of who gets what under a legal device called the *law of escheat*. What the law says is that, when no legal owner of property can be found and heirs cannot be located, ownership goes to the individual state after the state's statute of limitations has run.

Even though two or more people may co-own this type of property, each joint tenant-in-common owner may have different, *unequal* interests in the same property.

Arizona, California, Idaho, Louisiana, Nevada, New Mexico, Texas, and Washington, plus Wisconsin are called community property states. In these states, salaries and assets acquired during marriage are considered to be owned 50/50 by the spouses. When one spouse dies, his or her half of the property is disposed of by will or by the state's intestate laws, just the same as tenancy in common property. The results could be far different from the outcome you desired.

Because of the public attitude toward probate proceedings, techniques such as joint ownership (jointly owned property) have developed in order to avoid probate. Depending upon the type of ownership, jointly owned property is *not* a substitute for a will.

## LIFETIME DANGERS

So far, you have seen what happens after you die. But let us not overlook what joint ownership means while you are alive. It may seem like the answer to an economic partnership, giving harmony and peace of mind, utterly sensible and risk-free because a joint title does mean sharing control over the property.

But depending upon what is involved, your joint owner could exercise full control over the joint bank account, mutual funds, or brokerage accounts.

Joint ownership could be to your detriment when real estate or registered stocks are involved, and you are stymied in an attempt to sell if the joint owner does not approve.

Other problems develop with joint property when a married couple gets a divorce. And assets could be jeoparized if a creditor makes a claim against one of the joint owners.

Even more of a problem is the relationship of living together without being married. If you do not know your legal and economic position, you may face major problems later. This will be discussed later in the chapter.

## Tax Snarls

Too much jointly owned property may threaten your family's financial survival and your goal of minimizing federal estate taxes. That might not seem like much of a problem to you, because under current law you can leave an unlimited amount to your spouse free of federal estate tax plus an additional amount known as the unified credit to other beneficiaries or heirs before Uncle Sam takes a bit of your estate. The tax-free unified credit amounts are in addition to whatever you leave your spouse (which will be brought back into his or her estate for tax purposes when he or she dies).

For estate tax purposes, 100 percent of the value of jointly owned property will be included in the gross estate of a deceased joint tenant, except to the extent that the surviving joint tenant can establish an independent contribution to the acquisition of such property. However, a special rule applies to joint interest (in any form) held by spouses: only one-half of the property is included in the gross estate of the first to die, regardless of the consideration furnished by each spouse toward the purchase price, and the surviving spouse does not get a *stepped-up basis* for the one-half of the property that is excluded from the gross estate. The word *basis* is used by accountants. A very simplified definition would be the original purchase price that you paid for a piece of property. Generally, the basis of property acquired or passed from a decedent is the property's fair market value at the applicable estate tax valuation date. (See I.R.C. Sections 1014(a) and 1015.)

When someone dies, the I.R.S. allows what is called a *stepped-up basis* on the decedent's share of the property. This means that the property's fair market value on date of death now becomes the basis (or purchase price) of that property. In other words, it has been stepped-up to equal its fair market value. Therefore, it would make sense to own separately property that appreciates in value. There may be nontax reasons for owning property jointly, but there is rarely a tax advantage for joint ownership.

Since your estate will include the future growth of your net worth, and the rule is that only half the value of jointly owned property goes into the estate of the first person to die, this can and does result in increased taxes for the survivor. You may have avoided probate, but have you avoided taxes?

Assume that the husband and wife own their home jointly with right of survivorship. Assume that the original price (basis) was $75,000 and that, when the husband died, the fair market value of the house on the date of death was $250,000. Only half the property will be included in the husband's estate at death. This one-half gets a stepped-up basis and qualifies for the marital deduction; the other half does not. The wife holds the same basis in her half of the house ($37,500, which is half of the original purchase price of $75,000) plus the new basis from her husband's half ($125,000) to give her a basis of $162,500.

## Example of Jointly Owned Property

| | | |
|---|---:|---:|
| Original purchase price of home | | $ 75,000 |
| Fair market value at husband's death | | $250,000 |
| Original basis for wife | $ 37,500 | |
| Husband's stepped-up basis | +125,000 | |
| Wife's New Basis | $162,500 | |

Assume further that the wife sells the house for the fair market value of $250,000. The wife now has a reportable gain of $87,500 on which her income taxes will be based even though only half the value of the house was included in her husband's estate. If, however, the house is never sold, her basis (original purchase price) for estate purposes would be the $162,500. The difference between this basis and the property's fair market value on date of death would be what was included in her estate for tax purposes. The following example shows both this and what would happen if the wife later sells the house for its fair market value. The difference, however, is that, with appreciation, the house's fair market value on date of death may be even greater than it is right after the husband died.

## Example of House Sold by Wife for Fair Market Value

### "A TAX TRAP"

| | |
|---|---:|
| Fair market value of house | $250,000 |
| Wife's new basis | − 162,500 |
| Basis for tax gain (loss) | $ 87,500 |

Even though there were no estate taxes on the husband's one-half because of the unlimited marital deduction, there was a different tax that must be considered: income taxes!

Consider the same property, but this time the property is held in the husband's name alone as fee simple owner that he leaves to his wife via a will. The entire value would receive a stepped-up basis, equal to the fair market value at the date of the husband's death. Since the husband is now sole owner of the property, at his death, the basis of the property would be stepped-up to $250,000. On its subsequent sale, assuming a price of $250,000, no tax would be due. The wife has no reportable gain since she received a stepped-up basis when her husband died, and the property wasn't owned jointly.

## Example of Property Held in Husband's Name Alone

| | | |
|---|---:|---:|
| Original purchase price of home | | $ 75,000 |
| Fair market value at husband's death | | $250,000 |
| Sale of house for fair market value | $250,000 | |
| Stepped-up basis | − 250,000 | |
| Tax gain (loss) | -0- | |

As you can see from the examples, jointly owned property may have a lifetime of income tax consequences.

## Problems Involving Joint Accounts and Safe Deposit Boxes

Income from jointly owned bank accounts, mutual funds, or brokerage accounts is generally taxable according to the contributions of each owner. Where only one contributes money, a gift may occur on the right of the other joint owner to withdraw funds from the account (since only one has to put in the money). For example: Dr. and Mrs. Louis Zetter maintained a joint bank account into which they deposited all their money. Right before her husband's death, Mrs. Zetter made withdrawals totaling $20,000 and deposited this money into her own savings accounts. She considered the withdrawals as belonging to her. But after Dr. Zetter died, the I.R.S. included the $20,000 in his estate as a gift.

Joint bank accounts and safe deposit boxes may pose an even greater problem. Most states freeze accounts and seal safe deposit boxes at the death of one joint owner until opened by a Court Order (which is generally after the probate of a will). This poses the question: Are safe deposit boxes really safe? After the Court Order to open a sealed box is granted, a complete inventory is made of everything in that box. Most states have this law, even though some banks do not actively enforce it. And what happens if the will is kept inside and it takes days before a Court Order is issued? What if there are specific funeral instructions included?

Dr. and Mrs. Wright, for example, rented a safe deposit box in joint names. When Dr. Wright died, their state sealed the box until a Court Order was issued. With the Court Order, the box was opened by the bank authorities in the presence of Mrs. Wright.

An inventory was made of all the items in the box. Inside it was nearly $35,000 worth of gold coins and stock certificates. Dr. Wright's will left half his estate to his wife and half to be divided equally among his grown children. Mrs. Wright claimed everything in the box, since it had been held jointly with her husband.

The results: three years later, after thousands of dollars were spent on legal fees, the case was settled in favor of the children. Tax advantages, as you can see, aren't the only considerations when you are deciding what to do with joint property or whether to hold title jointly.

There are pluses and minuses of joint ownership. However, all the confusion in the Wright estate might have been avoided if the safe deposit box had *not* been rented jointly.

## Joint Ownership Not a Substitute for a Will!

Millions of people put all types of property in joint names. Are they building up the possibility that it might explode in five, ten, twenty, or more years from now, as in the Wrights' case? Jointly owned property can be transferred at death without administration, but not without taxes. And what would happen to the property if both of you were to die in a common disaster? Remember that jointly owned property is *not* a will substitute! Careful planning, keeping in mind the different kinds of situations that may arise and the different types of ownership, can maximize your tax and nontax advantages for the recipient of your property.

Since the state laws vary, and since what happens to your property will depend upon the state where the property is located, review the type of property ownership and your family's financial survival plan. After all, you may have avoided probate, but have you avoided taxes? The spouse you save may be your own!

## THE LEGALITY OF LIVING TOGETHER AND OWNING PROPERTY JOINTLY

As recently as a dozen years ago people seldom talked about it, and if they did, "living together" was discussed in whispers. Nice people would not think of such a thing, and nice magazines wouldn't touch the subject with a ten-foot pole. But times have changed, and so have attitudes. Today more than one-and-a-half million unmarried men and women are openly living together, and a substantial number of those who choose this alternative lifestyle are professional couples.

### Points to Ponder

Most couples who are living together or are planning to do so will say: "We're in love, and we've given this serious thought. We feel we don't need all the legal hassles that go with being married. We don't need a license and certificate to prove our love. We trust each other, that's enough!" It may be enough right now. Unfortunately, people and situations change. Suppose that four or five years—or even ten years—from now this ideal couple comes to the parting of the ways. Sadly, the results may bring them even more difficult legal hassles and trauma than a divorce.

For example, in the state of Washington, a certain couple lived together. The woman believed that they were legally married. However, the man had neglected to tell her that he was already married. The state Supreme Court ruled that this woman was entitled only to a share of the share of the couple's community property because there was an implied contract between them.

A better-known example is the case of actor Lee Marvin who was sued in 1976 by Michelle Triola Marvin for $3.6 million (half the money he earned during the six years they lived together).[1] She claimed that there was an

---

[1] *Marvin v Marvin*, 18 Cal. 3rd 660, 557 P.2d 106 (1976), 122 Cal. App. 3d 871, 176 Cal. Rptr. 555 (2nd Dist. 1981).

unwritten agreement—an oral contract—that the couple would share and share alike. This case set a precedent giving her the right to trial on that basis. She did not win her case, but the judge did award her $104,000 as a going-away token to provide her with "the economic means to re-educate herself and to learn new employable skills." This award was later overturned after a long legal battle and high court costs and attorneys' fees.

Actor Nick Nolte was sued by model Karen Eklund for a settlement based on their six years of living together. British rock star, Peter Frampton, also faced a suit brought by his former live-in companion, Penelope McCall, for the five years they lived together.

Granted, these cases involve celebrities, but the important thing is that these suits have set a precedent. In the past, such cases were not recognized as a basis for trial. Naturally, any individual in the high-income bracket is most likely to be the target of such a court suit. Doctors and other professionals are particularly vulnerable.

If you think living with another person without marriage is your lifestyle preference, then it is wise to document individual and joint possessions. Even though the media features movie stars and other public figures who are having these difficulties, it is not only the famous and wealthy who end up in court because of cohabitation or a meretricious relationship.

Presently, there is still discrimination against couples who are not married. However, if this live-in lifestyle continues to grow as it has during the past ten years, the laws are bound to change. Meanwhile, you must live with them as they are—which means that your own protection is largely up to you. The bottom line is that, if you and your companion are living together, you may be forced to recognize the legal implications of your relationship whether you want to or not.

## Other Problems

What happens if you are injured on the job? As a wife you would be entitled to workers compensation, but, if you are not married, you are out of luck. Each state has laws of intestacy (inheritance) and, although they differ from state to state, no state will allow a non-heir to receive a deceased's property. Again, you are out of luck. A live-in companion is not entitled to anything. Even if you do draw up a valid will, the inheritance tax on such legacies will usually be much higher than anticipated, since you will not be allowed the usual benefits allowed a married couple under the Federal Estate and Gift Tax law, such as the unlimited marital deduction.

## Palimony

You may think that you do not have any valuable assets, especially compared to the assets of a media celebrity. Think again. What about your television set? Your records, tapes, and stereo. Perhaps even your car.

If an agreement, expressed or implied, written or oral, can be shown to have existed, you may be subject to a palimony suit. What is *palimony*? It is an award or settlement given to an unmarried person if that person can show that there was an agreement to share property and earnings while that person and another lived together. It is easier to prove a case in which there is a written agreement rather than an oral agreement, however, an oral agreement *is* a valid contract in law. And, in some instances, the mere fact of cohabitation will imply a contract—even if there is no agreement of any kind—as long as it can be shown that a division of property was anticipated. Just "sleeping over" once in awhile is not the same as cohabitation. Generally it must be shown that the couple lived together and held themselves out openly (to others) as being married. The question as to whether a valid contract exists is still unclear in law today, but the principle that allows you to claim property rights when you are unmarried and living together in a meretricious relationship has been established.

Cohabitation claims have been considered by courts since the famous *Marvin* v *Marvin* case (122 Cal. App. 3d 871, 176 Cal. Rptr. 555 (2d Dist., 1981)) to distinguish between permissible contractual claims based on acceptable consideration and impermissible claims based solely on sexual services. In *Suggs* v *Norris* (364 S.E. 2d 1959 (N.C. App. 1988)), the court considered whether an unmarried but cohabiting partner may file a claim against the decedent's estate for services rendered to the couple's joint business. It reached the conclusion that a claimant may submit a claim using either an equitable trust or a quantum merit theory, which means that the claimant is to be paid the amount (in services or cash) contributed.

And, there may be other theories by which a cohabiting partner may prevail. In *Knott* v *Vachal* (752 P.2d 39 (Ariz. App. 1988)), the survivor claimed entitlement to property, alleging an express agreement to create a joint tenancy. The court agreed that unmarried cohabitants can contract to own property in joint ownership.

Living together, in some states, still attaches the label of bearing on moral turpitude. In Georgia, as in some other states, a divorced mother may not be able to get custody of her children if she is cohabitating with a man other than her husband. The same is true in Illinois as being against "public policy."

## Put It in Writing!

No one likes to think about death, injury, or even the possible breakup of a relationship. But from a legal standpoint, living together without being married may not provide a firm position *unless* some type of *written* agreement exists.

A written agreement may begin with a list of the major items that each person brought into the relationship. It is wiser to avoid joint ownership, but, if a couple decides to purchase items together, the proportionate shares of ownership should be spelled out. The question of settling debts should be decided at the beginning in case the partnership splits up, or if one moves out, and the other is left with the bills.

It is wise to consider having a waiver of all financial claims on each other, which would state clearly that:

- neither plans to share earnings and property with the other;
- property acquired while living together belongs to the person who paid for it;
- any agreements to share property must be in writing;
- compensation is not expected for services rendered the other;
- there is no obligation for either one to support the other.

The contract should be concerned only with *legal* obligations and identities, *not* with the love and affection each holds for each other while living together. Trust is wonderful, but don't misplace it. What is said in the contract is up to the individuals involved, but it must be clear, and it must be *in writing*. Remember, the best way to insure a lasting friendship is to avoid misunderstandings from the beginning. It is not a question of "Don't you trust me?" Instead, it is a positive step toward strengthening the relationship by clarifying what each expects, plus a protective device against bitter battles and expensive legal fees in case the couple separates.

You might consider putting in writing what each of you expects financially from the arrangement. If your lists are the same, you have a basis for an agreement. If they are not, this is the time to resolve the differences before they lead to bitterness later on. The economic, legal, and psychological point of view is invaluable.

Avoid unnecessary problems, keep separate bank accounts and credit cards. Keep a record of your expenses. These five areas deserve particular consideration:

- *Housing.* If you purchase a house together, make sure both names are on the deed and both have signed the mortgage. Each should be liable for one-half of the down payment, mortgage, insurance, and utility bills. If you sell, you should have it in writing that you will divide the proceeds equally. If just one of you wants to sell, the other should have the first option to buy the other's share.
- *Insurance.* Insurance companies look upon people's living together as a liability. A homeowner's policy may not cover the other person if he or she is not your spouse or an overnight guest, but instead is a boarder in the home. To make payment of claims easier, both names should be on the policy.
- *Taxes.* Here you have an advantage over married couples. Each of you is allowed a higher standard deduction than most married couples are allowed. Being unmarried, you can either itemize or not. Married couples

take the same deductions even if they file separately. Unmarried couples with large deductions can either split the deductions or shift them to the person who would get the bigger tax break. There are 19 states that prohibit cohabitation. However, taxation may not fall in your favor either. If one of you works and the other stays at home, the one at home does not qualify for the dependency exemption, or for any other deduction that may be allowed.

• *Separation.* It may appear that cohabitation has the advantage of offering the easiest way out—an open door. However, if the parting is not amicable, there are no reliable rules with which one may go to Court.

• *Survivor's rights.* What happens if the other person dies? Will you be out in the cold? If you are married, you will probably be entitled to a share of your spouse's estate, even if you are not mentioned in the will. When you are not married, you had better have a good will! Who is the beneficiary of the other's life insurance policy? Who is the owner of that policy? Some group plans sponsored by employers permit only spouses (and ex-spouses) to collect, so it is important to check those policies you are holding. Pension (or retirement) plan payments, also, may only be transferred to a surviving spouse.

You might find that trying to avoid those financial responsibilities of marriage has in reality created greater complications for you than if you married. Very few state courts have recognized that "all unmarried persons have the right to claim a share of property and earnings, if they can show that an agreement existed while they were living together. There may not have to be a written or spoken agreement; the fact of cohabitation itself can imply a contract." Courts in Illinois, Minnesota, New York, New Jersey, Oregon, Utah, Washington, and California (to name a few) have ruled in a similar way. Other states, like Georgia, have rejected this claim altogether.

Instead of just leaving your assets and the future to chance, you could take charge of your life with a written contract. And isn't that what most people want? If you are living with someone or plan such an arrangement, keep in mind that there are laws to protect marriage partners, but these same rights are in much dispute regarding unmarried couples. Since there may be no laws to protect you, it's up to you to protect yourself. These guidelines will help you.

• Draw up a written agreement before you move in together. This contract should spell out in detail who gets what and who pays what if there should be a separation later.

• List all property each party brought into the relationship. There should be two copies of each list, and both should sign both lists.

• Later, if one or the other of you buys an item during the relationship, the item, price, and date should be added to the list, and both should initial the addition.

- Do not buy anything jointly. In case of a breakup, it is easier if various items are owned outright by one or the other.
- Maintain separate checking accounts. If there should be trouble later, remember that one party can *legally* wipe out that account, and the other partner has no recourse.
- Do not have joint savings accounts, either. Of course, you can request two signatures for withdrawals, but even this can cause trouble. If the other party leaves in an angry huff, he or she can refuse to co-sign a withdrawal, thereby tying up your funds.
- If you are renting an apartment or house, both of your names should be on the lease.
- Do not have joint charge accounts or give the other person an additional credit card on your account. It is easier to keep track of finance charges if credit cards are kept separate.
- Do not co-sign the other person's loans, since that makes you responsible for his or her debt—even if you are no longer living together.
- You should have some life insurance naming your live-in companion as the beneficiary. The amount should at least cover your funeral expenses. In the event of an accident your companion should not be burdened with such expenses. (Remember that insurance carriers do not recognize a live-in companion as a spouse.)
- If yours is a serious relationship, be sure that your companion is included in your will, with clear instructions as to what you want your companion to have. If you do not do this, your family or relatives can make a solid claim on all your property.
- Be sure to include in your agreement, any pets you have acquired during the relationship. The decision as to who gets custody of a beloved dog, cat, or horse at breakup time can be traumatic psychologically as well as financially.
- Do not forget that laws vary from state to state. It is wise, therefore, to consult an accountant, banker, and attorney regarding the laws of your region.

A sample agreement for living together appears in Appendix C.

# 5

---

# DISPERSING YOUR ESTATE THROUGH GIFTS AND TRUSTS

There is a long list of credits, exemptions, deductions, and shelters that can reduce the amount of federal income tax that you pay annually. But when it comes to estate taxes, you can deduct only funeral and administrative expenses, losses during administration, charitable and marital deductions, and debts of the deceased.

So what can you do to reduce the estate tax on your money? Only two things: spend it or give it away. When it comes to spending or giving away money, your own present needs and desires are far more important than any amount of estate tax savings. But once your family earning pattern does permit some substantial gifts, you should consider making them to dependent parents, to children in anticipation of college costs, or to others.

## GIFTS

### What Constitutes a Gift?

Giving away property is not as simple as it sounds. There is more to it than just handing over cash or a stock certificate. To be sure, the I.R.S. does not concern itself with a $10 or $20 present. But gifts of substantial amounts can be tricky, and all kinds of tax pitfalls abound. Suppose, using this oversimplified example, that you buy a sweater for your son for his birthday. But you like it so much that you hang it in the hall closet and wear it occasionally yourself. Have you really made a gift? The I.R.S. would say, "no."

Making a gift means delivering the property, surrendering all rights and control over it, giving up all benefits and enjoyment of it, and not receiving anything of value in return. (See Chart 17 (Figure 5–1) at the end of the chapter.)

For example: Doctor Sleek opened savings accounts for his two children who were 18 years old and put $10,000 a year into each of them. The accounts were only in the children's names and under their social security numbers. When he died, the passbooks were found in his desk drawer where he had always kept them. The Tax Court held that these were not gifts and would be included in his estate. Why? The I.R.S. did not consider them completed gifts. Delivery, being one of the elements of a gift, had not been made since Doctor Sleek had kept the passbooks. Therefore no gift!

Another example: Doctor Grede transferred title to his personal home to his daughter and son-in-law but continued to live there until he died. The I.R.S. included the value of the residence in his estate for tax purposes on the basis of implied understanding that he had retained the right to use and possess the property until death.

## Primary Elements of a Gift

The primary elements of a gift include the following:

1. Delivering the property, irrevocably.
2. Surrendering all rights, title, and control over the property.
3. Giving up all benefits and enjoyment of it.
4. Not receiving anything of value in return.
5. An intention on your part to make a gift.
6. An acceptance by the person to whom you are giving the gift. Generally, gifts must be given from "detached and disinterested generosity" and not from business-related activities. They must be for affection, admiration, and respect; and, they must be given for no economic benefit.

All six factors above must be met for either a gift or a charitable contribution.

## Gift Taxes

A gift tax, according to the I.R.S., is an excise tax, payable on "the privilege of transferring property without consideration." What is *consideration?* In tax law, consideration is *money* or *money's worth*, not a trade or an exchange. However, as it may be used in legal documents, it means an *exchange* or *quid pro quo* (the Latin, meaning "this for that").

The gift tax definition actually came out of the case of *Commissioner of Internal Revenue* v. *Duberstein.*[1] This case was heard by the Supreme Court at the request of the Commissioner of the I.R.S. Mr. Duberstein had furnished helpful information to a corporation. In appreciation of this information, the corporation's president presented Mr. Duberstein with a new Cadillac, as a gift. Since it was a gift, Mr. Duberstein did not declare the value of the car in his gross income. The I.R.S. declared a deficiency in his income. The issue in the case was whether the Cadillac constituted a gift as interpreted by the Internal Revenue tax law. The Supreme Court indicated that a voluntary transfer of property by one to another without any consideration or compensation (though legally a gift) is not necessarily a gift within the meaning of tax law. If the payment proceeds primarily are from "the incentive of anticipated benefit of an economic nature, it is not a gift."

The Supreme Court held that the Cadillac given to Mr. Duberstein must be included in his gross income and was *not* a gift. After all, had Mr. Duberstein not furnished the corporation with helpful information, the corporation would not have given him the car.

There are many incentives for lifetime giving, but there are individuals who are unwilling to completely part with wealth while there is still a possibility they might need it during their lives. A gift is given out of the "goodness of your heart," without expecting anything in return. However, if you attach strings to your gifts, such as the power to change the beneficiary, the power to revoke a trust, or a reservation as to the scope of the enjoyment of the gift, you have not given up complete control over the property, and, therefore, it is not considered a gift for tax purposes.

Some strings might be all right under law, but reservations or control may cause the gift or trust to end up as part of your taxable estate. A gift must be one in which you have completely parted with dominion and control over it, with no strings attached.

The Federal Gift Tax is imposed upon transfers of property by gift where the amount is greater than the annual exclusion. It is imposed upon the person making the gift (the donor). If the donor does not pay the tax when due, the person receiving the gift (the donee) may be called upon to pay it to the extent of the value of the property received by him or her. Unless a gift tax return is filed, there is no statute of limitations on gift giving.

## Basic Gift Tax Rules

- Up to a certain point, you will not need to pay federal gift taxes on the money or property you bestow on your offspring and you will not have to pay any at all on things that you leave your spouse.

---

[1] 363 U.S. 278, 80 S.Ct. 1190 (1960).

Specifically, the law in 1990 allows you to give up to $10,000 annually to as many persons as you like without paying a gift tax. Thus, if you have four children, you can give $40,000, divided equally, without worry. But, if you make a gift that is over the annual exclusion you must file Gift Tax Form 709.

- If you are married, you and your spouse may combine your annual exclusion. Together you can give $20,000 (1990) to each person without paying a tax. In fact, if your spouse agrees to join in the gift giving, it is called a *split gift*. However, where the split gift is over the individual annual exclusion allowed, two gift tax returns must be filed and each spouse *must* consent to the gift-splitting by signing the other's gift tax form. Joint gift tax returns are not permitted. This will assure that one-half of the gift will not come back into your estate for tax purposes. In community property states (Arizona, California, Idaho, Louisiana, Nevada, New Mexico, Texas, and Washington, plus Wisconsin) gifts to third persons are automatically considered to be made half by each spouse. A gift made without proper regard for taxes may cause you or your children a great deal of grief later on.

- The unlimited gift to a spouse makes it possible for a married couple to postpone all federal transfer taxes until the death of the surviving spouse. In effect, it treats husband and wife as one person with respect to gift giving of property between them.

- Your generous impulses might be influenced by a single unified progressive rate schedule that is applicable on a cumulative basis to all types of giving—gifts made during your lifetime and gifts made (by will) at death.

- Many popular financial planning techniques involve shifting income from a parent to a child in a lower tax bracket. But there are limits to the use of these techniques. For example, Internal Revenue Code Section 677 provides that income payable to a child from such a trust may be taxable to a parent if it is used to discharge a legally enforceable support obligation. Income may also be taxable at a parent's tax bracket if the child is under 14 years old. Therefore, if you are thinking about using any of these devices, be sure to get good accounting and legal advice before setting the wheels in motion. With respect to community property life insurance, community property wills may contain a bequest "to my issue per stirpes my ownership interest in any policies of life insurance wherein my spouse is insured." By specifically leaving your community property interest in the policy to your children (or someone else), one-half of the proceeds should escape taxes on your estate.

## What Assets Should You Give Away?

Choosing what to give is often more difficult than deciding whether to give. Important tax and other practical consequences flow from this choice. Many factors have to be considered in each separate case, including purely psychological factors. Do you need the future income from the particular asset? Is it wise to give up control of a particular piece of property?

Since you are allowed to leave your spouse an unlimited amount without incurring any tax, let us look at gifts to your children, grandchildren, or others.

Give cash if you possibly can. All other things being equal, cash probably makes the best gift. For one thing, neither you nor your children will have to worry about whether the money has appreciated or depreciated in value, as you would if you gave stocks, bonds, real estate, or other property. And there are no problems of valuing the cash or exchanging it.

What else can you give besides money? Life insurance can make a fine gift. By giving policies away, you can reduce the size of your estate and thus reduce your estate taxes as long as all incidents of ownership are given away (or assigned) at least three years before your death. If you hold onto the policy or if you die before three years have passed since you gave the policy away (or assigned it), it will be later included in your estate for tax purposes at its face value.

If one of your children (not a minor) has an income of his own, he may be able to start paying the premiums right away. Be careful about continuing to pay them yourself. That, or the fact that if you die within three years of giving the life insurance policy away, will cause the policy to be brought back into your estate for tax purposes.

You might consider giving your children the money to pay the premiums. Just be sure that you do not specifically earmark it for that purpose. Otherwise, the I.R.S. may argue that the policy belongs to you and is, therefore, subject to estate taxes.

Two other points are worth noting about giving life insurance to children: first, once you give it away, you give it. The policy belongs to them irretrievably. Second, if you give life insurance to your children, do not forget your spouse. Make sure that the balance of your insurance and your estate are adequate for his or her needs.

Stocks and bonds make good gifts. And the best rule of thumb is easy to remember: give stocks or bonds whose market value is not much higher than it was when you bought them. Reason: your children won't have to pay a sizable capital gains on the securities if they ever want to sell them.

Suppose you bought 100 shares of Xerox when it was selling for $30 a share. If you give your children the stock now and they later want to sell it, they will have to list its cost as $30 and pay a capital gains tax on the difference between $30 and its market value at the time it is sold. However, if you leave the stock in your estate with your children as beneficiaries and they later sell it, the stock's cost basis for federal estate tax purposes would be the same as its market value at the time of your death. Here your children would get a stepped-up value and the capital gains tax probably will not be as high.

## Custodial Gifts Under the Uniform Transfers to Minors Act

Under the Uniform Transfers to Minors Act,[2] you can transfer common types of property to your minor children rather inexpensively. The gift is irrevocable and the property automatically belongs to the child when he or she reaches the age of majority (18 years, in most states).

You can give your children cash, stocks and bonds, set up bank accounts, and even life insurance policies. With the exception of Washington state, land is *not* a qualifying gift. Without using a trust, a custodial account under the Transfers to Minors Act (as it is often called) is the most effective and simplest form of a gift. It allows you to transfer any interest in property, whether during life or by will or trust or pursuant to a life insurance policy designation. If you are the person making the gift, name someone else as custodian. The reason for doing this is that, if you were to die before your child reached the age of majority, the gift would be taxed in your estate for tax purposes. If someone else (such as your spouse) were named as custodian and you died, the gift would not be included in your estate.

A custodian is similar to a trustee, but a custodian does not have legal title to the property as a trustee does. The custodian may withdraw or otherwise dispose of the account at any time for the benefit of the child so long as the funds are not used for a parent's legal obligation of support. The funds are a good way to save for college. (See Table 5–1.)

**Table 5–1.** Uniform Transfers to Minors Act (Custodial Gifts).

| ADVANTAGES | DISADVANTAGES |
| --- | --- |
| 1. Another as custodian. | 1. As custodian, taxes in your estate. |
| 2. Child taxed on income. | 2. Gift is irrevocable. |
| 3. Annual exclusion allowed. | 3. Property belongs to child at age of majority. |
| 4. Control over investments; accumulate for college. | 4. Cannot discharge legal obligation of support. |
| 5. Taxed to lower bracket taxpayer. | 5. Earnings are income to minor, taxable to minor. |

[2] In 1963, the National Conference of Commissioners on Uniform State Laws adopted a new Model Uniform Transfers to Minors Act to replace the Uniform Gift to Minors Act it had developed and which 23 states have adopted.

# Gift Tax Applications

A gift can be in many forms besides the familiar transfer from one person to another. It can take the form of the cancellation of a debt, the designation of a life insurance beneficiary, the setting up of a trust, the purchase of services for another's benefit, or the withdrawal of money from a checking account in which you have deposited money. What if you lend your child some money but you really intend for that loan to be a gift? What if you sell property to your child but you forgive the indebtedness? Have you really made a sale or is it a gift? Here is how the gift tax is applied to different types of gifts.

## Disguised Gift or True Loan?

If you make a loan to a family member, it may be transformed into a taxable gift when its collection is not enforceable under local law or if you never really intended to have the loan paid back and it is over the annual gift tax exclusion.[3]

No-interest loans (often referred to as Crown Loans) were used in the past by family members. These types of loans became popular after the Laster Crown case (67 TC 1066, 585 F.2d 234, 1978; and Rev. Rul. 1978-22). In this case, Laster Crown made loans in excess of $18 million to 24 trusts established for the benefit of various family members. The Tax Court held that the interest-free loans made to family members did not give rise to taxable gifts; however, in 1984, in the case of *Dickman* v. *Comm. I.R.*, 465 U.S. 330, the Supreme Court handed down a ruling that was a victory to the I.R.S. in that the interest-free loans are subject to gift taxes between family members on the use of transferred funds on a continuing basis until the loan is repaid.

Although planning opportunities for interest-free loans for extremely large sums of money have been reduced, such loans are still a viable planning technique. The $10,000 (1990) gift tax exclusion ($20,000 with gift splitting)

---

[3] At first, courts held that below-market demand loans created no gift tax consequences. *See Johnson* v. *United States*, 254 F. Supp. 73 (N.D. Tex. 1966); *Crown* v. *Commissioner*, 67 T.C. 1060 (1977), *aff'd*, 585 F.2d 234 (7th Cir. 1978). The I.R.S., however, maintained that such demand loans did carry gift tax consequences. Rev. Rul. 73-61, 1973-1 C.B. 408, 409. The United States Supreme Court resolved the issue in *Dickman* v. *Commissioner*, 465 U.S. 330 (1984), *aff'g* 690 F.2d 812 (11th Cir. 1982), holding that below-market demand loans do create gifts of the reasonable value of the use of the money lent. *Id.* at 344. The dissenting opinion in *Dickman*, however, indicated that the complexity of the gift tax computation imposes a heavy burden on taxpayers who conscientiously try to adhere to the Code. *Id.* at 347 (Powell, J., dissenting).

Below-market term loans were not quite as controversial as below-market demand loans. The I.R.S. view is that below-market term loans involve gift tax ramifications. Rev. Rul. 73-61, 1973-1 C.B. 408, 409. The court in *Estate of Berkman* v. *Commissioner*, 38 T.C.M. (CCH) 183 (1979), agreed with this position, holding that below-market term loans not made at arm's length involve gifts of the difference between the fair market value of the property and the fair market value of the consideration received by the donor.

might shelter gift taxes each year on these loans of about $100,000 ($200,000 with gift splitting) assuming a 10% interest income.

In order to have a good chance that your loan will stand up as a *bona fide* transaction for the I.R.S., keep these points in mind:

1. Structure your loan so that the value of the principal plus interest falls within the annual exclusion.

2. Make sure the loan is evidenced by a written promissory note, much the same as the bank draws up when you borrow money. The loan should have all the characteristics of an arm's length transaction.

3. There should be some evidence of repayment or the intent to make repayment so that the I.R.S. will not declare the loan to be a disguised gift instead of a true debt.

Crown loans have provided excellent means of shifting income from high-bracket taxpayers to lower-bracket ones in the past. However, because of their nature, the use of these loans may lead to unanticipated taxes. Use them with caution, be prepared to dot all your "*i*'s" and cross all your "*t*'s" to achieve your desired objective.[4]

### Disguised Gift or True Sale?

Let's say that you owned income-producing property that was valued at $144,000 and you and your spouse decide to give this property to your four children. Instead of giving it to them outright as a gift, you sell the property to them. Each of them would receive a deed or contract. In return for their interest in the property, they sign a promissory note in which they agree to pay off the indebtedness in annual $6,000 installments. Each time an installment comes due, you forgive the debt. By forgiving $24,000 in debts each year, you would complete the transfer of the property to your children in six years. However, will the property actually escape estate taxes? Probably not. Why? Because you have prearranged to forgive the indebtedness and, therefore, the sale is not really a sale but a disguised gift. In order to have a good chance that your sale will stand up as a bona fide transaction for the I.R.S., keep the following points in mind:

1. Put a realistic price on the property, one close to its fair market value and make some effort to collect.

2. Write down the terms on paper, including foreclosure terms in the event of default.

3. Be sure to keep the promissory note and all paperwork in proper legal form.

---

[4] See also *Elizabeth W. and Ritchie A. Snyder*, T.C. Docket Nos. 28964-87 and 28965-87, 1989; Regulation Sec. 25.2512-5(e) and -9(e).

4. State an interest rate. If the agreement doesn't specify an interest rate, the I.R.S. does have the right to impute interest (an amount that is stated in the Code). If the sale is structured as an installment sale, there are rules affecting the allocation of the purchase price for property between profit and basis recovery for the seller under I.R.C. Section 453.[5] For Section 453 purposes, only the portion of the installment payments that are considered to be principal (which may add to the purchaser's basis) may be treated as amounts upon which the seller may compute its profit and the recovery of its basis under one of the various methods provided in the regulations under Section 453. (See Section 453C in Appendix B.)

## I.R.C. SECTION 1060

Section 1060 of the I.R.C. was enacted under the Tax Reform Act of 1986. It mandates a method for allocating the purchase price as well as rules for determining the value of goodwill or going-concern value in the case of the distribution of partnership property or the transfer of a partnership interest.[6]

Prior to the enactment of I.R.C. Section 1060, sellers and buyers could contractually agree to an allocation that would result in a substantial tax savings for both parties. This often resulted in haggling over the allocation values of individual assets, and specific values were not always spelled out in the sales contract. This resulted in incorrect allocations and caused the I.R.S. to intervene and impose its own allocations.[7] The feeling was that, if a doctor does not arrange his own affairs so as to minimize taxes, he should not expect the courts to do so retroactively.[8]

This was one of the reasons behind the I.R.S. adoption of the "residual method" for allocating assets under I.R.C. Section 1060 and with limiting preferences for long-term capital gains. Section 1060 applies to "all applicable asset acquisition," and is defined as any transfer of a group of assets that constitutes a trade or business in which the buyer's basis is determined by reference to what the buyer paid. Asset acquisitions must be reported on Form 8594.

Under the residual method, the purchase price (in a qualified stock purchase treated as an asset purchase for tax purposes) is first reduced by

---

[5] The Tax Reform Act of 1986 and the Revenue Act of 1987 made changes to the law affecting taxpayers who use the installment method.

[6] See also I.R.C. Section 755.

[7] *Illinois Cereal Mills, Inc.*, 46 T.C.M. 1001, 1983; *Stryker Corporation*, 44 T.C.M. 1020, 1982; *Adventist Living Centers Inc.*, No. 88-2067, US Ct. of Appeals (7th Cir., 8/89).

[8] See *Markham and Brown Inc.*, CA 5, 6/25/81.

cash and cash equivalent assets, and then is allocated sequentially to two defined classes of identifiable tangible and intangible assets, but only to the extent of the fair market value of those assets, and any remaining purchase price is allocated to goodwill and going-concern value.[9] In other words, Section 1060 requires that the purchase price be allocated among assets other than goodwill to the extent of the fair market value of each, with the remainder being allocated to goodwill.

## CLASSES OF ASSETS

Assets that are transferred are classified into four categories: Class I, Class II, Class III, and Class IV assets.[10] The following are assets that belong to the different classes:

- Class I assets: cash, demand notes, bank accounts, savings and loan accounts, and similar items.
- Class II assets: certificates of deposit, U.S. government securities, readily marketable stock or securities, foreign currencies, and similar items.
- Class III assets are all assets not included in Classes I, II, or IV and consist of furniture, fixtures, land, buildings, leases, contracts, equipment, accounts receivable, covenants not to compete, and franchise, trademark, or trade name.
- Class IV assets are going-concern value and goodwill value.

### The Residual Method of Asset Transfer

Each class of assets should be assigned a separate value as a means for determining a buyer's basis in the acquired assets and the seller's gain or loss on the sale.

Assets that are transferred are categorized into the different classes as shown above. The purchase price is first reduced by the amount of any Class I assets. The remaining purchase price is allocated to Class II and then to Class III assets. Within any given class, the purchase price allocated to each asset may not exceed the fair market value of that asset. After allocation of the purchase price paid, reduced by Classes I, II, and III, any residual price is allocated to Class IV assets (goodwill and/or going-concern value).

Example: In 1989, S transfers to B assets with a fair market value of

---

[9] Samuel C. Thompson, Jr., et. al. "Issues Involved in Allocation of Purchase Price in Stock and Asset Acquisitions, Including Impact of Section 1060." Ninth Annual Georgia Federal Tax Conference, June 1–2, 1989.

[10] See Temporary Regulation 1.1060-IT(d); I.R.C. Secs. 1245 and 1250; Form 8594.

$56,000 plus goodwill. The purchase price of the practice is $65,000. B pays $50,000 in cash and assumes $15,000 in liability. The fair market value assets consists of the following:

| | |
|---|---:|
| Certificate of deposit (a Class II asset) | $25,000 |
| Equipment (a Class III asset) | 12,000 |
| Supplies (Class III) | 4,000 |
| Accounts receivable (Class III) | 15,000 |
| | $56,000 |

In the above example there are no Class I assets so $25,000 of the $56,000 is first allocated to Class II assets (i.e., purchase price $65,000 − $25,000 = $40,000). The remaining $40,000 paid is then allocated to Class III assets ($12,000 + $4,000 + $15,000 = $31,000). This exceeds the aggregate fair market values of the Class III assets ($40,000 − $31,000 = $9,000) and accordingly, this amount is the fair market value of Class III assets. After the allocation to the Class III assets, the balance of $9,000 is allocated to Class IV assets (i.e., goodwill).

If you are the party to a buy-sell transaction, you are required by I.R.C. Section 1060(b) to furnish information to the I.R.S regarding the consideration (money) transferred.[11] This would include any amounts transferred including the allocation among the assets transferred, as well as information concerning subsequent adjustments (increases or decreases) in the purchase price. And both the buyer and seller must each file asset acquisitions statements on Form 8594 with their income tax returns for the taxable year that includes the purchase date or the year in which later adjustments have occurred.

## PRIVATE ANNUITY—AN INCOME-SHIFTING DEVICE

Another type of income-shifting device is known as a *private annuity.* (This has nothing to do with insurance. *Annuity* simply means payments extending over a period of time.) A private annuity involves the transfer of property to a younger family member in exchange for his or her unsecured promise to make fixed payments to the parent (or older family member) for the parent's lifetime.

It is similar to an installment sale in which you sell property to your children at a fair market price. The amount of the money paid to you is actuarily determined from the Internal Revenue Code based on the fair market value of the property and your age. A private annuity is used as a means of moving appreciated property out of your estate and transferring

---

[11] I.R.C. 1060.

it to a loved one while providing you with cash prior to your demise. The annuity payments would be taxed to you, as you receive them.

Like an installment sale, an annuity involves a purchase of property at its fair market value. However, in the installment sale, the estate would collect the balance due at death. With an annuity sale, the payments due end at death. An installment sale with a cancellation clause (or forgiveness in a will) would work in a similar manner. Both types of transactions will remove property from your estate. This will help reduce your estate taxes.

There is a disadvantage to a private annuity sale. You do take the risk that you will outlive your life expectancy (from the actuary tables in the Internal Revenue Code) and have the property overpaid. Although a delicate matter, this would be a great way to beat the tax game, if you have a terminally ill parent who wants to save on estate taxes. Another disadvantage of the annuity sale is that there is no interest deduction for the payor. See I.R.C. Section 2036(c) regarding "enterprise" and the disucssion about private annuities.

A gift may take many forms besides the familiar transfer from one person to another, such as the setting up of a trust.

## TRUSTS—ANOTHER WAY OF GIFTING PROPERTY

What if you don't want to give up ownership and control over your property while you're alive? Or, what if you still want control over it long after you've gone? For that, you will need a trust.

A trust may sound complicated, but it is really quite simple if you consider this oversimplified example: As you leave for the office one morning, you hand your wife a $20 bill. "It's Uncle Bernie's birthday today," you tell her. "When you're downtown, pick up something nice and mail it to him."

Believe it or not, you have created a trust. Since you contributed the idea and the money, you are the "grantor" (settlor, creator, or donor). Your wife, who has to carry out your orders, is the "trustee." The instructions to buy and deliver the gift are the indenture. Lucky Uncle Bernie is the "beneficiary" of all the action. And after he has received the gift, the trust is terminated.

Suppose you telephone your wife later that morning and tell her, "Forget about the gift for Uncle Bernie. Maybe we'll take him out to dinner instead." Right then, the trust has been "revoked."

Or, suppose you had first told your wife in the morning, "You go out and get that gift no matter what, even if I phone you and change my mind the way I did last year." Now the trust is "irrevocable."

Since all this went on while you were hale and hearty, the trust was *inter vivos*, which means that it was created while you were living. But if it had been a wish in your will, it would have been testamentary.

That, in a nutshell, is what trusts are all about. To be sure, that is a simplified version. Highly oversimplified! But a trust agreement does not have to fill five pounds of legal foolscap. Although certain legal requirements must be met, the provisions can be just as simple or complex as you care to make them.

What can a trust do for you? Possibly nothing that you cannot do very nicely for yourself. Or, it may be able to transfer your assets in ways that you could not or would not want to handle yourself, under virtually any conditions you could possibly erect. This might be when your beneficiary comes of age, or marries, or has children, or needs help with educational expenses, or is mentally or physically handicapped, when you die or long after.

Under a will, your executor must conclude your affairs as swiftly and expeditiously as possible and pay out the cash to the beneficiaries. A trust, on the other hand, offers infinite possibilities regarding distribution.

Setting a trust in motion is a little like launching a guided missile. You set the dials to tell it when to start, where to go, what to do, and when to stop, just as you did with Uncle Bernie's birthday present. Of course, your objectives are likely to be far weightier and more detailed than that. And, your trustee can do only what is stated in the trust instrument, nothing else. Before setting up any type of trust, be sure to get competent legal and accounting advice.

Almost always, a trust is set up to protect someone from something. Maybe it is to protect your estate from taxes. Maybe it is to protect your mentally or physically handicapped child. Or it might be to protect your children from the spending habits of their spouses.

Each type of trust has its own special uses, advantages, and disadvantages. Which trust you will select depends almost entirely upon your objectives—what you want the trust for in the first place. (See Table 5–2.)

---

**Table 5–2.** Trusts.

TYPES OF TRUST:
Testamentary: In a will
*Inter Vivos:* Made during one's lifetime

CLASSIFICATION OF TRUSTS:
Revocable: Can be changed
Irrevocable: Cannot be changed

COMMON TRUST DEFINITIONS:
Donor, Grantor: Person who creates the trust
Beneficiary: Person who receives income from trust
Trustee: Person who carries out terms of trust; manages trust;
        has legal title to trust
*Corpus* or *Res:* Principal assets of the trust
Income: Interest accumulated or retained by corpus

---

## Taxation of Trusts

Are trusts taxed? A trust is a legal, taxable entity for which a tax return must be filed each year. Very simply, income that is to be distributed by the trust is taxable to its beneficiaries. Income that is retained and accumulated by the trust is taxable to the trust.

## Trust Considerations

Are the tax savings worth creating a trust? In many family financial planning situations, trusts may not be as feasible as they appear because the disadvantages might outweigh the advantages.

A trustee is entitled to a fee during the existence of the trust. That, along with the fact you must have a trust created, may be more expensive in terms of legal fees, administrative fees, trustee's fees, and the like, than are offset by subsequent savings in taxes. Since a trust is considered a legal entity, a tax return must be filed each year for the trust, just as you file a Form 1040 income tax return each year. A fee is usually involved.

## Trusts with Retained Interest

Some types of trust offer a tax break. Some do not. Generally, most trusts with retained interest do not. This is because there is a "string" or retained "right" and the elements (incidents of ownership) that control gift taxes also control the taxation of trust.

Below are two examples of commonly used trust transfers with retained life estates.

*Example 1:* Doctor Cullen Lowery creates a trust reserving the interest income for life to himself, and upon his death, the remainder will go to his son, James. In this example, the entire trust will be included in Doctor Cullen's estate when he dies because he has retained the "right" to use and enjoy the income even though the gift of the remainder will go to his son when he dies.

*Example 2:* Doctor Cullen creates a trust to pay the income to his wife for life, the remainder on his wife's death to go to their children. Doctor Cullen has retained the power to invade the principal of the trust for the children's benefit.

Here again in the second example, the entire principal of the trust will be included in Cullen's estate for tax purposes. This is because the doctor has retained the right to affect his wife's income by a possible invasion of the principal for the children's benefit. If Cullen had retained the power to revoke the trust at any time, change the beneficiary, or any other control over the trust, it would be included in his estate because he had not given up "dominion and control" over the property as we discussed earlier.

Some of the main purposes for a trust might be: to support an elderly parent, to take care of a physically or mentally handicapped child, to manage property, to give to charity, or simply to save on income taxes. In order to avoid its being included in your estate, you must give up "dominion and control" over the property. You cannot retain any type of string or right (any incident of ownership) in it. Be sure to look into all aspects before you act.

## An Irrevocable Living Trust

If you want to cut your estate taxes, you should consider an *irrevocable inter vivos* (or living) trust. This means giving the trust property away, once and forever, while you are still alive. The property is excluded from your estate just because you have given it away. But unlike a direct gift of property, the trust agreement controls how it is invested and paid out, the beneficiary cannot fritter it away, and you cannot later change it (as it is irrevocable).

Still, very few people can afford to give away sizable amounts of their property and the income from it while they are still alive, no matter what the estate tax savings might be. So consider the matter carefully before you do it, and be as certain as you can that you will not change your mind later on.

## Irrevocable Life Insurance Trust

Another planning technique is an irrevocable life insurance trust. An irrevocable life insurance trust generally provides for the distribution of trust income and/or corpus to, or for the benefit of, your spouse, children, or grandchildren. There are two basic types: a funded trust and an unfunded trust.

The benefits of these types of trusts have been complicated by recent changes in the tax laws, but have survived numerous changes in the tax law.[12] They are designed to (1) keep the proceeds of the life insurance policies owned by the trust from being taxed in the insured's estate, (2) transfer the insurance without adverse gift tax consequences, and (3) bypass taxation in the estate of the insured's surviving spouse and, sometimes, in the estates of the insured's children. These types of trusts can be used to solve a variety of estate problems, such as providing estate liquidity and providing income for family members.

In order to accomplish these goals, these types of trusts are always irrevocable and they are designed to be funded either with a life insurance policy or policies or with cash which the trustee may use to purchase a life insurance policy or policies. There should be money in the trust to allow

---

[12] See I.R.C. Sec. 2036(c), as amended by the Technical and Miscellaneous Revenue Act of 1988 and the Revenue Reconciliation Act of 1989.

the trustee to continue paying the premiums on the life insurance policies owned by the trusts (if not paid-up policies), or it would receive annual contributions that allow the trustee to pay the premiums generated by the policies owned by the trust.

While the irrevocable life insurance trust has appeal, it is not without its drawbacks.[13] Among those drawbacks is the insured's loss of control over the policy, including the right to borrow against or make use of the policy's cash surrender value. Another drawback is that the trust is irrevocable. Once you establish the trust, you give up the power to make changes. If you have an estate of less than $600,000 then this type of arrangement is not for you.

You must make gifts to an unfunded irrevocable life insurance trust if the trust is to have funds needed to pay the premiums. Such gifts are subject to gift tax if they are over the annual exclusion and if they are considered gifts of a present interest. Gifts of a future interest do not qualify for the annual exclusion. A gift will qualify as a present-interest gift only if the recipient has the unrestricted right to the immediate use, possession, or enjoyment of the property transferred. Therefore, if you pay the premium directly to the insurance company, or if you make a cash gift to a trustee who then pays the premium, the gift will be treated as a future-interest gift and will not qualify for the annual gift tax exclusion. Your unused unified credit is applied against the gift tax, thereby reducing the credit that will be available when you die.

The solution to the problem of gifts of future interest lies in what is referred to as a "Crummey Power."[14] Crummey powers are noncumulative withdrawal rights of the trust beneficiaries to reach the gift. If the beneficiary fails to exercise the withdrawal rights, the power lapses and the trustee then has use of the money to pay the insurance premiums. Actual notice must be given to the beneficiaries if the gifts to the trust are to constitute present-interest gifts, and a reasonable opportunity to exercise the Crummey Power must exist before it lapses. The maximum amount that a Crummey beneficiary may withdraw is generally limited to the greater of $5,000 or 5 percent of the value of the trust corpus (sometimes referred to as the "Five and Five Rule").

Your primary consideration for using an irrevocable life insurance trust is the potential for estate tax savings. Yet, Sections 2035 and 2042 may

---

[13] See "spousal unity" rule under Sec. 2036(c)(3)(C), which provides that a husband and wife are treated as one person for purposes of applying Sec. 2036(c).

[14] See *Crummey* vs. *Commissioner*, 397 F.2d 82 (9th Cir., 1968) in which the donors created a trust for their four children, two of whom were minors. Each beneficiary had a separate trust share and each had the right to demand a distribution of additional contributions made to his share during the taxable year. The Court of Appeals held that the additional contributions were gifts of present interest. If a minor can make demand for distribution, the transfer in trust is considered to be a gift of a present interest.

prevent your excluding the insurance proceeds from your estate. Under Section 2035, if you transfer a life insurance policy insuring your life to a trust and die within three years of the initial transfer, the policy proceeds will be included in your estate. For example, if you created an irrevocable life insurance trust in 1990 and funded it with insurance on your life, the insurance proceeds would be subject to tax in your estate if you died in 1991. (See also *Estate of Frank M. Perry*, T.C.Memo 1990-123 March 8, 1990.) Where the transfer took place more than three years prior to death, the proceeds will be excluded from your gross estate.

In addition, Section 2042 causes life insurance proceeds to be included in your gross estate if they are payable to, or for the benefit of, your estate. If the trustee is required under the terms of the trust to use the proceeds to pay any of your death costs, the proceeds will be included in your gross estate to the extent required to be used to pay those costs. A different result occurs in community property states. In community property states if the life insurance proceeds are payable to your estate or if you die with any incidents of ownership in the policy, the entire amount of the insurance proceeds is included in your gross estate.[15]

In case law, it is apparent that you can keep the insurance out of your estate if certain conditions are met. First, the trustee must purchase the insurance for the trust, not the insured! Next, the trust terms should not require the trustee to purchase insurance but can empower the trustee to make this kind of investment. The funds (not the exact amount) for the premiums should be paid by the insured to the trustee who can submit the premium payments to the insurance company.

It is clear that the irrevocable life insurance trust is a complex estate planning tool, so be sure to get competent legal and accounting advice before structuring it. It does remain a viable technique for solving a variety of estate problems.

## Revocable Living Trust

If you are looking for investment management for yourself, then for your wife and children after your death, you might set up a *revocable inter vivos* (or living) trust. Here there will not be any tax savings to your estate, but you could watch the trust in operation during your lifetime, and amend or revoke it at any time you wish.

After your death, the trust could continue to operate as it did before, distributing the benefits as you directed. In effect, the trust would take the place of a will for the property in that trust. And, you would have a sneak preview of how it all works out, with time enough to change the trust if it does not meet your expectations.

---

[15] See Letter Ruling 8928003; I.R.C. Sec. 2042.

## Grantor-Retained Income Trusts

A grantor-retained income trust (GRIT) is an irrevocable inter vivos trust in which you retain the right to receive all the income of the trust, or the right to use the property of the trust, for a fixed period of time. Upon the expiration of your retained interest, the trust property is either distributed to younger generation family members or is held in further trust for them.

Congress has constructed an elaborate statutory scheme under the Technical and Miscellaneous Revenue Act of 1988 (TAMRA) and Notice 89-99 published at 1989-38 I.R.B.4, August 31, 1989, (Notice) to discourage estate planning arrangements that attempt to reduce the overall transfer tax burden upon the transfer of property to succeeding generations. Because of this, the well-known Clifford trust is seldom used today. In the typical Clifford trust, the grantor gave away the income interest for a term of more than ten years and retained the remainder interest. In the GRIT, you, the grantor, retain the interest income and give away the remainder.

When you create the GRIT, you make a taxable gift to the remainder beneficiaries. Your retention of the income or use interest in the trust property reduces the value of the remainder interest gift. The amount of the gift is calculated by subtracting the actuarial value of your retained interests from the value of the property transferred to the trusts. (See Private Letter Ruling 8849067.) The value of your retained income or use interest is determined under I.R.S. actuarial tables. (Regulations Sec. 25.2512-5 and I.R.C. Section 7520) The use of the actuarial tables may produce a low or no rate of return. Still, Revenue Ruling 77-195, 1977-1 C.B.295, held that the tables could be used even if the income generated was less than the assumed rate.

### Position of the Internal Revenue Service

Notice 89-99 deals with, among other things, the definition of "enterprise," disproportionate appreciation, retained interests, "safe harbor" exceptions, the "spousal unity" rule, substantial interest requirements, and consideration. The Notice devotes nine pages to defining "enterprise" for purposes of I.R.C. Section 2036(c).

The term "enterprise" includes not only an active trade or business, but also an undertaking with respect to passive investment property. In other words, an "enterprise" is defined to include "a business or other property that may produce income or gain." A trust holding cash, securities, real property, or other passive investment property generally is considered an enterprise, although a decedent's estate is not. An important exception is created for what is called "personal use" property and includes life insurance and principal residences.

The Notice takes an exhaustive approach to what may constitute an "interest in the income of an enterprise," including for this purpose preferred equity interests, promissory notes, a life or term interest, employment agreements, retirement arrangements, and sale or lease agreements. The extent to which reversionary interest can be used in GRITs is clarified in the Notice. The retention of a reversionary interest is generally considered to be a right to receive an amount that is not determined solely by reference to income. The Notice provides that the reversionary interest (reverter) will not taint a GRIT if its value does not exceed 25 percent of the value of the grantor's retained income interest.

GRITs have survived the enactment of Section 2036(c), as amended by TAMRA, provided they meet the conditions that are specified in that section of the Internal Revenue Code. GRITs are widely used as a means of maximizing the use of an individual's unified credit. Notice 89-99 indicates that the I.R.S. views every GRIT as an "enterprise" subject to the Section 2036(c)(4) deemed-gift rule, even though funded with cash or publicly traded securities. An exception for GRITs would be to use "personal use" property such as a principal residence.

A GRIT works if you survive the term of your retained interest. If you do not, the trust property is included in your estate under I.R.C. Section 2036(a). However, an advantage of using a GRIT is the ability to "leverage" the use of the unified credit since the value of the gift will be actuarially reduced by the value of your retained interests. For example, a ten-year irrevocable GRIT can be funded with over $1.5 million in property without exceeding the $600,000 credit equivalent amount (assuming a 10 percent rate of return under the I.R.S. tables). Neither you nor your spouse can be trustee under the spousal unity rule of Section 2036(c)(3)(C).

The best assets to use to fund a GRIT are those likely to appreciate substantially in the future. The reason is that the GRIT will freeze the transfer tax value of the assets and will pass them to the remaindermen at a discount due to the leveraging of the unified credit. Use "personal use" property to fund the GRIT, since such property is outside the scope of Section 2036(c). A personal residence and life insurance policies are conclusively presumed to be outside the scope of Section 2036(c) under Notice 89-99.

If you are unmarried or up in age, you are more likely to use a GRIT than is a young married couple. The reason: Unless you are very well off, you will probably want to keep all assets available for your use until the death of the survivor, since in using this technique you would be making substantial lifetime gifts.

### Private Annuities and Installment Sales

With a private annuity, G transfers property to A in return for the unsecured promise of A to make fixed payments to G for his or her life.

In a private annuity or an installment sale where the seller does not retain a security interest in the sold property, all future appreciation in the transferred property inures to the benefit of the transferee. The transferor in each receives a fixed right to future payments. The private annuity and the installment sale appear to remain available as planning options and, at present, should not be considered subject to Section 2036(c).

**Figure 5–1.** CHART 17: Deed of Gift.

*(A form, similar to the one below, can be used for deeding gifts to another. The words "love and affection" are considered good consideration that some value has been exchanged in return for the gift.)*

This deed of gift and conveyance made and entered into this ____ day of ____, 19__, by and between (YOUR NAME), party of the first part, and (NAME OF PARTY TO WHOM GIFT IS BEING MADE), the second party.

WITNESSETH: That the said party of the first part, in consideration of the love and affection he bears his son, has given and does by these presents give, grant, and convey to the said second party, all the right, title, and interest now vested in him to all those certain pieces of personal property described as follows:

*(Insert detailed list and description of property here)*

To have and to hold the same, together with any appurtenances thereto belonging, unto the second party, his successors, heirs, and assigns forever.

IN WITNESS WHEREOF, the said party of the first part has set his hand and seal the day and year first above written.

_____

(YOUR NAME), GRANTOR

_____ (WITNESS)    _____ (WITNESS)

# 6

# YOUR WILL

Doctor, a major part of planning your finances is considering the needs of your family after you die as well as while you are alive. The best and usually the only way to insure that your plans are carried out is to draft a will. Just remember that all arrangements need revision now and again.

When you wrote your will, you wrote it for that day and for your family's needs at that time. What about now? Are they the same? When was the last time you looked at your will? A will that was right then, may be wrong now.

To find out if it is time for a change, ask yourself the five famous questions of every good newspaper reporter: Who? What? When? Where? How? (See Table 6–1.)

Maybe the following scenario will help you determine one of the most important questions, it not *the* most important question, you will be faced with.

**Table 6–1.** Is your will invalid?

Believe it or not, your will may be invalid if any of the following events have occurred and your will has not been updated:

- Marital status altered because of marriage, separation, divorce, remarriage, or death.
- The birth or adoption of a child.
- Moving to another state where the laws are different.
- Making changes to your will by erasing, scratching out, adding words, or by not following the formalities as required by your state laws.

## WHO WILL EXECUTE YOUR WILL? CHOOSE YOUR EXECUTOR CAREFULLY

The executor—not just any executor, but Doctor Cowart's best friend!—refused to serve! It was unthinkable!

"What," asked the city gossip with malicious undertones, "would Dr. Cowart say if he could come back? It just goes to show," she added philosophically, "you never know a person until after you're dead."

What *would* Dr. Cowart say? In this case, it is possible to find out. So infuriated, hurt, upset was the late Doctor Cowart that he asked for and was granted a brief return to Earth to find out what had prompted Marc, in whom Doctor Cowart had the greatest confidence, to turn down the position of executor. We record the conversation for posterity—and for those who have yet to select executors of their own:

DR. COWART: So you refuse to serve. You are a louse! I pay you the highest of compliments and you turn it down!

MARC: Nuts!

DR. COWART: Is that all you have to say? I guess I'm wasting my time.

MARC: You stick around. You've caused me enough grief. First you have to up and die, leaving me without a best friend, and without a doctor, too. Then I learn, for the first time, that I'm to be your executor.

DR. COWART: Well, what's wrong with that?

MARC: Don't you think you might have asked if I'd serve before you put me in your will?

DR. COWART: Well, naturally, I assumed. . . .

MARC: That's where you made your first mistake. Executor! What do I know about the job? Photography is my strong suit.

DR. COWART: What do you have to know?

MARC (*whispering*): Now he asks. I spend a week studying a copy of your will, swimming in hereinafters, remaindermen, life estates, and counting "per stirpes" in my sleep. And you wouldn't spend five minutes to find out whether I'm qualified for the job.

DR. COWART: Well, it seemed simple enough. All you had to do, I thought, was take care of my affairs after I'm gone.

MARC (*very sarcastically*): Is that all? Just a moment while I get the paper that I picked up at the bank last week. Here it is. These, my departed friend, are some of the duties an executor is supposed to perform.

(MARC reads the following list):

### BASIC AREAS OF EXECUTOR'S RESPONSIBILITIES

• Probate will after it is found;

• Fulfill legal obligations such as securing "Letters Testamentary" from the Court and notifying creditors;

• Pay estate taxes;

• Carry out wishes in will and distribute assets.

MARC: The basic areas of an executor's responsibilities don't look like much at first glance, but take a closer look at what's involved . . .

(MARC reads on): Although the details of these problems may vary from state to state, many of the tasks that an executor must perform will depend on what the will of the decedent provides, as well as on the types of estate assets.

I. Preliminary steps
   1. Locate will and study it.
   2. Help with funeral arrangements, if required.
   3. Have an attorney handle the legal matters, prepare petition for probate, and be ready to defend the will if necessary.
II. Arrange for probate of the will
   1. Locate witness if there is no self-providing declaration attached to the will.
   2. Notify creditors by placing an advertisement in the official legal newspaper in the county of the deceased's residence.
   3. Arrange for bond and obtain court authority over the property.

   Many states insist that your executor post a bond and submit regular reports of inventory to assure the court of the faithful performance of his duties, unless your will has specific provisions exempting the executor from that requirement (which the majority of states will recognize).

   4. Have the attorney file the petition to probate.
III. Assemble, inventory, and protect assets
   1. List contents of all safe deposit boxes in the presence of bank or legal representatives and make an inventory for tax purposes.
   2. Take possession of all personal effects.
   3. Manage, dispose of, or distribute all real estate . . . as directed by the will.
   4. Examine, secure appraisals, and manage or sell any privately owned business or professional practice that you control (and let me tell you, selling a professional practice is a lot different from taking photographs).
   5. Ascertain if property is owned in another state.
   6. Examine insurance policies on real estate or personal property and have the policies endorsed to whomever they were left. Check the coverage.
   7. Collect all life insurance proceeds due the estate.

8. Determine what is to become of patient records: are they to be sold to another licensed professional or should they be held in custody for the time period of the statute of limitation?
9. Destroy all unused prescription blanks, stationery, and controlled substances from the doctor's practice.

IV. Study financial records of decedent
1. Send notification of death to concerned insurance companies.
2. Decide what is to be included for marital deduction purposes.
3. Obtain all brokerage records and have brokers arrange for the necessary paperwork in transferring ownership of stocks and bonds.
4. Study available employment contracts, deferred compensation plans, or retirement plan benefits to determine whether payments are due and to whom.
5. Secure appraisals for real estate, personal effects, or a professional practice where needed.
6. Determine whether the practice receivables (i.e., all amounts due the practice for which work has been performed) should be collected or sold.

V. Administer the estate
1. File Federal Estate and State Inheritance tax returns.
2. Request the post office to forward mail, if necessary.
3. File for Social Security and/or veteran's benefits.
4. Pay just claims against the estate.
5. Keep records of all transactions, income, and expenses in a separate "estate" checking account.
6. Keep beneficiaries and others with proper interest in the estate informed of progress of estate settlement.
7. Pay support for widow and children as required.

VI. Determine personal and estate tax liability
1. Secure federal and state estate tax releases so that distribution may be made as promptly as possible.
2. Get I.R.S. approval to close out any qualified retirement plans so distribution can be made.

VII. Distribute estate and make final settlement
1. Distribute assets of the estate according to the will or state law, if there is no will or if provisions were not made for the assets.
2. Prepare information for final accounting, including all assets, income, and disbursements.

(There is a moment of silence after Marc finishes reading.)

MARC (*wearily*): I probably would have messed up your affairs beautifully as your executor. And, after breaking my neck doing the best job possible in the limited time at my disposal, I could have been sued for what the court might consider gross negligence of duty. Then I'd have to sue myself for neglecting my own business. What do you have to say to all this?

DR. COWART (*whispering*): Oh.

MARC: Is that all?

DR. COWART: I am sorry. You are still the best friend I have . . . er, had.

MARC: Shake on that before you go!

The two friends shake hands warmly and Dr. Cowart departs. Marc is left alone, somewhat conscience-stricken, because he had neglected to make a confession to his friend. He had named Doctor Cowart executor of *his* estate. Had he been the first to die, Dr. Cowart would have been in the same predicament.

## EPILOGUE

Of course, you have heard of an executor. You may even believe you know what he or she does. That is the person who sees to it that the directions in a will are properly carried out, isn't it? Whom have you named in your own will as executor? Perhaps a relative, your spouse, or a close friend? And she or he may have named you as executor of hers or his. After all, what are friends for?

If you have entered into any such reciprocal arrangement with a friend (and millions of people have), both of you owe it to yourselves to find out about the specific and complex duties that an executor must perform. While you may trust your friend to do the "right thing" for your survivors, good intentions are not nearly enough when it comes to executing a will. Once you understand what is involved in the job, you and your executor may both have a change of heart.

The listing of an executor's duties by Marc does not begin to explore the possible complications in settling an estate. A seemingly simple thing like locating the actual will can require hours, if not days, of searching. Once it is found, the executor must take the will before the proper court and prove that it is genuine and in accordance with the laws of that state.

If you fail to name someone who is willing and able to serve as executor, the court will appoint an administrator. Your executor or administrator is your personal representative for purposes of terminating your financial affairs and seeing that your assets are properly distributed.

You might consider naming a co-executor or a successive executor to take over if your named executor is unable to serve because of death, disability, or any other reason. An accountant and attorney should give your executor the technical knowledge and advice the job requires. So, should you choose your attorney as executor? I would not recommend it. The American Bar Association does not really say "no" but they do feel that . . .

> A lawyer should not consciously influence a client to name him as executor, trustee, or lawyer in an instrument. In those cases where a client wishes to name his lawyer as such, care should be taken by the lawyer to avoid even the appearance of impropriety. *Source:* American Bar Association's *Code of Professional Responsibility,* Canon 5.

Take a look at Table 6–2 for an idea of what you should expect to pay for an executor's or administrator's fees.

## IMPORTANT QUESTIONS TO ASK ABOUT YOUR WILL

### Who Will Be Beneficiary?

Have there been any changes in *who* should be the beneficiary of your estate? Births, deaths, marriages, divorces, and adoptions in your family are all sure signs that it is time to review and update your will.

### Who Will Care for the Children?

If something should happen to you, *who* will care for the children? Vague thoughts and a casual request expressed to relatives can be forgotten when it comes to reality. The best way to have your wishes carried out for the best interest of your children is to name a guardian.

If you do not name someone, the court will. The named guardian must post a bond . . . that must be renewed each and every year that the children are minors. Besides that, periodic reports must be made to the court each and every year that the children are minors.

Selecting a guardian is probably the hardest decision you will have to make. Divorced parents usually have a more complex situation. When a mother has custody of the children, they will normally be returned to the custody of their father on her death (or vice versa). If she has remarried, and her new husband has not yet adopted the children, but would like to, there could be problems.

Why so many parents get hung up over the selection of guardians is a problem in itself. In most cases, they are confused about the duties of a guardian and do not understand what choices they have.

Setting up a guardianship for your children involves two main jobs. The first is to provide for the care of the children themselves, seeing that they have a good home, clothes to wear, proper meals to eat, and supervision

**Table 6–2.** Executors' and administrators' commissions.

| | |
|---|---|
| Alabama | Such commission as court may deem just and fair, not to exceed $2\frac{1}{2}$% of monies received plus $2\frac{1}{2}$% of monies paid out (plus expenses)[1,2] |
| Alaska | A reasonable commission is permitted |
| Arizona | A reasonable commission is permitted |
| Arkansas | 10% on first $1,000 of personal property; 5% on next $4,000; 3% on balance over $5,000[3] |
| California | 4% on first $15,000 of estate value; 3% on next $85,000; 2% on next $900,000; 1% on balance over $1 million[2] |
| Colorado | A reasonable commission is permitted |
| Connecticut | Probate court sets reasonable commission |
| Delaware | Percentage varies for estates under $100,000; over $100,000 percentage begins at $4\frac{1}{2}$% and decreases to $2\frac{8}{10}$% over $500,000 |
| Florida | A reasonable commission is permitted |
| Georgia | $2\frac{1}{2}$% on monies received plus $2\frac{1}{2}$% on monies paid out (plus expenses)[3] |
| Hawaii | 4% of first $15,000 of estate value; 3% of next $85,000; 2% of next $900,000; $1\frac{1}{2}$% of next $2 million; 1% of excess over $3 million; 7% of first $5,000 of estate's yearly income; 5% of balance[3] |
| Idaho | A reasonable commission is permitted |
| Illinois | No statutory rate. Commission is set by the probate court |
| Indiana | No statutory rate. Commission is set by the probate division of the circuit court |

**Table 6–2 (continued).**

| State | |
|---|---|
| Iowa | Reasonable fees not to exceed 6% on first $1,000 of estate value; 4% on next $4,000; 2% on balance over $5,000[3] |
| Kansas | A reasonable commission is permitted |
| Kentucky | Reasonable fees not to exceed 5% of value of personal estate plus 5% of income received thereon[3] |
| Louisiana | $2\frac{1}{2}$% of appraised value of estate[2,4] |
| Maine | A reasonable commission is permitted |
| Maryland | Such commission as court may deem appropriate, not to exceed 10% on first $20,000 of personal property; 4% on balance[5] |
| Massachusetts | No statutory rate, but $2\frac{1}{2}$%–3% on personal property up to $500,000 and 1% on balance is usually considered not unreasonable. |
| Michigan | A reasonable commission is permitted[3] |
| Minnesota | A reasonable commission is permitted |
| Mississippi | Commission is set by the probate court, but in no case may it exceed 7% of value of entire estate |
| Missouri | At minimum, 5% on first $5,000 of estate value; 4% on next $20,000; 3% on next $75,000; $2\frac{3}{4}$% on next $300,000; $2\frac{1}{2}$% on next $600,000; 2% on balance over $1 million |
| Montana | A reasonable commission is permitted, not to exceed 3% on first $40,000 of estate value; 2% on balance[2,6] |
| Nebraska | A reasonable commission is permitted |
| Nevada | 6% on first $1,000 of estate value; 4% on next $4,000; 2% on balance over $5,000[2,6] |

106

| State | |
|---|---|
| New Hampshire | No statutory rate, but court will award reasonable compensation |
| New Jersey | Principal of estate: 5% on first $100,000; on the balance such percentage as set by probate court, but in no case more than 5%. Income from estate: 6%[5,7] |
| New Mexico | Up to 10% of first $3,000; up to 5% of balance, unless otherwise ordered by court[8] |
| New York | For receiving and paying first $100,000, 5%; next $200,000, 4%; next $700,000, 3%; next $4 million, 2½%; sums over $5 million, 2%[9] |
| North Carolina | Commission is within discretion of clerk of court and may not exceed 5% of monies received and paid out[10] |
| North Dakota | A reasonable commission is permitted |
| Ohio | 4% of first $100,000; 3% of $100,000–$400,000; 2% above $400,000 |
| Oklahoma | 5% on first $1,000 of estate value; 4% on next $4,000; 2½% on balance over $5,000[2] |
| Oregon | 7% on first $1,000 of estate value; 4% on next $9,000; 3% on next $40,000; 2% on balance over $50,000[2] |
| Pennsylvania | No statutory rate but usually 5% of principal and income on estates under $100,000; 3% if estate is $100,000–$200,000, decreasing to 1% as estate exceeds $3 million |
| Rhode Island | Probate court sets just compensation |
| South Carolina | 2½% on appraised value of personal assets received and 2½% on personal assets paid out plus 10% of interest on money loaned[2] |
| South Dakota | 5% on first $1,000 of personal property; 4% on next $4,000; 2½% on balance over $5,000[8] |
| Tennessee | Probate court sets reasonable commission |
| Texas | 5% of all monies received in cash plus 5% of all monies paid out in cash[11] |

107

**Table 6–2 (continued).**

| | |
|---|---|
| Utah | Commission may not exceed 5% on first $1,000 of estate value; 4% on next $4,000; 3% on next $5,000; 2% on next $40,000; 1½% on next $50,000; 1% on excess over $100,000[3] |
| Vermont | Court sets reasonable compensation |
| Virginia | A reasonable commission is permitted, usually 5% on monies received and property sold; 2½% on tangible or intangible property distributed in kind or retained in trust |
| Washington D.C. | Probate court sets reasonable compensation |
| Washington | Probate court sets reasonable compensation |
| West Virginia | A reasonable commission is permitted, usually 5% on monies received |
| Wisconsin | 2% of inventory value and gains to principal[2] |
| Wyoming | 10% on first $1,000 of estate value; 5% on next $4,000; 3% on next $15,000; 2% on balance over $20,000[2] |

(1) 2½% of value of lands sold for division, but no more than $100 if the lands are not sold under terms of a will.
(2) Probate court may permit additional compensation for extraordinary services.
(3) Probate court may permit additional compensation for extraordinary services or for services in connection with real estate.
(4) If more than 1 fiduciary, compensation is apportioned by the probate court.
(5) Unless the will provides for a larger commission.
(6) If there is more than 1 fiduciary, one commission is divided equally among them.
(7) If there is more than 1 fiduciary, commission on principal may be increased up to 1% per each additional fiduciary. If administration of the estate lasts more than 25 years, additional compensation may be granted, up to ½ of 1% for each additional year.
(8) Probate court sets the commission, if any, on real estate.
(9) If there is more than 1 fiduciary, commission is divided among the fiduciaries as follows: (a) if the value of the estate is $100,000 or less, the commission for one fiduciary is divided among the fiduciaries; (b) if the estate is over $100,000 but less than $300,000, 2 fiduciaries get a full commission, but more than 2 share the total of 2 full commissions; (c) if the estate is $300,000 or more, 3 fiduciaries get a full commission, but more than 3 fiduciaries share 3 full commissions.
(10) The clerk of the probate court may set the commission if the estate is $2,000 or less.
(11) Total commission can never exceed 5% of the gross fair market value of the estate.
*Source:* Adapted by permission from *You and the Law,* pp. 693–695. Copyright © 1984 by The Reader's Digest Association, Inc.

until they reach the age of majority. The second is to manage in a reasonable way the property and money left to them.

In most states, you can name one person to handle both jobs, or you can name separate people or institutions to handle these distinctly different jobs. And, instead of putting your children's inheritance in the hands of a guardian, you could establish a custodial account or trust fund for them, either as part of your will or as a separate document.

If you children are mature enough, ask them to help choose their guardian if something should happen to you. Much to most parents' surprise, there are no fears or tears in such a situation and children get a sense of closeness in being involved in this mutual decision.

You should select one person as guardian and name at least one alternative. Guardians can become ill, disabled, or even die. A substitute should be named as a precautionary measure.

## What Does a Will Do for You?

One of the most important papers that you will ever sign is your will. But, Doctor, do you know *what* it does for you?

First and foremost, a will allows you to leave your property to anyone you please. You may want to leave your spouse everything, or you may want to stipulate that certain things are distributed to specific individuals named by you, such as your boat to your son and your stamp collection to your daughter. You may wish to include a clause stating that if none of the named beneficiaries survive, that another named person take their share.

A will can save unnecessary expenses. For example, as a general rule your executor must post a bond, making periodic reports, and give an inventory to the court, unless your will relieves them of this duty. This of course, saves money.

A properly drawn will can help protect your family's welfare. Mistakes can create unnecessary complications. They did just that for the father who left a yearly income to his married daughter "as long as she is above the ground." When the daughter died, her husband installed her in a mausoleum "above the ground." Guess what? The husband collected the money for the rest of his life!

You are all-powerful when it comes to your will. You are making a legal document that, upon your death and after probate, becomes law in the sense that you have the right to dispose of your property the way you see fit.

There is certain property that you cannot dispose of in your will. Jointly owned property with the right of survivorship automatically goes to the surviving owner upon your death. You cannot dispose of life insurance benefits unless you have named your estate as beneficiary. Pension and profit sharing plans cannot be given away in your will, since you have already designated beneficiaries for them. Naturally, you cannot dispose of property that you expect to inherit but have not actually received. Nor can you devise any assets over which you have no control, such as income from a trust that you receive only during your lifetime. If you do, the courts will simply ignore these provisions.

## What If You Die Without a Will?

If you don't have your own will written, *what* will happen? The state will do it for you. Every state has a code of laws governing the disposition of property of those who die without writing their own formal, legal directions. There is no "justice," and "needs" are not considered in the rules of inheritance when a person dies intestate (without a will). And these rules are binding.

If you do not have a will, your estate will be divided according to the laws of your state. And, your estate may have to pay higher estate taxes than necessary to meet needs; your administrator (probably your spouse) may have to post a bond and give frequent records to the court; and your family may have to follow the rigid requirements set by your state. (For an example of what may happen when the state disposes of your estate, see Chart 18 (Figure 6–1) at the end of the chapter.)

## When Is a Will Probated?

A will should be probated *when* you die. State laws vary but most claim it should be probated within a "reasonable" time after your death. It is probated to prove the fact of your death so that title to your property may go to the proper person.

The word *probate* merely means *to prove.* Actually, your will isn't probated, your estate is—with or without a will. Probate should take place in the state and county where you are domiciled (your legal residence) at the time of your death. If you have real estate in any other state, then a probate procedure should take place in that state and county where the property is located in addition to your place of domicile in order to transfer the title to its new rightful owner.

When you write your will, just remember that personal property is governed by the law of the state where you are domiciled at the time of your death and real estate is governed by the law of the situs (location) of that property. If you own property in more than one state, your will must comply with the laws of all those states.

For example: Doctor Barrie was a resident of Sterling, Illinois, when he signed his will leaving 160 acres of his property in Iowa to four named beneficiaries, including the First Presbyterian Church. When he died, his will was found with the word *VOID* written across the top of the first page and on the envelope in which it was found. The Illinois court claimed that this was a revocation of his will and his property in Illinois was to be distributed to his heirs at law. However, the Iowa courts admitted this same will into their probate courts and upheld it, claiming that the state in which real property is located governs the testator's capacity or incapacity to give the will its due effect. Doctor Barrie's personal property that was located in Illinois was distributed among his heirs-at-law, while his real estate in Iowa went to the named beneficiaries who would otherwise be unable to claim it under Illinois law.

Have there been any changes in where you live or where your property is located? If you or your property have moved, it is surely time to check your will.

Obviously, tax and other probate laws vary from state to state. A will that does what you want it to under the laws of, say, Florida, where you used to live, may not do so under the laws of California (a community property state). There are no uniform laws pertaining to wills. And, states do not have to recognize a will made in another state. This is because states are not governed by the "Full Faith and Credit" clause under the Constitution.

Or, if you move, maybe you should choose a new executor for your will. Perhaps your brother was an ideal person when both of you lived in Pennsylvania. Now he is still in Pennsylvania but you are in Washington. Will he still be able to handle your estate, collect money owed to you, sell your practice—all at a distance of 3,000 miles?

Believe it or not, more than half of the people in the United States die intestate, that is, without a valid will. Many of these people who die intestate obviously intended to get around to having a will drafted, but, for one reason or another, never found the time. On the other hand, some of those who did draft a will were under the mistaken impression that a will was not something that needed to be updated.

Take Senator Robert Kerr of Oklahoma, for example. He was a pioneer in tax reform. He wrote his will in 1939 and had thought about updating it for years, but never quite got around to it. In his will he left a trust in which his wife was to get $9,000 a year.

I'm sure that in 1939 that might have been a lot of money, but what about inflation and today's cost of living? Thirty years later when the senator died, his estate was worth $20 million dollars and his estate taxes were $11 million. His wife was locked into an income of $9,000 a year and had to borrow money to pay taxes. Had he undated his will, a lot of time, energy, and expense could have been saved.

## When Are Common Law Rights Recognized?

There are still some states that recognize the old common law right of "dower" (for a woman) and "curtesy" (for a man). These rights are recognized *when* they are not released (in writing) by the spouse if the property is sold. They entitle a surviving spouse to an interest in the decedent spouse's real estate, regardless of what the will says, for his or her life. These rights are created by operation of law in some states. Take a look at Table 6–3 to see what your state does or does not recognize.

## Where Are the Witnesses?

Give a little thought as to how your estate will be administered. For example, even if you decide that you have no other changes to make in your will itself, ask yourself, *where* are the witnesses who signed your will? If they are all dead or vanished, maybe you should update your will with new witnesses.

Or, you might consider a "Self-Proving Declaration" (recognized in most states) at the end of the will itself. The purpose of a Self-Proving Declaration is to presume that your will is valid even without witnesses' being present when it is probated—provided, however, that your will is not contested. Otherwise, you may simply add to your executor's work by his having to account for the missing witnesses and making sure of their signatures. You may even risk having your will thrown out of court.

Some states require two witnesses to a will for that will to be properly signed and witnessed; others require three. Most states claim that if one of the persons who signs is an "interested witness" (that is, also named as a beneficiary in the will), that person will lose his or her share of what was left them in the will. A spouse is generally the only person who is excluded from this provision. Not fair? Maybe not, but do check your own state laws before selecting witnesses to your will.

Most states have fixed by statute (law) the age at which you may make a will. The most common fixed age is 18 or 21, but in some states the fixed age is lower, as in Georgia where it is 14. A few states accept holographic (handwritten) wills. However, most states do not recognize them at all. A holographic will is one that you write yourself, date, and sign in your own handwriting. See Table 6–4 for valid will requirements.

## Where It Cannot Be Determined Who Survived?

If you and your spouse were killed in an accident where it could not be determined who survived the other, what would happen to the property that qualified for the marital deduction? In order for the marital deduction to be available, it is necessary for there to be a surviving spouse. Where there is insufficient evidence of who died first, there is a presumption (supplied by local law) that each predeceased the other. If each predeceased the other, there is no surviving spouse. And, with no surviving spouse the marital deduction would be lost.

**Table 6–3.** Your right to part of your spouse's estate regardless of the will.

| | Rights of Curtesy & Dower[1] | Right of Election | Community Property[2] | What You Are Entitled To | Time Limit for Filing |
|---|---|---|---|---|---|
| Alabama | Wife only | Wife only | No | Dower[1] plus intestate share of personal property[3] | 6 months after will admitted to probate |
| Alaska | No | Yes | No | 1/3 of augmented estate[4] | 6 months after notice to creditors |
| Arizona | No | No | Yes | 1/2 net community property | Filing not required for 1/2 net community property owned by surviving spouse |
| Arkansas | Yes | Yes | No | Curtesy or dower[1] | 1 month after expiration of time for filing creditors' claims |
| California | No | No | Yes | 1/2 net community and net quasicommunity property[5] | Filing not required for 1/2 net community property owned by surviving spouse |
| Colorado | No | Yes | No | 1/2 of augmented estate[4] | 6 months after notice to creditors or 1 year after spouse's death, whichever is sooner |
| Connecticut | No | Yes | No | Use for life of 1/3 real and personal property | 2 months after expiration of time for filing creditors' claims |
| Delaware | No | Yes | No | $20,000 or 1/3 elective estate,[6] whichever is less | 6 months after issuance of letters testamentary |
| D.C. | Yes | Yes[7] | No | Dower[1] plus 1/2 personal property; or intestate share not to exceed 1/2 net estate[8] bequeathed and devised by will | 6 months after will admitted to probate |
| Florida | No | Yes | No | 30% of net estate[8] except real property outside Florida | 4 months after date of notice of administration |
| Georgia | No | No | No | But spouse entitled to 1 year's support from decedent's estate in amount not less than $1,600 | Within 3 years of spouse's death |
| Hawaii | Yes[9] | Yes | No | 1/3 of net estate[8] | 9 months after death or 6 months after probate of will |
| Idaho | No | Yes[10] | Yes | 1/2 net community property and, if elected, 1/2 net quasicommunity property[5] | For 1/2 quasicommunity property share, 6 months after notice to creditors; filing not required for 1/2 community property share owned by surviving spouse |
| Illinois | No | Yes[7] | No | 1/3 of net estate[8] if descendant(s); 1/2 if no descendant(s) | 7 months after will admitted to probate |
| Indiana | No | Yes | No | 1/3 of net estate[8] | 10 days after expiration of time for filing creditors' claims or 30 days before final determination of pending litigation |
| Iowa | No | Yes | No | 1/3 of net estate[8] | 6 months after second publication of notice of admission of will to probate |
| Kansas | No | Yes | No | Intestate share | 6 months after will admitted to probate |
| Kentucky | Yes | Yes | No | Curtesy or dower[1] | 12 months after will admitted to probate |
| Louisiana | No | No | Yes | 1/2 net community property | Filing not required for 1/2 community property share owned by surviving spouse; if spouse dies rich by comparison to surviving spouse, latter may claim a portion of the estate up to 3 years after spouse's death |
| Maine | No | Yes | No | 1/3 of augmented estate[4] | 6 months after will admitted to probate or 9 months after spouse's death, whichever is later |

# Table 6–3 (continued)

| | Rights of Curtesy & Dower[1] | Right of Election | Community Property[2] | What You Are Entitled To | Time Limit for Filing |
|---|---|---|---|---|---|
| Maryland | No | Yes | No | Intestate share | Within 30 days of expiration of time for filing creditors' claims, unless extended by court order |
| Massachusetts | Yes | Yes | No | Intestate share, not to exceed $25,000 plus income of balance for life; but if no issue, $25,000 plus 1/2 of net estate[8] | 6 months after probate of will |
| Michigan | Yes | Yes | No | 1/2 intestate share reduced by any recent transfers to surviving spouse | 60 days after date for presenting creditors' claims or after date surviving spouse was served with estate inventory, whichever is later |
| Minnesota | No | Yes | No | Intestate share, not to exceed 1/2 of estate | 9 months after spouse's death or 6 months after will admitted to probate |
| Mississippi | No | Yes | No | Intestate share, not to exceed 1/2 of estate | 3 months after will admitted to probate |
| Missouri | No | Yes | No | If issue survive, 1/3 of net estate[8]; is no issue, 1/2 | Within 10 days of expiration of time for contesting will; or if in litigation, 90 days after final determination |
| Montana | No | Yes | No | 1/3 of augmented estate[4] | 6 months after notice to creditors or 1 year after spouse's death |
| Nebraska | No | Yes | No | 1/3 of augmented estate[4] | 6 months after notice to creditors or 1 year after spouse's death |
| Nevada | No | No | Yes | 1/2 net community property | Filing not required for 1/2 community property share owned by surviving spouse |
| New Hampshire | No | Yes | No | If issue survive, 1/3 of net estate[8]; if kindred but no issue, $20,000 plus 1/2 remainder; if no kindred or issue, $20,000 plus $4,000 per year for life and 1/2 remainder | 6 months after appointment of executor or administrator |
| New Jersey | No | Yes | No | 1/3 of augmented estate[4] | 6 months after appointment of personal representative |
| New Mexico | No | No | Yes | 1/2 net community property | Filing not required for 1/2 community property share owned by surviving spouse |
| New York | No | Yes | No | If issue survive, 1/3 of net estate[8]; if no issue, 1/2[11] | 6 months after appointment of executor or administrator |
| North Carolina | No | Yes | No | Intestate share, not to exceed 1/2 estate | 6 months after appointment of executor or administrator |
| North Dakota | No | Yes | No | 1/3 of augmented estate[4] | 9 months after spouse's death or 6 months after will admitted to probate |
| Ohio | Yes | Yes | No | Intestate share, not to exceed 1/2 estate | Within 1 month of notice of right to election |
| Oklahoma | No | Yes | No | Intestate share | Prior to final distribution or settlement of estate |
| Oregon | No | Yes | No | 1/4 of net estate[8] | 90 days after will admitted to probate or 30 days after filing of inventory, whichever is later |
| Pennsylvania | No | Yes | No | If issue survive, 1/3 of net estate[8]; if no issue, 1/2 | 6 months after will admitted to probate |
| Rhode Island | No | Yes | No | Use for life of spouse's real estate | 6 months after will admitted to probate |

114

| State | Wife only | Wife only | Dower[1] | Prior to final distribution of estate |
|---|---|---|---|---|
| South Carolina | No | No | Not more than $1/3$ of augmented estate[4] or $100,000, whichever is greater | |
| South Dakota | No | Yes | $1/2$ of net estate[8] | 2 months after first publication of notice to creditors |
| Tennessee | No | Yes | | 6 months after will admitted to probate or 9 months after spouse's death, whichever is later |
| Texas | No | No | $1/2$ net community property | Filing not required for $1/2$ net community property share owned by surviving spouse |
| Utah | No | Yes | $1/3$ of personal estate or, if no issue, intestate share; or, if surviving spouse so chooses, $1/3$ of real estate if issue, $1/2$ if no issue | 6 months after probate of will or 1 year after spouse's death |
| Vermont | No | Yes | Curtesy or dower,[1] plus $1/3$ personal property if issue survive, or plus $1/2$ personal property if no issue | 8 months after will admitted to probate |
| Virginia | Yes | Yes | $1/3$ of net estate,[8] reduced by testamentary devises to spouse | 1 year after will admitted to probate or later if extended by court |
| Washington | No | No | $1/2$ net community property | Filing not required for $1/2$ net community property share owned by surviving spouse |
| West Virginia | Yes | Yes | Intestate share as if decedent died leaving children | 8 months after will admitted to probate |
| Wisconsin | Yes | Yes | $1/3$ of augmented estate,[4] multiplied by fraction representing ratio of decedent's marital property[12] to the gross estate | 6 months after spouse's death or later if extended by court |
| Wyoming | No | Yes | Intestate share, not to exceed $1/4$ of estate if issue survive and $1/2$ if no issue | 3 months after will admitted to probate or 30 days after notice of right to election, whichever is later |

(1) Curtesy denotes the husband's marital share; dower, the wife's marital share; dower, the wife's (although in some places, such as the District of Columbia and Maryland, dower refers to both shares). In most states these rights apply only to real property, but in Arkansas and Kentucky personal property is also included. A typical curtesy or dower interest is $1/3$ of the spouse's real estate for life if children survive, and $1/2$ interest absolutely (that is, the interest can be passed on) if there are no children. Where unpaid creditors exist, the $1/2$ share may be reduced to $1/3$.

(2) Generally, a surviving spouse in a community property state who elects to take under the will is also entitled to his community property share. But in some cases, the decedent can write his will in such a way that the surviving spouse must choose one or the other (that is, the terms of the will or the community property share).

(3) If no lineal descendants and personal estate exceeds $50,000, widow may elect first $50,000 of personal property, and balance will be distributed according to the terms of the will.

(4) The augmented estate is the gross estate less: funeral and administrative expenses, the homestead allowance, family allowances and exemptions, enforceable creditors' claims and various real estate transfers.

(5) Quasicommunity property is all personal property, wherever located, and all real property located within the state which would have been community property had the parties (the decedent and the surviving spouse) been domiciled in the state at the time the property was acquired.

(6) The elective estate is approximately the adjusted gross estate minus certain transfers made by the decedent during his lifetime with the written consent or participation of the surviving spouse.

(7) Technically, a "right of renunciation."

(8) The net estate equals all of the decedent's real and personal property, reduced by funeral and administrative expenses, homestead and other exemptions and, in some states, by creditors' claims against the estate.

(9) But only for rights that accrued before July 1, 1977.

(10) But elective right applies only to surviving spouse's $1/2$ share of quasicommunity property.

(11) But certain provisions in the will may diminish right of election.

(12) Marital property includes all property acquired by decedent during the marriage except that acquired by gift, devise or descent, or that purchased with assets derived from these sources.

**Table 6–4.** Valid will requirements.

| | Individual State Requirements | | |
| State | Age (to dispose of property) | Number of witnesses | Holograph Wills Recognized? |
| --- | --- | --- | --- |
| Alabama | 19 (real)[1] | 2 | No |
| | 18 (personal) | | |
| Alaska | 18 | 2 | Yes |
| Arizona | 18 | 2 | Yes |
| Arkansas | 18 | 2 | Yes |
| California | 18 | 2 | Yes |
| Colorado | 18 | 2 | Yes |
| Connecticut | 18 | 2 | No |
| Delaware | 18 | 2 | No |
| Florida | 18 | 2 | No[3] |
| Georgia | 14 | 2 | No |
| Hawaii | 18 | 2 | No |
| Idaho | 18[4] | 2 | Yes |
| Illinois | 18 | 2 | No |
| Indiana | 18[5] | 2 | No |
| Iowa | 18 | 2 | No |
| Kansas | 18 | 2 | No |
| Kentucky | 18 | 2 | Yes |
| Louisiana | 18[6] | 2 | Yes |
| Maine | 18 | 2 | Yes |
| Maryland | 18 | 2 | No[5] |
| Massachusetts | 18 | 2 | No |
| Michigan | 18 | 2 | Yes |
| Minnesota | 18 | 2 | No |
| Mississippi | 18 | 2 | Yes |
| Missouri | 18 | 2 | No |
| Montana | 18 | 2 | Yes |
| Nebraska | 18 | 2 | Yes |
| Nevada | 18 | 2 | Yes |
| New Hampshire | 18[4] | 3 | No |
| New Jersey | 18 | 2 | Yes |
| New Mexico | 18 | 2 | No |
| New York | 18 | 2 | No[5] |
| North Carolina | 18 | 2 | Yes |
| North Dakota | 18 | 2 | Yes |
| Ohio | 18 | 2 | No |
| Oklahoma | 18 | 2 | Yes |
| Oregon | 18[4] | 2 | No |
| Pennsylvania | 18 | None[7] | Yes |
| Rhode Island | 18[8] | 2 | No[5] |
| South Carolina | 18 | 3 | No[5] |
| South Dakota | 18 | 2 | Yes |
| Tennessee | 18 | 2 | Yes |

**Table 6–4** (*continued*)

| State | Individual State Requirements | | |
|---|---|---|---|
| | Age (to dispose of property) | Number of witnesses | Holograph Wills Recognized? |
| Texas | 18[4,5] | 2 | Yes |
| Utah | 18 | 2 | Yes |
| Vermont | 18 | 3 | No[5] |
| Virginia | 18 | 2 | Yes |
| Washington, D.C. | 18 | 2 | Yes[2] |
| Washington (state) | 18 | 2 | No |
| West Virginia | 18 | 2 | Yes |
| Wisconsin | 18 | 2 | No |
| Wyoming | 19 | 2 | Yes |

(1) For real property; 18 for personal property. (2) But witnesses are necessary. (3) But courts have recognized holographic wills as valid if it is proved that testator had sufficient "testamentary intent." (4) Younger if married or widowed. (5) But exceptions are made for servicemen on active duty outside the U.S. or during armed conflict, and for mariners. (6) But 16 if near death. (7) If the will is actually signed, not merely initialed, by testator; otherwise, 2 witnesses are necessary. (8) But if under 21, only for personal property.
*Source:* Adapted by permission from *You and the Law*, p. 635. Copyright © 1984 by The Reader's Digest Association, Inc.

So what can be done? Your will should contain a "Simultaneous Death Clause." This clause—which relates to the time of the deaths—is a reverse presumption and is controlling regardless of the local law's presumption. Then the marital deduction would be saved. This could mean the difference in thousands of dollars for your children's benefit if both of you were to die at the same time.

In common law states, the spouse with the larger estate frequently provides in the will that the spouse is presumed to be the survivor if they die simultaneously. This provision splits the property in order to take advantage of the unified credit available to both estates.

In community property states, the property is already split (unless separate property is involved). To avoid separating the estate, the will should give the property to the spouse only if the spouse survives the testator by a certain period (less than six months to avoid marital deduction disqualification).

If both spouses have large estates, then the survivorship clause should be conditioned on survival by as much as six months. The reason is that some states and the I.R.S. [I.R.C., Sec. 2056(b) (3)] require a person to survive by a set time period (six months, by the I.R.S.) in order to be considered an heir-at-law. This will not adversely affect the ability of the deceased spouse's estate to claim the marital deduction and property will go as directed by the will instead of by state law.

A "Common Disaster Clause" relates to an "event" and is trickier to use than a simultaneous death clause. With a common disaster clause, the beneficiary is deemed to have predeceased the testator "if their deaths arise out of or result from a common disaster or accident."

A common disaster provision operates very well if the testator and beneficiary die within a short time of each other. But, if the beneficiary lingers in life, factual issues surrounding the cause of death may arise. This "result of" clause could result in an extended deferment of the question of survivorship and the loss of the marital deduction if the surviving spouse is still alive at the time of auditing the decedent's return. Then, no property interest would pass to the spouse and consequently no question would arise concerning the availability of the marital deduction.

To prevent an extremely narrow survivorship condition's being placed in your will, you might consider something like the following:

> In the event that my wife and I die under circumstances wherein it cannot be determined which of us survived the other, it shall be presumed for purposes of this will that my wife survived me and this will shall be construed upon that presumption; and
>
> If my spouse does not survive me by six months, then I leave all the rest, residue, and remainder of my property to be divided equally among my children, Leslie Bradley, Marc Bradley, and Tracy Bradley.

## How Should Codicils Be Drafted?

Do not try to change your will yourself with pen and ink—even slightly. Unless these changes are made in a new will or in a codicil in a rather technical manner, they will be ignored. A codicil is an addition or change to your will. If you try to make changes—scratching out, writing over, erasing, crossing out—a court will decide that the whole will should be thrown out on the ground that you really intended to revoke it and it is invalid. So changing your will is a job for your attorney.

And, even though you may not have thought of any changes you want in your will, have it reviewed periodically by your attorney (at least once every five years). The tax laws are constantly being amended in ways that may affect you. It is your attorney's job to keep abreast of those changes, and to show you how to turn them to your own best advantage.

## How Should the Will Be Executed (Signed)?

First, read your will carefully to ensure that its provisions meet with your satisfaction. If your will is satisfactory, ask two (or three, depending upon your state's requirements) adult persons to witness the signing of your will. Witnesses should not be members of your family or beneficiaries under your will.

When you are ready to sign your will, you must tell the witnesses that the document you are about to sign is your will and that you are asking them to witness your executing it.

Then, in the presence of the witnesses, initial or sign your will in the margin or at the bottom of each page. Date and sign the last page of your will and the "Self-Proving Declaration" (if there is one). When you sign your name, sign it exactly as it is typed below the signature line.

After you have dated, initialed, and signed your will, the witnesses should sign their names (addresses are optional) on the last page of your will and on the Self-Proving Declaration page. You must be present when the witnesses are signing your will *and* each witness must be present while the other witnesses sign. You now have a valid will.

## How Can You Elect Against a Will?

If you are left an interest in property and you do not want it, you may "disclaim" that property. In most states, rather than accept the terms of your spouse's will, you may choose either to disclaim your inheritance or "elect" to follow the state laws that would normally become effective if your spouse died intestate (without a will). (See Table 6–3.)

A disclaimer is a formal method of repudiating the legal or beneficial receipt of the property before any rights in the property have vested in the recipient of the property. Generally, I.R.C. section 2518 provides a method for making disclaimers for both gift tax and estate tax purposes; however, in order to have a proper disclaimer, each of the following tests must be met.

1. The refusal must be in writing.
2. The refusal must be received by the transferor of the interest, the legal representative of the transferor, or the holder of the legal title to the property to which the interest relates within nine months after the latter of:
   a. The day on which the transfer creating the interest is made, or
   b. The day on which the disclaimant reaches age 21.
3. The disclaimant must not have accepted the interest or any of its benefits.
4. As a result of the refusal, the interest must pass without any direction from the disclaimer to either:
   a. The spouse of the decedent or,
   b. A person other than the disclaimant.
5. The refusal must be irrevocable and unqualified.

According to the I.R.S., the nine-month period for making a disclaimer generally is determined for each taxable transfer. For a lifetime transfer, the period begins on the date the transfer is a completed transfer for gift tax purposes. For a transfer by will, it begins on the date of the decedent's death.

Why would you disclaim something that is left to you? One such instance may be where a QTIP (qualified terminable interest property) trust has been established and the surviving spouse does not want the property taxed in her estate when she dies since she does not have the right to determine who is to get the property. A QTIP trust would give the surviving spouse interest income for life, and, when she dies, the remaining trust would be distributed to the person to whom the testator designated as beneficiary, not to whom the surviving spouse designated.

## How Are Attorneys' Fees Determined?

People often put off going to a lawyer's office because they do not know *how* attorneys' fees are determined and they are afraid of what it is going to cost them. Lawyers do charge in various ways: by the hour, by the case, as a percentage of the money you recover in a case, or as a percentage of a decedent's estate. The fees shown in Table 6–5 will give you an idea of what to expect for probate fees.

I am sure that at one time or another, we have all heard someone's hair-raising story about how their lawyer charged an exorbitant amount for representation. And, it is not uncommon for you to believe the aggrieved client.

Abraham Lincoln reminds us that "a lawyer's advice is his stock in trade." And, unlike that of a doctor, the attorney's work is accomplished when the client is not present. The advice you are given in a few minutes and the multi-page trust drawn up on your behalf are actually products of many hours of work. Compounding the problem is the fact that most people feel legal fees are a blind expense.

Avoid unnecessary surprise and expense by first talking with your

**Table 6–5.** Attorney's fees for probating a will.

| Size of Estate | Attorney's Fee | Expense Percent |
|---|---|---|
| $  75,000 | $  3,450 | 4.6% |
| 100,000 | 4,600 | 4.6 |
| 200,000 | 9,200 | 4.6 |
| 300,000 | 13,800 | 4.6 |
| 500,000 | 22,500 | 4.5 |
| 750,000 | 33,000 | 4.4 |
| 1,000,000 | 43,000 | 4.3 |
| 3,000,000 | 126,000 | 4.2 |
| 5,000,000 | 215,000 | 4.3 |

attorney. Negotiate fees in advance. Arrange for itemized bills to be sent to you, and insist on being informed and kept up to date on what your attorney is doing for you. You can do this if you have kept your financial affairs as suggested in this book.

Using these questions: Who? What? When? Where? How? check your will and see whether a change is called for. If you need advice, your attorney is ready to help.

## How Can Wishes Be Stated More Personally?

How would you like to appear personally before your relatives or a court of law and directly state your intentions about your property after you are gone? You can, via videotape.

Law firms currently using videotape feel that the medium is a cost-effective legal tool that has almost limitless uses in any law practice because of its impact and trustworthiness. Videotape has been found to be valuable in recording depositions, civil and criminal trials, defendants' statements and confessions, line-ups, criminal transactions, and accident scenes. And yet, there are few practitioners today that have experimented with the medium in the field of wills.

Video wills should only act as a supplement to the standard written will, so that it leaves little room for questions of duress or mental incapacity. Since videotaped evidence incorporates both picture and sound, its evidentiary value is enormous and its effect is powerful.

If you are contemplating recording your will and its execution there are several steps you should follow. First, prior to the recording session, have your attorney prepare your written will just as he or she normally would. Set up a video cassette recorder (VCR) and any other essential accessories. Then, once you have read and re-read your written will so that your oral delivery duplicates the writing verbatim, you are ready to record. Not only should the will be completely spoken, but its execution (signing) should be completely recorded.

Caution: A written will and the videotaping of it should be done concurrently. The tape without a written will is not legal. If you want to change your will, a new tape should be made. The tape should be used merely to indicate mental clarity at the time changes are made.

Recording the reading of the will along with its execution will eliminate questions as to the authenticity of signatures and the presence and proximity of you, the testator, to the witnesses. The videotape will confirm that the state's statutory laws were obeyed. There would be little doubt that the instrument was authentic. The testator's mental capacity would be visually recorded at the time of execution of the will.

For example, in one recent case, a woman decided to leave her son only a token amount in her will with a "no contest" clause because she felt her son had caused her a lot of irritation all during her lifetime. Her legal counsel and the bank (who was administering the trust) felt that such a significant clause in her will should be recorded on videotape. They felt that videotape would demonstrate her sound mind, her understanding of the event, her satisfactory memory, as well as lessening any chance that the will would be contested.

Video specialists feel that it is not possible to successfully alter a videotaped will because any splicing, cutting, or editing of the tape would be obvious to the eye or could be detected by a video technician. Videotaped recorders with time and date generators indicate the exact time and date of recording directly onto the tape. Tampering would be obvious because any later modifications, whether by erasure or recording over the tape, would be visible not only in the testator's presentation but also by the prior recording of both the time and date.

Video uses are limitless. You might even want to go as far as videotaping the division of your personal property. On camera you could indicate which articles are to be left to which individuals. Some insurance companies already use a tape of video inventory service for insurance claim purposes. This same application applied to wills and property going into trusts could be significant.

One of the greatest advantages of video is that it shows people when they were alive, with facial expressions, sarcasm, nervousness, tears, and expressions of all kinds of emotions. Although the video is "live" keep in mind that it is not considered an exact duplicate of real life by the courts. Videotapes are only technical attempts to record and preserve mechanically your physical impressions.

Presently neither the Uniform Probate Code nor most state probate statutes recognize the use of videotaped wills as testamentary documents. Most states' statutes claim that your will must be typewritten complying with that state's formalities. Some state legislatures are studying the possibility of modifying their statutes in order to make videotaped wills legitimate as instruments for probate purposes.

Seeing someone on tape would raise lifeless words from the paper and give expression to a person's desires more dramatically than the written word could ever do. Television attests to that fact. Video could preserve, and does preserve, evidence in a solid way. In other proceedings, the courts believe that the accuracy of a demonstration tape requires that it demonstrate conditions resembling those at issue. In other words, does the tape accurately portray what it purports to portray? And are the circumstances sufficiently similar to those existing at the pertinent time as to be relevant? When the tape passes these two tests affirmatively, there are no significant problems to presenting videotaped wills in court.

In recording a will, both the testator and the witnesses should record an acknowledgment at the end of the cassette, indicating that the tape accurately captured the sequence of events. Then the written will, the video cassette, and the written Self-Proving Clause should be sealed inside a plastic cassette container. The document and cassette should be enclosed in an envelope or heat-sealing plastic bag and stored to insulate the tape from environmental changes. Safeguards should be taken to protect the recorded information so that it will not be damaged until the contents are needed.

Estate planning and writing a will should be more than a contemplation of death. It is planning your family's financial and emotional survival, not only while you are alive but also when you are no longer around. Videotaping offers you this opportunity.

The use of videotape is becoming more widespread. It is opening a new frontier.

## SUMMARY CHECKLIST FOR YOUR WILL

1. The marital deduction is available via (1) outright transfers to your surviving spouse; (2) a general power of appointment trust; and (3) a qualified terminable interest trust (known as QTIP under I.R.C. Section 2056(b) (7)).

2. Specific bequests give you an opportunity to make special gifts to those to whom you wish to leave certain items.

3. Simultaneous death clause is a provision clearly setting forth which party is presumed to survive if the testator and a beneficiary should die under circumstances in which it cannot be determined who survived. The correct choice of presumption will help preserve your testamentary wishes and defer costs and tax liabilities.

4. The residual clause concerns all the rest of your estate including any real estate. The correct choice to preserve your estate against a common disaster would be to require that your beneficiary survive for six months in order to receive anything under the terms of the will. This avoids increasing your estate if your beneficiary survives you but dies within that time period. If your beneficiary does not survive by six months, the rest, residue, and remainder of your estate should be bequeathed to another named beneficiary.

5. An appointment of executor should name your original and successor executors. A successor is named in the event that your original choice is unable to serve. The "Powers and Duties" of the executor should be broad and flexible, waiving any requirements of filing inventories, bond, and appraisals with the Court.

6. An appointment of guardian should not be overlooked if you have minors. You might consider appointing the surviving spouse as

the original guardian and also a successor guardian, if both of you should die during the minority of any of your children. The rights, duties, and responsibilities of the guardian should be provided along with a statement relieving them of the necessity to post bond or other security, inventory, or appraisals with the Court.

7. A disclaimer clause might be considered for the husband's will, if he is the major breadwinner. The clause would declare that the wife owns all of the personal effects and confirms the wife's ownership of the household items in an attempt to keep these items out of the husband's larger estate for tax purposes. Please note: this has nothing to do with divorce—it is only for the purpose of the will!

8. A self-proving declaration should not be forgotten because this clause presumes that your will is valid even without witnesses being present as long as your will is not contested.

Please note, this summary is not complete by any means, but it will help you to not forget the more important clauses that possibly should be included in your will. Do not forget to consult your attorney!

**Figure 6–1.** CHART 18: The Intestate's Will.

Being of sound mind and memory, I, _____, do hereby publish this as my Last Will and Testament:

FIRST—I give my wife only one-third of each of my possessions and I give my children the remaining two-thirds.

(a) I appoint my wife as guardian of my children, but as a safeguard I require that she report to the probate court regularly and render an accounting of how, why, and where she spent the money necessary for the proper care of my children.

(b) As a further safeguard, I direct my wife to produce to the court a performance bond to guarantee that she exercises proper judgment in the handling, investing, and spending of the children's money.

(c) As a final safeguard, my children shall have the right to demand and receive a complete accounting from their mother of all of her financial actions with their money as soon as they reach legal age.

(d) When my children reach age 21, they shall have full rights to withdraw and spend their shares of my estate. No one shall have any right to question my children's actions on how they decide to spend their respective shares.

SECOND—Should my wife remarry, her second husband shall be entitled to one-third of everything my wife possesses. Should my children need some of this share for their support, the second husband shall not be bound to spend any of his share on my children's behalf.

(a) The second husband shall have sole right to decide who is to get his share, even to the exclusion of my children.

THIRD—Even though my wife should predecease me or die while any of my children are minors, I do not wish to exercise my right to nominate the guardian of my children; rather my preference is to direct my relatives and my wife's relatives to get together and select a guardian by mutual agreement and, in the event that they fail to agree on a guardian, I direct the probate court to make the selection.

FOURTH—Under existing tax law, there are certain legitimate avenues open to me to lower death taxes. Since I prefer to have my money used for governmental purposes rather than for the benefit of my wife and children, I direct that no effort be made to lower taxes.

FIFTH—I appoint my wife to handle my estate, but, as a safeguard, I direct that she give a performance bond to guarantee that she does everything exactly as she should.

IN WITNESS WHEREOF, I have set my hand to this my Last Will and Testament this ___ day of _____, 19___.

Sovereign State of: _____

For _____

# 7

# INSURANCE:
# A HEDGE AGAINST
# THE INEVITABLE?

"Just give me a minute of your time, Doctor, and I can show you how to save a lot of money!"

Young Dr. Bradley had been bombarded with the message in letters and phone calls—both at home and in his new office—since he had started practicing. Life insurance agents are tireless. Finally, the young doctor agreed to sit down after dinner with a patient who sold insurance. After spreading impressive tables and charts across the coffee table, the agent produced a dazzling display of numbers and projections. "You see," he told the doctor and his wife, "this plan is tailor-made just for your special needs!"

When the Bradleys hesitated, the congenial salesman continued, "In addition, this plan will produce security for your retirement years. In fact, it will save you money!" The "package deal" was too good to pass up, and Dr. Bradley signed on the dotted line.

It was not until years later that he finally realized that the overpriced policy he had bought was for far more coverage than he needed. "Tailor made"? Far from it! It was just a standard policy that would pay the agent the highest commission, in the fastest way possible.

This is not to say that there are not honest, well-informed insurance agents. Unfortunately, however, the Bradley's case is not an isolated case. Doctors are prime targets, since the majority of them are not informed on the subject of insurance. Because they feel on the defensive, it is difficult for them to resist the agent's persistence and his or her impressive display of math.

With the current tax law, most doctors will not need as much life insurance or a large death benefit to help ease estate taxes. Because of this, it is well to remember that some agents may feel threatened that their livelihoods are in jeopardy. They may try to convince you with other ploys about what you need, only because they are selling it.

At one time or another, most people have experienced the frustration of trying to find their ways through the maze of life insurance language. Certainly, it is a complex subject, and there is much to learn about it. But instead of spending a lot of unnecessary time reading what you do not have to know, concentrate on this basic guide. You will find that it is the only life insurance guide you will ever need.

## DETERMINING THE NEED FOR
## AND AMOUNT OF LIFE INSURANCE

If you have dependents who will suffer financially if you died, then you should consider having some type of life insurance. *Otherwise, you do not need any!* It is as simple as that.

In determining how much life insurance you need, be aware first that, like most people, you plan according to the needs of the moment. You are providing for your family according to their needs, but periodically you may need to reevaluate. (Charts 19 and 20, Figure 7–1 and Figure 7–2) at the end of the chapter will help you determine your current insurance expenses and your life insurance needs.) What was right then may not be right now. And a computer is not needed for the job. Just follow these steps:

- List the face value of all your policies, and add them up.
- If you have borrowed against any of them, deduct that amount.
- Once you have totaled the face values, multiply that figure by 5 percent. I use 5% because economists tell us that 5% is still the most stable rate of return in a regular savings account, which is where many people put their money. And, even in times of inflation, a regular savings account is not much higher than that.
- The total would be the interest that that money would earn yearly in a savings account without any of the principal having been withdrawn.

If your dependents needed cash to live on, they might not be able to invest that money for a higher interest for a long period of time, because then that money would be unavailable to them when they needed it. Without touching the principal, could your dependents live on the interest? If money were needed, the principal would be reduced when it was withdrawn, which, in turn, would reduce the interest. Do you have enough other assets or do you need to consider insurance?

Take a look at this example to see how it works.

Example: *Do you have enough life insurance?*

Face Value of Insurance Policies

|  |  |
|---|---|
|  | $150,000 |
|  | 75,000 |
|  | 50,000 |
|  | 25,000 |
| Total Face Value of Policies | $300,000 |
|  | ×5% |
| Interest, per year | $ 15,000 |
| (without touching the principal!) | |

If you have $300,000 in life insurance proceeds put away for one year at 5 percent interest, could your dependents live on the $15,000 interest *without* touching the principal?

## TYPES OF INSURANCE

What type of life insurance should you buy? Renewable term insurance—for the *lowest* available premium that you can find.

### Term Insurance

Term insurance is the easiest insurance to understand. Just think of it as plain ice cream, without any toppings. It is a death benefit that gives you protection only for a stated number of years. The policy expires at the end of the term. Since every company offers term insurance with protection for a different number of years, it would be wise to compare policies and prices. It is not difficult to compare prices with only the following information: your age and your sex.

### Whole Life

Think of whole life and all other types of insurance plans as ice cream *with* various toppings. Whole life insurance provides insurance for as long as you live. It accumulates cash value, which is the money that you would get back if you gave up or *surrendered* the policy. Whole life comes with interesting names and high premiums that mean two things: (1) plain insurance, and (2) savings plan. The payments are much higher in earlier years (five or six times as expensive), because most of the premiums are put toward savings to keep them from increasing in later years. You are actually paying for the same death protection as you get with term insurance, but you are turning over large sums of your money to the insurance company for them to invest at a low rate of return to you.

In July 1979, a report was made to the Federal Trade Commission (FTC) from the Bureau of Consumer Protection. The report concerned life insurance policies that built up cash value each year at a specified rate. The FTC report said:

"Consumers are losing a great deal of income each year since keeping savings in life insurance policies carries an average return of only 1.3 percent compared to bank accounts that usually pay at least 5 percent."[1]

## Disadvantages of Whole Life and Other Plans

The disadvantages of whole life insurance and similar plans are:

• A poor rate of return on many of these savings plans.
• Difficulty in comparing policies to distinguish good ones from bad ones.
• Adequate whole life protection is too expensive for young parents to afford.
• The penalty for early withdrawal is enormous.

## Universal Life Insurance

Universal life insurance combines term insurance with a tax-deferred savings account that earns interest at bond-market rates. It seems to be a most attractive tax-shelter. But choosing just any universal life policy will not do! Many such policies come loaded with fees and hidden costs, *including high commissions.*

The big question you must face is whether to use life insurance as a form of savings at all. An individual retirement account (IRA) will do the same thing for you. Universal life policies do disclose the interest rate the company pays. Most pay interest *only* on the cash value left *after* the first year's fees. The quoted rate often is not paid on your total cash value. In addition, there are often annual fees as well as fees for withdrawals. For basic insurance protection, annual renewable term insurance is still cheaper.

Do insurance agents agree with this conclusion? The answer to this question is simple: Insurance agents sell life insurance. Insurance agents argue tirelessly that whole life policies are great for people who lack the discipline to save. Often they are right, because many people do not know how to save money. You could be hurt buying inexpensive renewable term

---

[1] *The Wall Street Journal* 7/11/79.

insurance *if* you fail to reinvest the money that you have saved by doing so. With universal life, the main consideration is whether you think the policy's tax-deferred yield is a satisfactory alternative to other investments—stocks or bonds, for example. *Keep in mind that a whole life or universal life agent gets a larger commission than the term agent!*

What you save by purchasing term insurance instead of other types of plans should be put toward some type of retirement plan. But this takes less discipline when you know how much more you would have to pay in taxes if you did not. Unlike life premiums, contributions to a qualified retirement plan lower your income taxes.

## COMMON QUESTIONS AND CONCERNS ABOUT LIFE INSURANCE

### Is It Better to Purchase Insurance While You Are Young?

Comparing whole life with term insurance, you will see that the premiums for term do increase periodically. Term does get more expensive. But for the same coverage, your payments for whole life are slightly over double. For what you would pay for whole life, you could double your term coverage.

It is important to invest the money you are saving by purchasing term rather than whole life. In this way, you can build up assets for retirement and still be able to afford term insurance later in life when it is more expensive (if you still need it). If you invest the difference, you are better off at any age purchasing term (and investing the difference) rather than purchasing whole life or some other type of policy.

### What If Your Health Fails?

If your health fails, then your payments will be higher. If you have purchased renewable term insurance, the company is stuck with you. As the name suggests, renewable term policies are renewable for the term of the policy as stated in the policy, some to age 65, some to age 70, and some to 100.

### Where Should You Purchase Insurance?

You should purchase insurance from any reputable company that offers you a good rate. Shop around. There are a number of companies that offer low-cost renewable term insurance, and, if one agent does not carry the policy you want, check with companies that are rated A or A+ by A.M. Best Companies (companies that keep you informed). But this should not be a major concern if you are buying term insurance.

## Should You Switch Your Insurance Policy?

If you purchased your policy when rates were not as low as today, you should almost always cash it in *after* you have secured coverage to replace it. You can find term insurance with a competitive premium that may be significantly lower priced than what you paid for your previous plan.

If you have purchased a whole life policy that does not pay dividends and whose prices are not competitive today, cash it in *after* having first secured elsewhere the coverage you need. If it does pay dividends (and if you still need insurance), you probably should keep it. But consider borrowing every cent of cash value, so you can invest it elsewhere if you are able to earn more after taxes than you would be charged for the loan (generally around 5 to 8 percent). You do not need to replace a policy loan— it will be subtracted from the death benefit, so do not throw it away either! If you take out a loan, you may be offered "credit life." Do not buy it— unless you are very old or very ill.

## What About Other Types of Policies?

"Reversionary term" insurance allows you extremely low rates. However, there is a catch! You must have a physical examination every five years or so. If you remain in good health, your premium remains low. If your health deteriorates, your rates will increase considerably. Whether it is right for you depends on what type of gambler you are.

## What About Riders?

The waiver-of-premium rider will keep a policy in force if you become disabled, and the inclusion of this rider makes sense. Some riders insure your children's lives, and some pay double for accidental death. These are poor buys because the children are young and the chances of something happening to them are extremely thin. This is how insurance companies make money.

### CONSIDERATIONS IN EVALUATING YOUR POLICY

Doctors are now beginning to take a hard look at their life insurance policies. After paying large sums into their policies for a good many years, they are realizing that similar policies may be bought at relatively low rates. For instance, Dr. Frank, now 45 years old, bought his $50,000 whole life policy 20 years ago. Like many young doctors beginning practice, he considered the $1,000 premium high. But he was persuaded because the policy built up cash value, paid dividends, and was a forced savings for his retirement, and it gave him a sum to borrow from at low interest rates.

Today, Dr. Frank wonders if he made a mistake. He can now find policies with a face value of $50,000 for less than the $1,000 he is paying annually. And there are much better ways to invest for retirement. In today's market the numbers favor replacement. Why are the prices lower? Because insurance companies are losing customers to more competitive investments. Like Dr. Frank, many others are bypassing whole life policies in favor of term insurance that provides only death benefit protection at far less cost. Tax-sheltered retirement funds and other types of investments are being used. Term insurance on a $100,000 policy is being offered for only a $100 yearly premium.

Dr. Frank's policy with a face value of $50,000 has $20,000 worth of cash value after 20 years. If he cancels this policy and invests the money in a Certificate of Deposit (C.D.) paying only 10 percent, he will have a return of $2,000 a year in interest before taxes. Today he can replace that $50,000 policy with one at lower premiums. The interest on the C.D. pays the premium with some left over, and he still has the same death benefit. Keep in mind that when Dr. Frank cashes in his old policy, any cash value exceeding what he has paid in premums is taxed as ordinary income.

## Who Should Own Your Insurance Policy?

Switching a policy's ownership from yourself to your beneficiaries can cut estate taxes. But you should know the rules before you do it. The unlimited marital deduction reduces or eliminates estate taxes payable on the first spouse's death. The unlimited marital deduction, however, only defers estate taxes, and it does not reduce them. In fact, it may increase them when the second spouse dies. Switching ownership may save money for your heirs because of the way the tax laws are written. The death benefits of life insurance—the amount the company pays the beneficiary when the insured dies—are not subject to income taxes, but they are included in the insured's estate for federal estate tax purposes.

Transferring life insurance can be an easy way to avoid estate taxes if you leave assets to someone other than your spouse such as your children if you are married, or, if you are single, to other heirs. It removes the value of the death benefits from your estate. For example, if you assign your policy on your life to your grown children, the proceeds at your death will not be included in your estate, and they will be free of both estate and income taxes. Assigning insurance is a relatively simple procedure. Your insurance agent can provide you with the forms.

When transferring ownership, you must give the new owner all the "incidents of ownership." These include the right to change beneficiaries, cash in the policy, cancel it, borrow against the cash value, or make another assignment.

If you continue paying premiums, those payments will count as gifts.

If your gift to each person remains below the gift tax exemption allowed each year, there will be no federal gift tax involved.

If you have transferred ownership of your life insurance policies and die within three years of the transfer, your estate tax benefit is nullified. The proceeds will be included in your estate for tax purposes.

## Survivor Joint Life Insurance

*Survivor joint life insurance* is another option. It is an insurance policy covering the lives of two insureds with the death benefit payable on the second death. This policy is an attractive way to pay the estate taxes due at the second death, especially in cases where the unlimited marital deduction coupled with the unified credit were utilized to eliminate estate taxes due at the second death. It also eliminates the need to guess who will be the surviving spouse because the survivor joint life insurance policy is payable only at the second death.

## Insurance as a Gift

When you give a cash value policy as a gift, the insurance of older policies is valued for gift tax purposes at an amount roughly equal only to the cash you would receive by surrendering the policy. The cash sum is not nearly as much as the policy's face value. Group term policies have no gift value since they do not accumulate cash values.

If you have transferred ownership and the new owner dies, the policy becomes part of the owner's estate. In most instances, the policy will then revert to you.

If you have transferred ownership to the beneficiary, what happens if he or she changes beneficiaries? Assume that the new owner, your wife, for instance, eliminates herself as beneficiary and substitutes your children. If you die while your wife is still alive, the policy proceeds (not the cash value) will be considered a gift made by your wife to your children.

## The I.R.S.

For the I.R.S. to recognize someone other than you as owner of your policy and to claim the estate tax savings, you must give up all rights and control over the policy. You must give away the policy *irrevocably*.

If life insurance is taken out as separate property in Arizona, Louisiana, New Mexico, Wisconsin, and Texas, it remains separate even though the premiums may be paid out of community funds. In the other states (common law states) and in California, Washington, and Idaho, ownership depends upon the source of payments.

Rev. Rul. 82-145 makes it clear that, if your controlled corporation owns insurance on your life, the proceeds will be taxable in your gross estate when (1) the corporation has the right to borrow against the policy, and (2) the proceeds are payable to any beneficiary other than the estate. This ruling modifies and expands the ruling by attributing "incidents of ownership" of the corporation to the stockholder. (The owner is the person who purchased the policy normally; however, the owner might not be the same person who is the beneficiary.)

## Does a Woman Need Life Insurance?

Whether the woman is married or single, a breadwinner or not, has or has not children, life insurance should figure into financial planning. The decision to purchase life insurance depends, of course, upon individual circumstances, *not* gender. The same guidelines that apply to a man apply to a woman. Just be sure to adapt your insurance to realistic needs, including your pocketbook.

Some other basic questions that need answering are: Do you have minors who are dependent upon your income? How long before they are grown? What other support will be available? Who will take care of your minor children if you are not around? How much will it cost to pay for all that you do in the household?

Remember that the prime purpose of life insurance is financial protection, it is an attempt to replace at least part of your economic value: your income, your services, etc. Your primary concern should be your dependents' economic needs until they can manage on their own. But, if a wife and mother is lost, someone must take over the labor she performs. This might entail hiring a housekeeper and baby-sitters, and it could mean that the breadwinner might have to work fewer hours. It will also mean the loss of an income tax deduction, and it might even result in the payment of inheritance and estate taxes if the estate is sufficiently large.

## Who Will Get Your Insurance Proceeds?

That seems easy to answer until you consider the ways that your intended beneficiaries could lose out because of careless wording in a policy.

- Ben Harris is a widower with two children, Michael and Karen. He marries Joanne, who has one child, Jane, from a previous marriage. In Ben's policies he has listed "my children" as beneficiaries. When he dies, will the proceeds of the policies be paid to his own two children or to all three? Ben may want the three to share the proceeds equally, but the way the policy is worded, only Michael and Karen are considered his rightful beneficiaries. *They* are Ben's children. Jane is Joanne's child. Ben's intent would have been clear if he had named all three children.
- George is a new father. He designates his newborn son, John, as one of the beneficiaries of his life insurance by "my son, John." But

George may have other children, and, if he dies before amending the policy, the other children will be cut off from the proceeds.

Phrasing of beneficiary statements often involves surprisingly complex issues. As a policy owner, you can name anyone you choose as beneficiary, but make sure that your intent is correctly worded.

The primary beneficiary is the one who gets the policy proceeds if the insured dies. The secondary or contingent beneficiary receives the proceeds if the primary beneficiary predeceases the insured and the insured fails to name another. Husbands and wives usually designate each other as primary beneficiaries with their children as secondary beneficiaries. Generally life insurance is not considered part of your probate estate even though it is included in your estate for tax purposes (in your taxable estate). If you have named no beneficiaries, or if they have predeceased you, then the proceeds will be paid to your estate, and the money goes through the probate process the same as if your estate were named beneficiary of your policy.

## Does Your Policy Say What You Mean?

If your policy does not say what you intend it to say, your intended beneficiary could be cut out by careless wording. When you name an individual as a beneficiary, be sure to state the person's relationship to avoid ambiguity. For instance: Karen G. Watzman, my sister; or Harvey Gartner, my brother. In identifying your spouse, be sure to identify him or her by the given name, such as "Cheryl Lewis, my wife," and not as "Mrs. Brian Lewis." Divorce and remarriage are common, and naming "Cheryl" eliminates any doubt about which wife Brian had in mind.

Sticky questions may arise about ostensibly clear-cut beneficiary designations. State laws often have provisions for situations, such as whether Brian and Cheryl were divorced, and who would get the money should Brian die before Cheryl. Even though Cheryl would no longer be Mrs. Brian Lewis after the divorce, many states require that the proceeds be paid to her as long as she is named a beneficiary of the policy. Other state laws may automatically terminate her interest in the policy after the divorce.

State laws and insurance company beneficiary forms often differ in terminology, but, subject to those reservations, here are some common forms to consider when naming children:

- "Children of the insured, Marc Bradley." All of Marc's children from all marriages would be included at the time he dies. Posthumously born, adopted, illegitimate, and stepchildren may or may not be included. If not, statements could be adjusted to include them.
- "Lawful children of the insured, Marc Bradley" normally means natural as well as adopted children but excludes illegitimate children.
- "Surviving children of the insured, Marc Bradley" more specifically

includes a posthumously born child and makes it clear that a deceased child's share should be distributed among the surviving children.

- "Children born of the marriage of Marc and Tracy Bradley" excludes children born of other marriages as well as those legally adopted children and stepchildren.

*Per capita* and *per stirpes* are Latin terms that refer to two significantly different ways of distributing insurance proceeds as well as other estate payments. By using *per capita*, all beneficiaries share equally. A *per stirpes* arrangement distributes according to representation in family lines. In other words, if Leslie is named as a beneficiary and all beneficiaries take *per stirpes* if Leslie is deceased, then Leslie's children (or members of her family) would be paid "in place of" Leslie—that is, they would divide her share equally. Whereas, per capita allocation means that the proceeds are divided equally among survivors.

## Possible Legal Problems

Legal problems may arise if the proceeds of your insurance are to be paid to a minor child. A guardian may have to be appointed by a court to receive the money if no guardian or trustee is named in the policy or in the insured's will.

The majority of states have laws providing that, if both spouses die simultaneously or under circumstances where it cannot be determined who died first, the policy proceeds are to be distributed as if the husband had survived the wife. In that case, the children would get the money. But what if the wife does not die until some time after the husband? Under many state statutes, she would be deemed to have predeceased him if she dies within 120 hours after his death. What would happen if she lived longer? Unless there is a contrary presumption in the policy, the will, or any trust agreements, the money would be paid to the administrator of the wife's estate. The funds would then be distributed according to her will or the state's intestate laws if she did not have a will. As a result, the children might not receive all that their father intended them to have. A clause in the beneficiary designation of the policy, such as "Connie Elder, wife of the insured, if living on 30 (or 60) days after the death of the insured," will reduce the chance of this happening.

It is important to keep your beneficiary arrangements up to date. Any major event may require a change, such as divorce, remarriage, death of one of the beneficiaries, purchase of additional insurance, etc.

## Updating Beneficiary

A policy owner can change the beneficiary of a policy merely by completing a form obtainable from the life insurance company.

## HOW DOES YOUR RETIREMENT PLAN AFFECT YOUR INSURANCE?

Assuming that you are part of the overwhelming majority of doctors in private practice who have set up Keogh or corporate plans, it is worth considering how the growing sum in your retirement plan affects the kind and amount of life insurance you need. Limitations on withdrawing money from your retirement plan apply to you and not to your beneficiary if you should die before reaching retirement age. That means that your plan is increasing your life insurance policy whose death benefit equals its cash value.

As your retirement plan grows, your life insurance becomes less important in your financial planning. Life insurance is needed to protect your family until your retirement plan and other assets have grown enough to take over the job. Agents suggest that life insurance be held as a retirement plan asset. It should not be. Your life insurance policy should be outside your retirement plan. Once your children are no longer young, your need for insurance is likely to drop because your family has acquired other assets to fall back on. If an insurance policy is part of your retirement plan, it is more difficult to cut back unneeded coverage than if the policy stands on its own, outside your plan.

Also, you may be limited in the amount of insurance coverage you may obtain. You may be required to purchase an amount that fits the formula devised by the insurance company; and the laws governing your type of retirement plan limit the amount and the kind of insurance. True, premiums are tax-deductible, but since pure insurance is considered an "excise" death benefit, the I.R.S. will tax whatever portion of the premium goes to pay for insurance rather than to build up cash values. Furthermore, the I.R.S. will not let you discriminate against employees in providing coverage.

## INSURANCE YOU DO NOT NEED

You do not need these unnecessary and overpriced policies that can cost you hundreds of thousands of dollars a year. Examples are:

- *Credit life* is one of several types of insurance known as "sleeper" insurance. It is said that people buy it so they can sleep at night rather than because the policy meets any real need for protection. Such policies are varied, but they do have certain characteristics in common. They appear inexpensive, but coverage is limited. In addition, many of these policies duplicate coverage that people already have under homeowners' or group health policies. Banks, loan companies, car dealers, etc., sell such policies, which pay off loans when the borrower dies or becomes disabled. "It is only a few dollars a month," you are told. Actually, the cost is included in the total amount repayable, and the borrower pays interest on his insurance premium. What looks like a small charge may in fact turn into a large percentage loan.

- *Cancer insurance* is sold to those fearful of this catastrophic illness. Most would do better to increase major-medical insurance coverage than to buy insurance against cancer or other specific diseases. Often the expensive, continuous costs of treating cancer patients, such as at-home nursing care, are not covered by these policies. They do pay part of the hospital costs, which a recent study has shown is not more than two weeks' stay on the average for a cancer patient.

- *Life insurance for children/college students* is pushed because of low premiums and easy payment plans. Unless your child is providing income to the family, life insurance simply isn't necessary, and a student with no dependents rarely needs life insurance. It's faulty reasoning to consider buying it just because premiums are lower for young people.

- *Flight and travel insurance* is sold by credit-card companies, by gasoline companies, and in airport vending machines. Why should a person be insured for more in the case of an accidental death than for death from natural causes if the needs of his or her beneficiaries would be the same? If you are underinsured, an airport vending machine is not the place to remedy the problem.

- *Rental-car insurance.* Resist the temptation to purchase collision damage waivers on rental cars. There is generally a charge. This charge insures you against having to pay the deductible on your own car. If it is less than theirs, then avoid this waiver. Your own car's policy will pay the difference between the deductibles. The fee you pay for this waiver becomes expensive, especially if you calculate it on a yearly basis. The premium in this case would be three times the amount insured.

## CHOOSING THE CORRECT INSURANCE PAYOUT OPTION

Getting the right amount of life insurance is important, but so is making sure that the money will be distributed in a way that best suits your family's needs. Life insurance payouts involve a choice: to receive the proceeds in one lump sum, or to take them in installments, according to one of the several "settlement option" plans.

• *Lump sum* is usually preferable since the beneficiary can personally decide how to use or invest the money. Under a settlement option, the insurance company handles the funds. The yield on funds handled by the insurance company may not be as high as if the beneficiary handled the funds alone or with the guidance of advisors.

There are options available, however, which you should know about in order to decide what is best for your situation. Talk over the advantages and disadvantages of settlement options with your accountant or other advisor in order to explore the various opportunities open to you.

Here are some of the choices the insurance company may offer you other than receiving the proceeds in one lump sum:

• Interest option. The proceeds of the policy are left on deposit with the insurance company. Interest payments are made to the beneficiary periodically. Arrangements for either partial withdrawal or withdrawal of all the principal can be made with the insurance company.

• Fixed-period option. Funds are paid out in installments—proceeds plus interest—over a fixed time (months or years, whichever you select).

• Fixed-amount option. The money is paid out in specified amounts, rather than for a specific period of time. The fixed amount is paid out each month until there is no principal left. Excess interest will not increase the amount of each installment but will increase the length of time of the payments.

• Life-income (or annuity) option. A life income from the funds is guaranteed to the beneficiary. The amount of each installment payment depends upon the beneficiary's age and sex. The proceeds are paid out based on a table set forth in the policy. Excess interest will add to the amount of each payment. Any unpaid installments will be paid to secondary beneficiaries when the primary beneficiaries die.

Basic options are similar among insurance companies, but some companies offer more flexible plans than do others. Interest rates also vary. Compare various policies and the options they offer.

Generally, life insurance proceeds are not taxable as income to the beneficiary. Lump sum payments of proceeds are free from income tax. But when proceeds are paid under one of the options, you must calculate the portion of each payment that represents death proceeds. That portion is exempt from income tax when received, the balance, that is, the interest earned on the fund is taxable.

• With an interest-only option. The interest payments are fully taxable in the year they are received.

- With installment and life annuity plans. The surviving spouse (but *no other* beneficiary) gets a tax break: each year, up to $1,000 in interest received as part of installment payments can be excluded from taxable income.

It is possible to have your insurance proceeds placed in a special trust arranged either during your lifetime or in your will. The advantages and disadvantages should be discussed with your attorney and other advisors.

## INSURANCE SALES PITCHES

You cannot learn all the insurance sale pitches, but it is wise to know four of the most important ones—those that may confuse you and could cause you unnecessary expense.

1. "Buy insurance while you're young, because it's cheaper!" Insurance agents frequently tell you that if you purchase whole life insurance before age 30, your annual premiums will be low, giving the policy a low annual cost. "If you wait," he tells you, "the older you get, the higher the premiums will be, and it will cost you a lot more!"

For example, he might say that if you were to purchase whole life with a face value of $200,000, it will cost you about $1,170 a year. By the time you are 65, it will have cost you $41,000, but, because you have built up $52,000 in cash value in the policy, you will now have a profit of $11,000. But if you wait until you are 40 years old or older, your premiums will be higher—$1,800 at age 40. You would have paid $45,000, giving you only $45,800 in cash value.

It sounds persuasive, doesn't it? What the agent does not tell you is that term insurance is much cheaper and offers higher death benefits for the same premium until a person reaches about age 60, then the term premiums greatly increase. Besides, if you took a term policy for about one-half the premium cost, you could invest the difference. Even at only 10 percent, by the time you are 65, you would have a cash fund probably over $170,000. Additionally, your insurance needs may be quite different when you are older than they are when you are young. If you have a cash fund, your family will have funds to draw on if something should happen to you.

2. "Term is much more expensive than whole life insurance." Again, with fast-sell techniques, the agent may try to convince you that over a period of 20 years, you would pay only a small amount for the actual cost of whole life insurance compared with term. "Whole life builds up a cash value," he says, "and, if you paid $42,000 for whole life, your cash value would be approximately $40,000, so your actual cost would be only about $2,000 for a $200,000 policy. But with term insurance, you will pay about $8,000 over 20 years for the same policy with no cash value."

You are told that it is plain to see that your term policy would cost you a lot more than whole life: $2,000 whole life actual cost against $8,000 for term. Here again, have you considered the investment return that you would get on the annual savings in premium if you purchased term over whole life? Even paying income taxes on the interest in savings, you would probably still come out ahead. And, if you put that money in your retirement plan, you would compound the interest tax-deferred each year. Besides, generally a person in his or her 30s can get three or four times more term coverage than whole life for the same premium.

3. "Whole life is permanent while term is temporary insurance." Actually, term is something like car insurance or any other type of insurance—when you stop paying, it expires. It terminates. The idea that some agents try to convey is that you are buying whole life or permanent insurance, that is, you are getting something for nothing because it lasts forever, even if you stop paying premiums. Agents think that because they are drilled in mathematical sleight-of-hand tricks by their companies.

But this just is not the case. By purchasing whole life, you are actually paying for the same "death protection" as with term. And in addition, you are turning over large sums of your money to the insurance company for *them* to invest. The return they give you is only 3 or 4 percent, at most.

4. "This insurance plan will be customized just for you!" Countless agents claim that they will "analyze your needs" in order to "create a tailor-made plan" just for you. If you did some checking and talked with two or three agents before making a decision, you might find that the *special* plan you were offered is just an off-the-rack package, regardless of your wants or budget. Keep in mind that an agent with an impressive record of belonging to the million-dollar round table club or some similar "golden" group may have earned that outstanding record because he or she does business with only one company. He may not have a variety of insurance products with which to serve your particular needs.

For the most part, insurance agents actually believe in what they sell. Because of that, the public becomes the unwitting victims of their good intentions. Remember, commissions are structured by most companies to give agents a higher percentage for selling whole life rather than term insurance. Whole life is hardly ever a good buy, especially in times of inflation.

There really is not any secret in selecting the right type and amount of insurance you need. You are actually gambling when you purchase a policy: you are betting that some catastrophe is going to happen, and the insurance company is betting that it won't. Insurance is not the best investment, but the only thing worse than paying for insurance is not having it when disaster occurs.

**Figure 7–1.** CHART 19: Fixed Living Expenses.

| Description | Annual or Semi-Annual Expenses (Amount) | Date Paid | Date Paid | Date Paid |
|---|---|---|---|---|
| INSURANCE PREMIUMS: | | | | |
| Homeowner's | | | | |
| Auto 1 | | | | |
| Auto 2 | | | | |
| Boat | | | | |
| Jewelry | | | | |
| Life | | | | |
| | | | | |
| Major Medical | | | | |
| Disability Premiums | | | | |
| HOSPITALIZATION | | | | |
| Federal Income Tax | | | | |
| PROPERTY TAXES: | | | | |
| City | | | | |
| County | | | | |
| Tags for Cars | | | | |
| | | | | |
| MORTGAGES OR LOANS: | | | | |
| Home | | | | |
| Auto | | | | |
| Other | | | | |
| | | | | |
| Monthly House Payment: Weekly Housekeeper Expenses: | | | | |

**Figure 7–2.** CHART 20: Your Life Insurance Needs.

1. Annual family living costs                               ——————————

2. Spouse's annual income from employment       ——————————

3. Annual income needed (line 1 minus line 2)     ——————————

4. Capital required to meet cash needs (at 6 percent return, multiply line 3 by .06)                      ——————————

5. Other capital needs (college tuition, mortgage loans, estate taxes)                              ——————————

6. Final expenses                                        ——————————

7. Total capital needs (add lines 4, 5, 6)         ——————————

8. Other capital available (life insurance proceeds, stocks, bonds and other property which may be liquidated)                       ——————————

9. Additional life insurance needed (line 7 minus line 8)                    ——————————

# 8

---

# DISABILITY
# INSURANCE: HOW
# GOOD IS YOURS?

"Look, Murray, these are the facts. You have cancer, and there's nothing we can do for you." In stunned silence we listened as the doctor concluded, "We are not sure how long you have—maybe a year, maybe a couple of months."

What now? What do you do when you are 34 years old, with a highly successful professional career, a wife, three young children, and a sentence of death?

Murray began preparing me for widowhood. He was at a high point in his practice, and his yearly earnings were substantial. In the past, he had told me, "If I were ever disabled for any length of time, I have enough disability insurance and overhead coverage to carry us so there would be no financial disaster."

Murray worked on a part-time basis until one week before he died. His patients whom he continued to treat never knew he was ill. And our family was fortunate in that, even though he worked only on a part-time basis, he was still able to collect proportionate disability benefits. This gave some measure of relief to the economic disaster that followed.

People are rarely totally disabled for a long period of time. Why? Because like Murray they do not live very long. I now speak and write about the stark reality of contracts and agreements, because of my experiences as the young wife in this story. The knowledge I have gained has been firsthand along with the later legal training.

You may now make sure that you will never have to face such unexpected financial catastrophe. You can do this by arming yourself with some basic knowledge that will help you to provide for your future security.

## READ YOUR POLICY

Have you ever read your disability policy? Or, are you like most professionals who buy a disability insurance policy and never read it until it is too late—*after* they are disabled?

Granted, reading the fine print of a policy is a chore and a bore. But you will not find it as difficult as you think if you follow this four-point guideline and acquaint yourself with the seven terms included.

## EVALUATING THE POLICY

Most doctors carry life insurance not only to protect their families in case they die, but they also carry insurance in case of a disability—a heart attack, cancer, or arthritis, or an accident—that may interrupt the flow of income long enough to be financially disastrous.

After evaluating a good many disability policies, I have come to realize that most doctors will not be as fortunate as Murray, who was able to collect partial disability benefits.

How about you? Could you and your family survive if you had to take a cut of one-half of your gross income? Will your disability policy pay if you are disabled and return to work unable to generate as much income as you had before, because you are working only for short periods of time? And will your policy pay for work in your *own* profession?

The value of a disability income policy lies in the insurance company's promise to protect you against loss of income resulting from an accident or sickness. You buy this promise with your premium payment. In order to evaluate a company's promise to pay you benefits, answer the following five questions, giving special attention to question number 5:

1. *How much?* Most policies will not exceed a stated percentage of your gross earnings, generally 60 to 80 percent of it—no more. The premium you pay is directly proportionate to the amount of benefit yielded by the policy. *If you are between ages 35 and 65, there is a 50 percent chance you will be disabled before you reach age 65.* With each passing year, the chance of disability increases, and so do the premiums. In order to collect benefits you must show a 20 percent or more loss of income until you get back to earning 80 percent of your prior income.

How is prior income determined? Prior income is determined on the basis of either (1) the previous 6 months or (2) on the previous 12 months, generally. Some policies give you a choice of the previous 6 months before the disability or any 2 consecutive years out of the previous 5. With such a choice in your policy, you have the opportunity to establish your prior income base as high as possible. This is important, since all future partial payments are determined by it.

2. *How soon?* Most policies begin benefit payments after what is called the *elimination period*. Elimination periods are 30 days, 60 days, 90 days, 6 months, or 12 months *after* you are disabled. This determines how soon you will start receiving benefits.

3. *How long?* The benefit period determines how long your benefits will continue. Most professionals carry disability payable to age 65. After age 65, the policy usually becomes prohibitively expensive.

4. *Is your policy noncancellable? Does it guarantee that the premium will remain the same until age 65?* What good is the policy if it can be taken away from you or changed without your permission at the whim of the company?

5. Under what circumstances? In other words, what is the definition of the word *disability* in your policy? Every company has its own definition of disability and it is *not* just any phrasing coined by an agent that determines what benefits will or will not be paid to you. Read it carefully, with special attention as to the way *disability* is defined.

## TOTAL DISABILITY

Typically, the policy definition of disability might read something like this one: *Total disability* means (1) the inability of the insured to perform any of the duties of his occupation; and (2) the insured is not receiving any earnings for performing any work or services; and (3) the insured is under the regular care and attendance of a legally licensed physician; however, after the first 12 months of benefit payments, the insured must also be unable to engage in any work or service for which he is reasonably qualified by education, training, or experience.

The definition of *disability* is the most important part in your policy! It determines whether you will be entitled to any disability benefits as a result of an accident or illness.

Let us examine a few more definitions typically found in policies:

### Disability Definitions

1. *Inability to engage in your own occupation during an initial period, and thereafter, inability to engage in any occupation.*
   Query: Do you have to be a vegetable to receive benefits?

2. *Inability to engage in your own occupation during an initial period, thereafter, inability to engage in any occupation for which you are reasonably qualified by reason of education, training, or experience.*
   Query: As a doctor, would you sell shoes?
3. *Inability to engage in your occupation during an initial period, thereafter, same definition, and not actually engage in any other occupation or profession.* (This is clearly the broadest definition.)
   Query: Will you be able to collect partial disability benefits (also known as "residual disability benefits") if you are able to perform only *some* of the duties of your profession?

## PARTIAL DISABILITY

If your policy requires less than full time at work to be partially disabled, you will *not* receive partial benefits! After all, you can still practice—maybe just not as fast as before. Some policies require your inability to perform a *certain portion* of your prior duties in order to qualify for benefits.

The catch here may be that total disability may be defined by some criterion other than loss of income. You may have a loss of income, therefore, without ever being totally disabled for a long enough period of time to trigger the partial disability provision. The best policies are concerned with loss of income upon returning to your practice.

What is considered "income" once you have returned to your practice? Some companies use a loss-of-income test for partial disability benefits. "Income" should be only that which you actually earn from your practice. After all, you did buy such insurance to protect your income. If your policy considers such items as Social Security, rental income, pension plan payouts, or any other type of income, you will be penalized.

### Partial Benefits

The length of time of your total disability could keep you from collecting any partial benefits. You may have a policy that provides for an elimination period, and, if you become partially disabled prior to the expiration of the elimination period, you would not be entitled to any payments for partial disability. You will not be collecting benefits if your contract requires a long period of total disability before you become eligible for partial benefits.

## PRE-EXISTING CONDITIONS

If you disclose a pre-existing health condition to the company when you apply for disability insurance, chances are that you are covered for any disability arising from that condition. However, read the policy, because some policies will not cover pre-existing conditions, whether you disclose it or not.

Some companies will not pay benefits for two years if you had a pre-existing condition and did not disclose it. What is or is not a pre-existent health condition will depend upon the individual insurance company with which you are dealing. Some companies consider only conditions for which symptoms existed during the previous two to five years. Others have no time limit at all (and could go as far back as your childhood).

## RIDERS

### Cost-of-Living Rider

A cost-of-living rider may appeal to you. Such a provision will adjust your benefits according to some measure of inflation, often the Consumer Price Index. Benefits may be adjusted automatically by raising your benefits each year that you are disabled. There is usually a limit to such adjustments.

### Option to Purchase

Another rider you may consider is the so-called "option to purchase." This rider gives you the right (but not the obligation) to purchase more insurance in the future, generally in specified amounts at specified intervals, regardless of changes in your health.

## CALCULATING THE AMOUNT OF DISABILITY INSURANCE NEEDED

It is not hard to calculate the amount of disability insurance needed. Just follow the steps in Chart 21 (Figure 8–1) at the end of the chapter.

1. Since disability benefits are generally tax free, calculate only your take-home (after-tax) pay. Estimate this from your last year's federal income tax return by subtracting the taxes paid, including Social Security taxes, from your gross earned income (salary only). Divide this total by 12 to get your monthly take-home pay.

2. Estimate government and other benefits. Include, if you qualify, Armed Services Disability Benefits, Veterans Administration Pension Disability Benefits, Civil Service Benefits, etc.

3. Add up any monthly disability benefits to which you are entitled.

4. Subtract these from your current take-home pay. The result will show the monthly disability benefits you will need in order to maintain your present after-tax income.

I hope that these guidelines will help you so that you will not fall into those small-print loopholes that could swallow your whole future. Policies are a dime a dozen in the marketplace, and that is just about what some of them are worth. No matter what the cost, what is it worth if it will not pay you when you need it most?

## DISABILITY INCOME INSURANCE

In some ways, disability income insurance is even more important than life insurance. Income needs are likely to be even greater if you are disabled than when you were hale and hearty. But disability income insurance is a much trickier form of coverage than life insurance.

For one thing, there is not much doubt about whether a person is alive or dead. There may be a lot of questions about whether you are disabled to the point that you are unable to work.

Also, life insurance policies may not be cancelled by the company once your health deteriorates. But many disability policies can be cancelled, and you may be dropped just when you need the coverage the most.

The best disability income policy should be noncancellable and guaranteed renewable to age 65. Some disability income policies stipulate that they are cancellable at any time, while others are guaranteed *continuable*—but with no guarantee that the premiums will not increase. Furthermore, much disability insurance is sold with the verbal promise that it is non-cancellable and guaranteed renewable. This is often the case with group or franchise policies, where the stipulation is made that the individual's policy cannot be cancelled. However, the entire group may be dropped, or the premiums increased, when the cost to the carrier becomes prohibitive. Verbal or half-way guarantees are not as good as an iron-clad contract.

A good disability income insurance policy must replace your earning power during periods when your ability to earn money has been suspended. The primary object of the coverage is to enable you to meet your living expenses during that period when no income is coming.

Disability income insurance must begin to pay when you begin to need money—and it should continue to pay for as long as your financial need is likely to continue. There is much debate over when payments should start, and for how long they should continue. Most insurance people agree on the following points:

- A disability policy should insure you for at least five years for sickness, and five years for an accident. Longer coverage is even better.
- The elimination period (the time between the day the disability manifests itself and payments begin) should be 60–90 days for a solo practitioner, longer for an incorporated practitioner. The one-month

waiting period assumes that any practicing doctor has enough money to meet expenses for that period. The longer period for an incorporated doctor assumes that the practice will continue to provide income after the onset of the disability period without undue hardship.

• A good disability income policy should include a first-day hospital rider—a stipulation that payments begin on the first day if you are hospitalized. Reason: Hospital expense can eat into your savings at an alarming rate.

• A good disability income will include a recurrent disability clause. Stories abound of doctors who became ill, recovered, and resumed practice, only to contract the same illness nine months or a year later. Many of these doctors have discovered, to their dismay, that their coverage picked up where it left off, rather than beginning benefits again from day one of the new claim.

• A top policy has a clause stating that you will be paid if you cannot practice your regular occupation or profession. Too many policies stop paying as long as you can perform any job, rather than the job for which you have been trained. So it is that many doctors have found that their payments have been cut off because they have taken a job in a laboratory or hospital, but are as yet unfit to resume the practice of medicine or dentistry. You have been trained as a doctor, and a good disability income insurance policy will pay until you can resume practicing your profession.

• Coverage should begin when the disability first manifests itself. As many doctors have discovered, some policies stipulate that a disability that existed before the policy became effective is not eligible for payment even though the disability was unknown to the policyholder. For example, a disability that is the result of a tumor that may have been present prior to the effective date of the policy but not discovered until after the policy was issued may not be covered. If your policy does not stipulate that you are covered from the day a disability first manifests itself, you may find that you are not covered in certain situations.

Here are some of the questions that you may have about disability insurance:

*Is disability income insurance really necessary?* Definitely. Statistics show that 1.2 million Americans between 20 and 65 years of age are disabled each year for three months or more due to illness or accident.

*Does the individual run the greater risk from illness or injury?* From illness. Some 86% of all disabilities result from illness, 14% from accidents.

*Will social security pay any disability income?* Yes, if you do not have the ability to contribute anything from wage, profit, or remuneration and have worked and contributed to Social Security. The disability must be proved to last one year or more. In this case, you would be paid retroactively, starting generally with the seventh month.

*What types of disability income policies are available?* Broadly speaking there are (1) individual policies, (2) group policies (usually written for a group of people working for the same company), and (3) franchise policies, which are usually written for people in the same profession (in many organizations, franchise policies are also called group policies).

*Can a professional corporation obtain disability insurance for its employees?* Yes, but it must be a formal plan. An agreement and a policy are substantial evidence that a formal plan exists.

*Are payments to the doctor during a period of disability taxable?* Generally not. But, as a rule, premiums are not tax deductible. However, under a professional overhead contract, which is a policy on your business expenses only, the tax situation is exactly the reverse—that is, premiums are deductible and payments are taxable. Professional overhead contracts are useful when you cannot get a professional disability income policy that fully suits your needs. Professional overhead policies usually pay for a two-year period during a disability, with the payments geared to cover only your business expenses during the two-year period. It is a good, low-cost way to supplement your protection, but it should not be the keystone of your coverage.

## SOCIAL SECURITY DISABILITY BENEFITS

Your social security is also a disability income policy and may provide benefits if you are incapacitated. The waiting period is 5 months before you can collect. Your dependent children, who would be eligible for a 50% benefit if you had retired, will receive 75% of your monthly benefit in case of death. There is a maximum sum that can be paid to a single family, so these benefits may be reduced and benefits are based on your salary.

According to the Social Security regulations, your disability must be so severe that you cannot do any kind of work that will provide you with a livelihood in order to collect Social Security benefits. Another requirement is that the conditions must have existed for at least a year or must be expected to result in death.

The amount you collect as a disability benefit each month is the same amount you would receive as an old-age benefit at age 65. This benefit may, however, be reduced if you are under 62 and are getting worker's compensation. Disability benefits collected before age 65 are reduced.

## VETERANS ADMINISTRATION

If you have a disability that is total and permanent, you may be entitled to Veterans Administration (V.A.) benefits. To be eligible, you must have served at least 90 days in the armed forces and have received an honorable discharge. The disability does not have to be service-connected in any way. They also have a small monthly benefit that your surviving spouse may be entitled to if he/she has minor children and if you served in the armed forces during any war, even if you were not directly involved in the war.

You need to evaluate your disability and office overhead insurance carefully. Remember, the friendly insurance agent who called you, explained the basics of your policy to you, and helped you establish a financial plan is a member of the company's sales force. It is the Claims Department that oversees payment. Do not rely on the salesman's promises alone.

Finally, make sure your policy keeps pace with your changing financial needs. An annual review of your disability coverage is time well spent. Chart 22 (Figure 8–2) will help you evaluate your disability coverage.

## EMERGENCY CARE AGREEMENT: INSURANCE MONEY CAN'T BUY!

(This scenario could easily happen to you, Doctor).

One sunny afternoon, an Orlando, Florida, doctor hurried on his way to the tennis courts. Earlier that day it had been raining, and, as he approached the courts, his foot touched a slick spot in the pavement and he fell. The last thing the doctor remembered was a flash of pain in his side. Several hours later he found himself in a hospital bed, numbed by pain and drugs, and imprisoned in a cast all the way from his neck to his legs.

Yes, he had insurance to cover the medical and hospital expenses of this prolonged disability, but what was to happen to his practice? What would hold it together during his long recovery period? Usually nothing. But this Florida physician had anticipated just such a problem. When he had regained consciousness, he whispered a few instructions to his wife who went immediately to the telephone.

She got more than sympathy from the person on the other end of the phone—she got help. Her injured husband was a member of a study club that provided emergency office coverage while he was recuperating.

This emergency coverage plan had been set up a few years earlier by a formal agreement, prepared by an attorney, covering all aspects of the program and signed by all doctors and their spouses who were participating in the program.

This coverage continued throughout the doctor's recuperation. When he was finally able to return to work, he found his practice intact and waiting for him.

The plan took an entire year to set up. During that time, the plan was able to step in and help disabled doctors on five different occasions. Disabilities ranged from broken legs to heart attacks. Two of the members died and the plan directors helped the widows dispose of the practices at fair prices.

The nice thing about this type of plan is that, when you help a fellow doctor, you also help the patients. And patients appreciate the way doctors stand in for one another.

An effective program requires cooperation from other professionals in your community, especially if you are a solo practitioner, in the event of a prolonged illness, or in the disposition of your practice in case of death.

One such plan might contain some of these elements:

1. Fees earned in the continuation of the practice should remain in that practice.

2. The time each is to contribute to keep the practice active should be determined (the half day you take off each week would be ideal time).

3. Patients of record remain the property of the practice.

4. A predetermined period should be agreed upon so that each will have some idea as to the length of time needed to maintain the practice. In the case of the doctor's death, allow enough time for the surviving spouse to find a buyer (with the study club's help). One to two months is the average time allowed in which your practice will hold its value. Giving notice to all graduating seniors of a dental school in or near your area is a good idea.

One study club on Long Island, New York, used these features as guidelines: When a member is disabled, a panel of four practitioners fills in at the disabled member's office. Each contributes one-half day a week on a regular schedule. Even the busiest doctor could give that much time. With the four members on the panel, it adds up to four half days a week, which is considerable help.

Panel members are taken in turn from a roster. The initial list was set up by drawing lots. After a member serves, his/her name drops to the bottom of the list. The plan director records the time contributed by each panel member. This is necessary because some panels might serve only for a week or two, while others could last for several months.

Minor illnesses of short duration are not covered. For major accidents, the panel starts filling in as soon as possible, but no later than one week after notification. Benefits for each emergency last a maximum of two months. By that time, the group believes, the dentist has had a reasonable opportunity to hire an associate to help in the practice.

Though participation is normally decided on a roster basis, when the list has been exhausted, it begins again with the first name. New members are added to the end of the roster.

All income goes to the disabled doctor's practice or the widow, and the work is performed in the disabled doctor's office with his/her own assistant and auxiliary personnel.

A three-member administration board settles questions involving interpretation of the agreement. Its decisions are binding unless overruled by a two-thirds vote of the members.

According to the American Dental Association's Code of Professional Conduct, Section 20: "Use of the name of a dentist no longer associated with the practice may be continued for a period not to exceed one year."

Could such a plan work out in your local medical or dental society? In the words of a disabled doctor: "This type of protection can't be bought—not from any company, not at any price!"

**Figure 8–1.** CHART 21: Work Sheet. Calculate the Disability Insurance You Need.

1. Estimate amount of current monthly take-home
   (after-tax) pay .................................................. $_____

2. Estimate existing disability benefits:
   * Government benefits                           $_____
   * Company programs                             $_____
   * Group disability policy benefits              $_____
   * Other benefits                                $_____

3. Total existing disability benefits ............................... $_____

4. Subtract existing benefit from current take-home pay .......... $_____

5. Monthly disability benefits needed............................. $_____

**Fig. 8–2.** CHART 22: Enough Coverage?

| | Monthly amount |
|---|---|
| 1. Your personal expenses | _____ |
| 2. Independent income | _____ |
| 3. Spouse's income | _____ |
| 4. Disability income insurance | _____ |
| 5. Additional disability income needs (line 1 minus lines 2, 3, 4) | _____ |

# 9

## PLANNING FOR THE PREVIOUSLY MARRIED

The world is changing rapidly, and one of the major changes today is the greatly increased number of those who have been previously married. Some of these have remarried, some are still single. Either way, there are rights and responsibilities that exist because of these prior marriages and they must be taken into consideration in your financial planning.

Those who were previously married may fall into one of these categories: (1) the single widow or widower; (2) the single divorcee, or (3) the remarried.

### NECESSARY DOCUMENTS

Obligations either to an ex-spouse or to children cannot be overlooked. In order to plan your financial survival effectively, it is necessary that you keep the following documents (if they apply to your situation).

- Any court order establishing legal obligations from a prior marriage,
- Divorce decrees and settlement agreements,
- Prenuptial or postnuptial agreements,
- Life insurance policies with all beneficiary designations,

- Annual summaries of employee benefits and beneficiary designations,
- Recent income and gift tax returns,
- Business contracts: buy-sell agreements, partnership agreements, deferred compensation arrangements, and the like, and
- Current wills and trusts.

## THE SINGLE WIDOW OR WIDOWER

The widow or widower no longer can anticipate the estate tax marital deduction at the spouse's death. This loss may be a significant problem in avoiding or minimizing estate taxes payable by a widow or widower with an estate in excess of the $600,000 unified credit.

As a solution, the widow or widower should consider gifts to children using the annual $10,000 exclusion per beneficiary, the transfer of life insurance policies to children, or an irrevocable insurance trust.

Suppose you are a widower whose estimated estate tax at death would be $750,000. Since you are allowed the unified credit, the first $600,000 will be sheltered from the estate tax. Your estate will pay $55,500 in federal estate taxes. If, however, you gift a $150,000 life insurance policy to an irrevocable trust, its death benefit would be removed from your taxable estate provided you lived three years longer. The unified credit would then be sufficient to shelter your remaining assets and no tax would be due. You have saved your children (or other family members) a great deal of tax.

Although other assets may be used to fund the irrevocable trust, life insurance is preferred because you give up no present income and you use up no part of your unified credit. In order to be assured of sheltering the trust assets from estate taxation you should avoid several traps: (1) you must not retain any beneficial interest in the trust; (2) you must have no reversionary interest in the trust assets; (3) you can have no power to revoke the trust; and (4) if the transfer of assets to the trust is within three years of your death, the assets would be included in your gross estate. (See the section "An Irrevocable Living Trust" in Chapter 5 for more details.)

For the younger widow or widower, with a greater possibility of a future marriage and additional children, establishing an irrevocable trust should be reviewed carefully. One word of advice: be sure to obtain competent legal advice in reaching your goals.

The widow or widower should not forget to review carefully any will or trust left by the predeceased spouse as well as any nonprobate assets in which the surviving spouse may have an interest. Life insurance and retirement proceeds that were payable to the surviving spouse and that may have bypassed the probate estate are nonetheless included for tax purposes in the deceased spouse's taxable estate.

A recently widowed person is eligible to file a joint income tax return for the year in which the deceased spouse died. This will generally result in income tax savings.

As you get older, you may want to execute a power of attorney granting authority to a relative or close friend to handle affairs in the event of a debilitating accident or illness not immediately resulting in death. Likewise you might want to consider a living will in the event of a terminal illness.

The living will would indicate that if you can be kept alive only by artificial means, it would be your direction that life-sustaining procedures and mechanisms should not be used or should be discontinued. A living will may be of great comfort to a widow or widower who, if incapacitated, has no spouse to make such decisions. Each state has a slightly different requirement under the Right-to-Die Statute, so make sure your living will meets the requirements of your state.

If the widow or widower has children or other dependents to support, it may be wise to look to insurance—life and disability. Choice of executor, trustee, and guardian for children should be given thoughtful consideration as well.

## IF YOU ARE DIVORCED AND SINGLE

If you are in the midst of a divorce, be sure to amend your will to name parties other than the estranged spouse as a primary beneficiary. If you are already divorced, it is likely that your will has already been revoked by your state by operation of law.

In drafting a will subsequent to a divorce, be sure to rethink your choice of executor. If you have minor children, but don't want your ex-spouse to control any assets you may leave for their benefit, consider a trust with a relative, friend, or bank trust department to manage the children's assets. Upon your death, the ex-spouse will automatically serve as natural guardian for the children unless such rights have been previously relinquished or forfeited in a legal proceeding.

A divorce will not automatically invalidate the beneficiary designation on your life insurance policies. It may be necessary to file a new beneficiary designation with each life insurance company unless you are prohibited from making such a change under a court-ordered divorce settlement.

There are other concerns such as what payments, if any, will continue following the death of an ex-spouse, property settlement arrangements, and the amount and conditions of child support. Alimony generally stops upon the spouse's death unless the decree specifically provides that alimony will continue or otherwise shall be charged against the estate of the deceased.

Until the statute of limitations has run out (generally 4–6 years unless fraud is suspected), a divorced person may be liable for past taxes, interests, and penalties on prior joint income tax returns or on an estate tax return, if something happens to one or the other. It would be wise to have the settlement agreement contain a provision that would indemnify you in the event of any claim for back taxes by the I.R.S.

There is a likelihood that a divorced person will remarry and may possibly have additional children. An irrevocable trust should be set up in light of the possibility of future children. (See the discussion of gifts and trusts in Chapter 5.)

If living with another without marriage is planned, consider having an agreement drawn up determining each other's assets, liabilities, and responsibilities. (See Appendix C.)

## IF YOU ARE REMARRIED

For couples planning a subsequent marriage, the protection of pre-owned assets may be an important consideration. A prenuptial agreement is an agreement negotiated between a couple about to be married that determines, in advance, the disposition of certain property and income in the event of a divorce or death. It is not uncommon, especially in community property states, for marital property agreements and prenuptial agreements to classify and reclassify assets and to establish separate rights to future income or appreciation that would otherwise be treated as community property. This becomes increasingly important if you want to preserve assets for children of a prior marriage. Postnuptial agreements are used in community property states to change ownership rights of spouses.

A previously married person who has decided to remarry must consider how much (if any) to leave any or all of the spouses, and how to assure that a portion of his or her estate ultimately goes to children of any prior marriage. If a remarried spouse wishes to provide for a new spouse but also wishes to make sure that the bulk of the estate goes to the children of any prior marriage, there are two possible alternatives: a life estate and/or a QTIP trust (qualified terminable interest property).

In a life estate, you would leave all or part of your assets to the surviving spouse, with the estate to terminate upon the death or remarriage of the surviving spouse. Life estates have been popular with those entering into a subsequent marriage.

A QTIP trust is a testamentary trust that provides for certain assets to be held, invested, and used for the benefit of a surviving spouse. The property held will qualify for the marital deduction at your death even if the property interest terminates at your spouse's death. But the qualified assets would be included in the surviving spouse's estate for tax purposes at the spouse's eventual death.

Those who have recently remarried would be wise to carefully consider the following:

- The choice of executor, trustee, and guardian,
- Trust assets and distribution of corpus,
- Division of personal property,
- A prenuptial agreement, and
- The designation of beneficiaries of life insurance, retirement, and other benefits.

If you have remarried it is likely that you need a new will. Prior wills that often contain special provisions to protect your children may no longer be valid under your state laws. Also, review your life insurance to determine what changes ought to be made as a result of the remarriage. Other considerations may be a custodial account, an irrevocable trust, or a funded revocable trust.

Common problems for the previously married and those who have remarried is the treatment of multiple groups of children. This may lead to potential estate disputes if you have not planned properly. The distribution of personal property and other assets is a sensitive issue and you need to make some provisions to avoid future animosity among such offspring.

Transferring ownership of your personal life insurance policies to your children (if they are no longer minors) is one type of planning for the previously married. Transferring a policy's ownership from you to someone else may decrease estate taxes, because your personally purchased and owned life insurance is included in your estate for tax purposes even when the proceeds are payable directly to a named beneficiary. The owner is the person who purchased the insurance policy and that person may or may not be the person who is named as beneficiary under the policy.

For the I.R.S. to recognize someone other than you as owner, you must give up all incidents of ownership over that policy. You must give up all rights and control over the policy. You cannot change beneficiaries, surrender or cancel the policy, convert from group to individual, assign or revoke the policy, cash it in, pledge it, or borrow against the cash value. All transfers of life insurance, however, made within three years of death, will be included in your estate even though the three-year rule on most other transfers will not be included in your estate. If a beneficiary dies before you, the policy will revert in most instances to you or to your estate and will be included in your estate for tax purposes. Generally, ownership of a policy depends upon the source of the payment. In Arizona, Louisiana, New Mexico, and Texas, life insurance remains separate if taken out with separate property. In California, Washington, and the common law states, ownership depends upon the source of payment.

## ONCE IN A LIFETIME EXEMPTION—
## A POSSIBLE TAX TRAP FOR THE REMARRIED

For millions of older married U.S. citizens, working harder can be a losing proposition. Twists in the tax laws may cause married retirees (55 years plus) to lose the special exclusion of gain that is provided by I.R.C. Section 121. This section provides that individual taxpayers may exclude up to $125,000 (or $62,500 for married persons filing separate returns) realized on the sale of a personal home if they have reached age 55 prior to the date of sale and have owned or used the home as a principal residence for at least three years during a five year period ending on the date of the sale.

This once-in-a-lifetime exclusion is an elective provision that will allow a taxpayer to use it alone or to couple it with the deferral of gain as provided for in I.R.C. Section 1034 if the taxpayer invests in a more expensive home.

In fact, senior citizens could end up losing this once-in-a-lifetime tax exclusion for homes they sell if they divorce, are widowed, or remarry.

### Unmarried Taxpayers

If you are unmarried and have reached age 55 before you sell your home, you are entitled to a full $125,000 exclusion. You are entitled to this full exclusion even if you own this home jointly. This tax law is a detriment to those who are unmarried and want to cohabitate.

If you are an unmarried senior citizen who owns a home, you may wish to sell your home *before* marrying or remarrying. This way two exclusions are available if both of you sell your homes before marriage but only one exclusion if the homes are sold after the marriage.

### Married Couples

If you are married and own a home jointly (with the right of survivorship, by the entirety, or community property), and meet the age, ownership, and use tests, you are limited to an exclusion of up to one-half of the maximum exclusion amount on a separate return. If you file a joint return, as a couple you are entitled to the full exclusion of $125,000. Once claimed (no matter what type of return is filed, joint or separate), neither one of you can thereafter claim another exclusion. If you take this exclusion during your marriage and later divorce, no further exclusions are available to either you or your ex-spouse, or, if either of you remarries, to your new spouses.

Dr. Jerry Brown, a 55-year-old widower, has lived in his home for 25 years. He is anticipating marrying Nancy whom he met several years before, after his wife had died. Nancy is also 55 years old and owns her own home. If both homes are sold before the marriage, Nancy will have a gain of $80,000 and Jerry will have a gain of $100,000. This means that two exclusions (which would total $180,000) would be available. However, if only one of the homes is sold before the marriage, there will be no further exclusions available to either of them. If they decide not to sell either before the marriage, then only one exclusion will be available to them afterwards.

The same situation may present itself in a slightly different manner. If Jerry were married but thinking of divorcing, he should consider dividing his and his wife's marital assets in such a way that the home would go to one of them. After the divorce, the party receiving the home could sell it and take the exclusion. In this way, the other person would not be stuck with the ex-spouse's election to take the exclusion and would still be entitled in the future to his or her own once-in-a-lifetime $125,000 exclusion. If the home is sold before the divorce, both parties will be bound by the exclusion and then it would be binding on new spouses as well, if either or both of the divorced parties remarried.

If you are married and 55 years old at the time of the sale of your home, the rules governing the exclusion apply even if you later divorce during the same tax year.

*Example:* A 60-year-old doctor sells his home for $250,000 and does not intend to purchase another one. The original purchase price of his home some 20 years earlier was $100,000 and it has cost him $15,000 in selling expenses. His gain would be computed as follows:

| | |
|---|---|
| Sale price | $250,000 |
| Less selling expenses | − 15,000 |
| Amount realized | $235,000 |
| Less basis of home | − 100,000 |
| Gain realized | $135,000 |
| Less exclusion | − 125,000 |
| Gain realized | $ 10,000 |

This $10,000 gain would not be recognized and could be deferred if he were to purchase another home costing at least $60,000.

## ANTENUPTIAL AGREEMENTS

Dr. X was left financially depleted after two divorces. He had to pay his first wife $40,000 a year until the last of their four children finished college. She also was awarded the home, valued at $175,000, but Dr. X was still not completely free of obligation unless she remarried. His second wife received alimony and child support for one child plus the use of their $300,000 home until the child left for college. At that time, the home was to be sold and the proceeds divided.

Now Dr. X is contemplating a third marriage and he would like some type of premarital protection.

The answer is an antenuptial (or prenuptial) agreement. This unromantic document is an agreement between prospective spouses that states clearly, before the wedding, how the property would be divided after divorce or after death.

Dr. X's bride did not object to this agreement. She had been married twice before and was fairly well off in her own right. To her, this contract represented little more than an exercise, because she did not want to risk the possibility of her own children losing their inheritance from her.

An agreement was drawn up stating that, if the marriage were to be dissolved, each would retain what each had brought into it, and neither would seek any financial consideration from the other. Any property obtained while they were married would be divided 50–50. Each was represented by separate counsel and financial statements from each were attached to and made a part of the agreement.

An antenuptial agreement, in order to be enforceable, must be specific with no ambiguous terms. It must list each item of property and how it will be divided or disposed of. Nothing takes the place of a valid, legal agreement properly executed by both parties and witnessed, giving full financial disclosure. This contract must be prepared and signed before the marriage and will apply to nothing other than that which is covered by its specific terms. It is cheap insurance against losing your assets and your future earnings.

Antenuptial agreements are being used frequently, when the marriage is not the first, as an effective way of protecting children of a previous marriage from claims of another spouse.

When there are substantial differences in wealth between couples, such an agreement should be considered prior to the marriage in order to limit property rights—common-law, statutory, or community—of the parties to each other's estates or when one party is giving the other a substantial gift in consideration of the marriage.

This seemingly cold and calculating approach to drawing up an antenuptial agreement does nothing to enhance the romantic atmosphere surrounding a marriage. However, it is not uncommon for a family to require that the person about to be married execute an antenuptial agreement. This family contract may help the about-to-be-married person to overcome the natural tendency to avoid the subject as well as to give him or her a feeling of obligation to parents, brothers, and sisters. Courts are reluctant to enforce family agreements, holding that such mutual promises are not adequate consideration. Therefore, there might be a question of enforceability. Even though such agreements are not enforceable by the courts, you might consider their purpose as a means of introducing the subject and of insulating assets and/or income against later claims. It might help avoid embarrassment at a time when it becomes appropriate to suggest negotiating an antenuptial agreement.

A typical antenuptial agreement might involve any of the following:

1. One of the parties' parent's agreeing to give a gift to one or both right after the marriage,

2. A prospective bridegroom's father's agreeing to support the intended bride and any children in the event his son fails to do so,

3. In consideration of marriage, giving one spouse certain limited and specified rights to the assets of the other. This is generally coupled with a waiver of all other rights to the property of the wealthier spouse or even of both spouses, including dower, curtesy, and statutory or elective shares, as well as a waiver of the right to administer each other's estates.

Most states do recognize both ante- and postnuptial agreements as a way of divesting a spouse's statutory share by a written contract. Where the parties are residents of one of the community property states or may move to one in the future, an antenuptial contract should deal specifically with community property problems. It could:

1. Classify earnings of the prospective spouses as either "separate" or "community,"

2. Provide for control and management of all the couple's assets—before, during, and after marriage,

3. Preclude possible rights and conflicts when one of the parties devotes time and effort to separate property,

4. Provide a waiver of release of rights to community or quasi-community property. (Quasi-community property rights may be automatically acquired by spouses moving from a common-law state to one that recognizes community property rights. It would give each spouse a forced share at the other's death, or upon divorce, in that portion of his or her estate that would have been community property in such states as California, Idaho, or Arizona [but not at death in Arizona].)

5. Classify gifts as either "separate" or "community,"

6. Convert part or all of the property of either or both into one of the following: separate, community, joint (with rights of survivorship, by the entirety, or as tenants-in-common), and

7. Ultimately become available to other members of the family.

Antenuptial agreements cannot, however, modify certain federal or state property rights. For example, government life insurance is not assignable, and the ownership of U.S. Savings Bonds and certain other federal obligations may be changed only by complying with federally prescribed procedures.

In order to draw up a reasonable, equitable, and valid antenuptial document, both parties should fully disclose all their income and assets to each other, a disclosure similar to that required before entering into any contract settling property rights, including separation and postnuptial agreements. These disclosures as you can well imagine, have caused and may cause problems. Even the most trusting person may be somewhat leery because of a previous unfortunate marital experience, or, being paid in cash as part of the underground economy, does not want to report his or her entire income on a tax return and is reluctant to disclose income in a disclosure agreement.

## Contents of an Antenuptial Agreement

Generally, an antenuptial contract is based upon a promise to marry and may contain one or both of the following: (1) the relinquishment of marital rights in the bridegroom's estate, or (2) this relinquishment in exchange either for property to be transferred to the bride or the groom's relinquishment of marital rights in the bride's estate.

The agreement should be in writing. It should give the names of both parties and the date the agreement was entered into. It should cover the fact that it is based on a promise to marry. It should contain facts concerning the relinquishing of any marital rights, and the particulars of all property transfers should be clearly defined. Transfers of property may take place before marriage, after marriage, or at the deaths of the parties.

All terms should be clearly defined, including provisions setting forth any special matters to be put into wills or trusts of either or both of the parties. The terminology should be the same in all documents. There should be terms dealing with the execution of any additional documents, making minimum provisions for the prospective spouse, defining property rights in existing or after-acquired property, nullifying any property rights that may arise otherwise by operation of law upon marriage (thus superseding common-law and statutory rights). Finally, it should state any other relevant matters, giving special attention to identifying possible conflicts between the parties.

Local state law will give the requirements as to execution, acknowledgment, and recording of an antenuptial agreement as well as to its cancellation, if necessary. A sample antenuptial agreement appears in Appendix D.

## Presumption of Validity

There is a legal presumption that an antenuptial contract is valid and binding on the parties to it. In old common law, such an agreement was void because it was considered to have been invalidated by the marriage. However, in some instances there was an equitable remedy. In some states, the burden of proof that such an agreement is not valid because it is unfair or is not free of fraud or deceit, rests on the party challenging its validity. In order to ensure the validity of the agreement, both parties should be represented by their *own* separate, independent attorneys. This will ensure that the agreement was entered into freely and that it was signed voluntarily with competent legal advice and with full knowledge of each one's rights and each other's assets. Some states, such as Florida, do not require disclosures for the agreement to be valid. For the agreement to be deemed invalid, it must be proved, in most instances, to be unfair or that the circumstances surrounding its negotiation involved fraud or deceit.

## Support Obligations

A husband's traditional obligation to support his wife remains in most states today. If the marriage should become unstable or fail, this support obligation continues, except to the extent that it is modified by a separation agreement or a divorce decree, or until the wife remarries. In most states, the antenuptial agreement does not relieve the husband from the obligation of paying alimony, especially when the ex-wife cannot support herself or when she remains single if the support obligation continues after a divorce.

Cases upholding provisions in antenuptial contracts dealing with a future separation for divorce have been decided in the District of Columbia, Wisconsin, Tennessee, Arkansas, Michigan, Montana, Nevada, Oklahoma, Indiana, Massachusetts, Kentucky, Georgia, and California. States not following the new trend are Missouri and South Dakota.

Frequently a married couple may wish that they had entered into an antenuptial agreement. In this situation, it is possible for them to sign a *postnuptial* agreement with similar results. Such agreements are made between spouses to handle unresolved problems or to settle property interests during a move between a community property and a common-law jurisdiction or vice versa, or where the Uniform Marital Property Act (UMPA)[1] has been enacted, such as in Wisconsin.

Formulating marriage goals and systematically identifying potential conflicts by means of a written contract—an antenuptial agreement—will prevent later problems that may arise.

---

[1] The Uniform Marital Property Act was adopted by the National Conference of Commissioners on Uniform State Laws on July 28, 1983. It was enacted April 4, 1984, by Wisconsin, effective January 1, 1986. (1983 Wisconsin Act 186.)

# 10

## GETTING YOUR ESTATE IN ORDER

### CHARTING YOUR COURSE

Financial planning means playing a game of security to win. With proper understanding, you can make security actually happen, but it does take constructive suggestions, involvement, education, and preparation for the participation of others in the management of financial affairs.

Now that you are familiar with some of the intricacies of planning your finances, you should sit down and chart your course. Do not let nonexistent or misplaced documents or the lack of organization of dates and records hinder you. Use Charts 23 through 32 (Figures 10–1 to 10–10) at the end of the chapter to help you organize your records. The present is often so crowded with things to do that we put off making our most important decisions, but a basic ingredient in effective planning is time. Your responsibility is to make that time.

Death is among the most shattering realities that we will all face one day. If you are prepared beforehand, you will find the situation much more bearable. How well you prepare for the uncertainty of the future will determine how well you will be able to handle the numerous problems that will arise.

One planning device is to give someone you trust your power of attorney in the event that you are unable to attend to your own affairs. Another such device is to execute a "living will."

# LIVING WILLS

A living will allows you to state in advance your unwillingness to be subjected to life-prolonging medical measures in the event that an injury or illness leaves you with no chance of recovery. This, of course, is in addition to your will.

An organization called *Concern for Dying* first developed the living will. It was designed to express your wishes if you were to become terminally ill and to relieve others of the legal and emotional burden of making those decisions for you.

Most states today have some form of legislation regarding living wills and some have a form that is recognized only in that particular state. This means that your living will may not be binding in another state. Some states recognize living wills for a specific term. For example, in Georgia, a living will is valid for only seven years, unless revoked sooner. The term of the living will may be extended for an additional seven-year term by re-execution in accordance with the formalities required by the state.

Most of the state statutes do not permit an individual to designate another person to act on his or her behalf without a power of attorney. Using a power of attorney even makes it possible to name an agent to act on your behalf—whether for health-care purposes or for any other transactions—while investing that agent with business-type powers that would enable him or her to manage your financial affairs. However, if it is for health-care purposes, you should consider a "durable" power of attorney.

## Durable Power of Attorney

A durable power of attorney, recognized by legislative act in many states, designates someone else to make health-care decisions for you if you are unable to do so yourself. It gives your agent the power to consent to your doctor's not giving treatment or stopping the treatment necessary to keep you alive. It is called "durable" because it is not revoked if you lack mental capacity. This power for making health-care decisions will not be valid unless it is signed by two qualified adult witnesses who are personally known to you, who are present when you sign it, who are not related to you by blood or marriage, who are not your physicians, and who are not directly financially responsible for your medical care. Also, the document must be notarized.

# POWER OF ATTORNEY: SHOULD YOU OR SHOULDN'T YOU?

- "I'm a doctor, what good would it be to me?"
- "Power of attorney is for the millionaire chairman of the board of some big corporation who has more money than he can handle himself."

- "I've got a will, so I don't need it!"

These are just a few of the misconceptions I have heard about power of attorney. In order to clear up misinformation on the subject, let us begin with questions that people ask most frequently:

Q: *What is a power of attorney?*

A: It is a legal document in which you name one or more persons to act on your behalf by legally granting the person(s) the power as *defined* in the document to make decisions for you and to handle your affairs as *defined* in the document, when for some reason you cannot be present or are unable to make those decisions yourself. (See Chart 33, Figure 10–11) at the end of the chapter.) The person you name is actually regarded as your alter ego, and the acts that he or she performs are considered acts of you, yourself.

Q: *For what reasons would the average person need to grant power of attorney?*

A: There are many reasons, but here are the more common ones:

- If you should have to leave the country for an extended period of time, and you need a responsible person to take care of your business, property, etc., while you are absent.
- If you were to become too ill or disabled to manage your affairs, and you needed someone to take over for you until you recovered.
- If you were to have more business to manage than you can handle alone and wish to delegate some or all of the responsibility.
- If you dislike, do not want to be bothered with, or do not feel capable of handling some or all of your business affairs and want another person to do it for you.
- If you were to be called into the military service, and you needed someone to take care of your affairs in your absence.

Q: *Must the person you name be an attorney?*

A: No, and this is probably the biggest misconception regarding power of attorney. People seem to misinterpret it to mean an *attorney's power* and assume it must apply only to attorneys. On the contrary, you may grant this power to any person 18 years of age, or over. This then makes that person your *agent* or *attorney-in-fact*, as it is sometimes called. You are called the "principal."

Q: *Is it customary to give power of attorney to a member of the legal profession?*

A: Generally, most attorneys prefer to prepare the legal document and give counsel rather than administer the power.

Q: *Is it customary for an attorney to ask a client for power of attorney?*

A: It is not uncommon, but it should be for a *stated, limited special purpose* and *not* a broad power to handle all your affairs.

Q: *How do you grant a person power of attorney?*

A: Engage an attorney, and he or she will draw up a power-of-attorney document, designed to fit your needs.

Q: *Who is the best person to name?*
A: That is entirely up to you. But *carefully consider your choice!* First and most important, you must be absolutely confident of the person's honesty, integrity, and loyalty. It is also wise to select a person familiar with the area upon which he or she is given the power to act. For instance, if you grant power to someone to take care of your personal affairs, your spouse or a close relative would be the best choice. In other cases, you might want special matters handled by an expert or specialist in the particular field(s) you name.

If you name other than a specialist, you should ask yourself: Does this person have the expertise necessary to handle this (taxes, accounting, investment, management, etc)? Has the candidate ever acted as an attorney-in-fact before? How often? Were there varied and difficult problems, and how did he/she conduct himself or herself? Will he/she maintain strict honesty and impartiality in dealing and acting on your behalf? Will he/she be available to handle your affairs? Is he/she a financially responsible person that you can trust to keep careful, meticulous records without commingling of cash or property? And most important of all: Do you feel *completely* comfortable with the idea of this person being in charge of your money?

Q: *Is it customary to grant a power of attorney to the same person who is executor of your will, and would it be a wise thing to do?*
A: As long as there is no conflict of interest, and the person named executor is not also a beneficiary under the will, it would not necessarily be unwise.

Q: *What are the duties and responsibilities of the agent that you choose to grant a power of attorney?*
A: The agent holding this power is required to exercise ordinary care and diligence in conducting your business affairs. The relationship is classified as being that of a *fiduciary* (i.e., it involves a high degree of faith and trust as well as loyalty).

An agent may *not:*
• reap a personal profit from dealing with your property;
• take advantage of facts obtained in his confidential capacity, to your prejudice;
• compete with you, unless he does so with your consent and knowledge.

If your agent disobeyed your instructions and did not stay within the scope of the agency created, he/she would be liable for any loss suffered by you as a result of the violations.

An agent *does* have a duty to:
• keep accounts in a regular manner, supported by proper vouchers, and to render to you that which belongs to you;

• give notice to you of all material facts coming into his knowledge that relate to the relationship.

However, keep in mind that any notice to an agent, within the scope of his authority, is also notice to you and, as such, is binding upon you.

Q: *How do I know whether I need to give anyone power of attorney, and what are the advantages?*

A: If you have a joint venture or a partnership, you may find it advantageous for one of your associates to have such a power when you cannot be reached personally. Or if, due to advancing years, you no longer want to be actively involved in your financial affairs, you may prefer to have someone handle your business for you. Also, keep in mind that you may become ill or incapacitated, in which case someone could handle your affairs until there is a proceeding to appoint a legal guardian. The power of attorney terminates with your death.

Q: *Are there dangers or disadvantages in granting someone power of attorney?*

A: Yes, there are some dangers and disadvantages in granting someone power of attorney. Therefore, before making a final decision, remember this: Any time you give another person the authority to act for you, you are treading on dangerous ground! Before you decide, think it over long and carefully! The greatest danger, of course, is granting this authority to someone who proves to be dishonest. Naturally, most people consider the person whom they choose to be trustworthy—but you can never be completely certain. Sometimes a person who has always been conservative, modest, and thrifty with his or her own money may suddenly become an overbearing big spender with yours. The sudden control of money can have a peculiar effect on some people, especially when it is money that they did not earn. For that matter, the person may be basically honest, loyal, and well-intentioned but may overextend his/her new authority, abuse your trust, and lose your money.

For example, a 70-year-old woman planned to make a trip to Europe to visit relatives for six months. Since she owned a house and a small candy store, she wanted someone to take care of her business and property while she was gone.

A nephew she had raised seemed the ideal person, so she granted him a power of attorney. However, before his aunt even arrived at her destination, the impetuous nephew heard about a "can't lose" stock deal. He decided to *temporarily* borrow the money by mortgaging the house and candy store to "make a bundle" for the aunt he loved, and surprise her when she returned. He did surprise her. When she got back, she found herself homeless and bankrupt as a result of her well-meaning nephew's get-rich-quick dealings.

Q: *Are there other dangers?*

A: As unbelievable as it sounds, many people grant power of attorney, and then forget about. It is not unusual for people to grant this power to others, and not only forget about it but even lose all contact for years with the person named.

A good illustration of this is the case of the partners in business who had given each other a power of attorney eight years ago. Last year, however, the two of them had an argument, stopped speaking to each other, and one of them left town.

A few weeks following the departure, the remaining partner discovered that his former partner had sold property owned by their business. Indignant and angry, he went to his attorney to file criminal charges against his ex-partner. However, his attorney discovered that he had never revoked the power of attorney, so the other partner had legal right to dispose of any assets of the business.

Q: *Can you revoke a power of attorney and how do you do it?*

A: You have the right to revoke this relationship any time you wish. However, the revocation must be in writing, signed, notarized, and delivered to anyone interested in such power, including any person holding such power. In addition, it may be required that such release be recorded in the office of the court of the county in which your property or any part thereof is located. (See Chart 34, Figure 10–12, at the end of the chapter.)

In general, this relationship may be terminated by the acts of the parties themselves, or by operation of law. An agreement creating this relationship may contain a provision calling for termination of the agency upon the expiration of a stipulated time, the happening of a given contingency, or the accomplishment of the object of the relationship.

The relationship also terminates by operation of law in any of the following ways:

- By a subsequent agreement, you and the person to whom you have granted the power of attorney may mutually agree to terminate it;
- The death of either of you;
- Bankruptcy of either of you, if the bankruptcy affects the subject matter of the relationship;
- The destruction or loss of the subject matter of the relationship;
- A drastic change in business conditions (e.g., dissolution of partnership or corporation);
- A change in law causing illegality of the subject matter.

Q: *It sounds risky. Isn't there some sort of legal protection against the possibility of a dishonest or irresponsible agent?*

A: The wisest safeguard is naming a co-fiduciary. That is, someone other than the person named to hold the legal document. For instance, if you grant power of attorney to a person to handle your stocks, have a second person hold the actual certificates. In this case, the person granted the power of attorney would have to go to this second party to explain the reason behind his intention of using the power. If the co-fiduciary questions the proposal or believes it to be not in your best interest, he could contact you.

Q: *But suppose you were in the hospital in a coma?*

A: In such case the only thing that could be done would be to petition the court to have someone appointed as guardian or receiver or to initiate some other judicial proceeding terminating the power.

Q: *What is the difference between a general power of attorney and a specific power of attorney?*

A: A general power of attorney grants a person the authority to do almost *anything* on your behalf. It is a very broad power. A specific power of attorney means that you have granted the person power for a *limited* purpose (as defined by you in the document).

Q: *How long does power of attorney last?*

A: A power of attorney ceases to exist when you die. Persons who are under disabilities may not raise their status by the appointment of someone to act for them. The power of attorney does not cease when you lose your mental faculties, depending upon state law. Generally, it continues until there is a court proceeding to appoint a guardian or receiver.

Q: *What responsibilities should you give the person to whom you grant power of attorney?*

A: That is up to you. A power of attorney may be a combination of caretaker, order clerk, messenger, bookkeeper, or even an automatic reminder system. The person may be able to deliver or receive items for you; receive payment or make it. Of course, meticulous record keeping should be a must in all transactions.

Q: *Who would check these records?*

A: This is strictly a personal matter: either you, yourself, or you may want to have an accountant or a C.P.A. check records. But there is no necessity for either.

Q: *Could a bank be granted power of attorney, and, if so, is it a good idea?*

A: Yes, a bank could be granted power of attorney. Again, that is a personal matter. However, keep in mind that there are generally fees involved when anyone else handles your affairs for you. Find out what these are and any other administrative costs. A bank is an institution, and as such it would have a system of checks and balances, which could prove to be a safeguard for your affairs. But keep in mind that banks are not money managers as such.

Q: *Is the person granted power of attorney paid for his services, and, if so, how is the fee determined?*

A: Unless otherwise agreed, or unless the services rendered are obviously gratuitous, you must compensate the person you appoint. The amount of compensation depends upon the express agreement of the parties, or, in the absence of an agreement, upon reasonable value of the services rendered by the person appointed, considering the purpose, extent, and character of the service, and the fidelity of the person appointed.

The person appointed is entitled to reimbursement for money spent or advanced on your behalf and at your express request.

Q: *What time limit should you put on the power of attorney?*

A: You can set a time limit for the performance of tasks to be completed. But if you *do not* specify a time limit, the relationship continues for a reasonable time. What is considered *reasonable* is a question of fact for the courts.

Q. *Can you name a second party in the event that your first choice dies or becomes disabled?*

A: This relationship is strictly one of contractual capacity and you may do whatever is mutually agreed upon by you and the person or persons whom you choose to act in such a representative capacity. Any person, usually, may act for you who is capable of exercising authority. That person acts only as a medium or a conduit through whom the transaction passes or flows.

Q: *What kinds of power of attorney can a person grant?*

A: It depends upon the person's needs and the extent of power he wishes to grant. Most power of attorney documents list different areas in which you can grant power. Some of them are: real estate transactions; records, reports, and statements; stocks, bonds, and commodity transactions; operation of business; claims and litigation; insurance transactions; personal relationships and affairs; tax returns; and benefits from military service.

Q: *Is there a power of attorney in which you could grant a person authority to make medical decisions for you?* That is, if you were in the hospital paralyzed or unconscious, could this person make decisions as to whether you should or should not have surgery, be examined by a specialist, dismiss a doctor in favor of another one, etc.?

A: As long as you have not been declared judicially incompetent, a "durable" written power of attorney, unless expressly providing otherwise, shall not be terminated by your being paralyzed, unconscious, etc., in the hospital. (See "Durable Power of Attorney" earlier in this chapter.) The power to act as an attorney-in-fact for you remains in force until such time as it becomes necessary for a guardian or receiver or other judicial proceeding to terminate this power.

Q: *Suppose you are the only parent of a minor child and you are in a coma, paralyzed, etc., for a long period of time. Would the person to whom you granted power of attorney have authority over the minor child (regarding place of residence, etc.)?*

A. Not usually. There must be a court proceeding to have a guardian ad litem, as it is referred to, appointed on the child's behalf.

If you should become incapacitated, you should have someone preauthorized to act as agent. The document executed to appoint this agent can be simple. (See Figure 10–11.) A copy of it should be filed with your attorney, trust-officer, etc. This simple step might save you several thousand dollars.

## HOW TO SELECT ADVISORS

Screening possible financial planners and other consultants who can help you secure your estate is probably one of the most difficult things you will ever have to do. The reason is that there are so many people today who call themselves *consultants* or *financial planners*. To make matters worse, there are no licensing requirements for consultants or financial planners. And, you will find that a good many doctors leave medicine or dentistry and decide to retire, who, all of a sudden, become financial experts and consultants! These individuals charge various fees, but the most prevalent fee is a percentage of assets or an hourly rate.

Finding an attorney or accountant is another difficult task. The reason is that the majority of us today base our judgment on personality and our subjective opinions. Most attorneys have accountants with whom they like to work just as accountants have those attorneys with whom they work best. Because of these close working relationships, you may not be getting the independent advice you need. To solve this problem, you should hire an attorney who does not work with a certain accountant and hire an accountant who does not work with a certain attorney all the time. This will enable you to get independent advice from several sources.

Accountants are reluctant to give advice because they cannot practice law without a license. Therefore, they may or may not give you the advice you really want to hear. I have a solution you might try. When posing a question to your accountant, ask it in this manner:

> If this were your particular situation, how would you handle the matter? What would you do? And, naturally, I won't hold you to it.

The other thing you should never do is tell your accountant that your attorney said "this" or "that." Most accountants will not contradict your attorney's advice—and they are careful not to practice law without a license. If you want to know the answer to a particular question, pose that question as your own opinion or your own thought. Just remember, the only dumb question is the question not asked!

## TAX SHELTERS—A PLANNING DEVICE

Most people equate tax shelters with doctors and others whom they consider the super-rich. These tax-advantaged investments are not reserved for doctors but they also attract taxpayers who may have only $5,000 or $6,000 to invest. According to a recent study, citizens in the United States invest more than $9 billion in tax shelters each year.

A tax shelter is an investment of funds, at risk, to acquire something of value. Before the change in the law, such an investment generally reduced or deferred current taxes so that it would ultimately result in income and/or gains.

Congress believed that these types of special investments were being taken advantage of so they limited many of the specific tax advantages extensively.

Because of their limited use, tax shelters are not for everyone. First, a potential investor must have disposable income to invest. A non-recourse loan (secured only by the asset) enhances the attractiveness of the investment because there is no risk of personal liability on the loan. The adoption by Congress of the at-risk rules has, however, restricted the use of non-recourse financing in all investments except real estate.

One major pitfall to this type of investment is the buyer's lack of knowledge. Many buyers, especially those who are doctors, favor such investing without proper knowledge of the investment: its structure and operation, tax risks, benefits, advantages, or even specific information about the promoter of the shelter being considered. (See Table 10–1.)

**Table 10–1.** Ten guidelines for tax shelter investments.

1. Never rush into a tax shelter deal unprepared.

2. Never invest in a deal that would be unattractive if it were not for the supposed tax benefits.

3. If the deal seems too good to be true, it probably is!

4. Avoid deals that seem particularly offbeat. The more offbeat it is, the more likely it is to attract the attention of the I.R.S.

5. If the deal is so good, ask yourself why the offer is being made to you.

6. Stay away from deals that are based outside the United States.

7. Be aware that, if you sign a note as part of the purchase price of participation in a shelter, you may have to make good on that note, no matter how badly the deal has gone.

8. Be wary of boiler plate, direct mail, coupon response, and other questionable forms of solicitation for investment.

9. Non-securities offerings (that is, direct sale of energy-saving devices, patents, licenses, art works, and other "shelter" items) and offers to pay your accountant's or lawyer's review fee are all on the list of things to watch out for.

10. If the promoter promises half, or more, of your money back from investment tax credits, he has probably inflated the price of the asset and the tax credits will not stand up.

## Limited Partnerships

Most tax shelters are structured as limited partnerships. A limited partnership is not a taxable entity. Such an entity is a conduit by which taxes and obligations flow through the partnership to the individual partners, avoiding the double taxation problem associated with corporations. The limited partnership provides the best of the corporate and partnership worlds because losses flow through it as in an ordinary partnership, but the investor's liability is limited, like that of a shareholder, to the amount of the investment.

Limited partnerships allow an individual (limited) partner to be responsible to the partnership only up to the amount of his or her investment. Beyond that point, risk is borne by the general partner(s). The general partner is responsible for major decisions made for all members of the partnership, and for all management and control of the partnership. The limited partners are not bound by the obligations of the partnership and a limited partner does not become liable as a general partner unless he/she takes part in the control of the business.

Exactly what is a limited partnership? It is a partnership formed by two or more persons, having as members one or more general partners and one or more limited partners. The retirement, death, or insanity of a general partner dissolves the partnership, unless there is a right given to the remaining general partners under a written agreement (usually stated in the partnership certificate) or with the consent in writing of all members. On the death of a limited partner, his or her executor or administrator obtains all the rights of that limited partner for the purpose of settling the estate. The estate of a deceased limited partner is liable only to the extent of his or her investment as a limited partner.

## Evaluating a Limited Partnership Tax Shelter

Most limited partnership tax shelters focus on the anticipated tax benefits. But investors pay very little attention to or even disregard entirely the person or entity to whom they are giving their money. If you are about to write a check for a "great tax shelter," stop first and redirect your attention to the general partner(s)—the person or persons who will be in charge of your money.

Suppose someone approached you asking to borrow $50,000 or more. What would you do? Unless that person was extremely close to you or you knew exactly what was planned for this money, you would probably refuse. Most people are more careful about loans than about investments, so think of the limited partnership tax shelter as a loan. After all, you worked hard to earn that money. Isn't it worth a few hours of your time to check out the person(s) to whom you are turning over your money?

You should be aware that, as an investor, you risk the loss of your investment in the partnership plus whatever obligation for additional capital contribution that you have agreed to under the partnership agreement. These risks are appealing because the benefits of the early years' tax losses are passed through to the individual investor's income tax return, and, when the project turns profitable, income may be distributed without a "double" tax.

## Investigating the General Partner

What do you know about the general partner? Remember he is the one who will be in charge of your money. Before you release your check, evaluate him by following these check points:

• *Begin with the prospectus, or "offering memorandum" as it is sometimes called.* Ask your attorney and/or accountant to do a more technical search for you. The prospectus is an indispensable tool, a kind of information booklet. It describes the "Company's Business," its products, its competition, and what it plans to do with the money it raises. Once you have read the history of the company, turn to the "Capitalization" section. This section will give you a starting point for your math framework. It describes the company's current sources of capital (stocks, bonds, short-term notes or loans, or a combination of these). The "Selected Financial Data" section illuminates the ups and downs of the company's earnings and growth. Here you will find the balance sheet items: working capital, total assets, long-term debt, and shareholders' equity. Without this type of financial data, you will not be able to invest intelligently. (See Table 10–2.)

• *Is the general partner an expert at what he is doing?* In the table of contents in the prospectus, look up "Management." This will list the manager's credentials. (What sometimes turns up is shocking!)

• *What is his track record?* What was promised to past investors? What was delivered to them during the term of the investment and at the time of the sale? How much money were the investors required to invest, and how much did their investments earn? How long did it take for them to recoup their investments? What was the average annual return on their investments? The record is there. Take time to read it.

• *Does the general partner actually manage his project?* Or is he a wheeler-dealer? Meeting the general partner and some of his employees can help you decide. Your questions can be formulated from the prospectus. Do not forget to discuss the structure of the investment, past performances of deals he has put together, and his financial condition. Also ask about tax, legal, and accounting aspects.

• *How does the general partner handle questions about major problems?* Does he/she show a willingness to discuss some unexpected big expense or bad times? Is he/she confident of his/her ability to overcome these problems?

**Table 10–2.** How to read a prospectus.

You will find that about 90 percent of a prospectus is written in "boilerplate" language. To get to the meat of the proposed deal, find the following topics in the table of contents, and read them in this order:

1. Summary of Offering: This is usually found at the beginning of the prospectus. The project will be outlined in the summary, which may run anywhere from 5 to 25 or more pages. This section also describes the company's business, its location, how it differs from its competitors, and what it intends to do with the money raised from the offering.

2. Tax Implications/Accounting Projections/Selected Financial Data: Read the footnotes under this section, also. What are the tax considerations? This section describes how well or how poorly the company has done recently in its earnings and growth. This tax section will tell you where the real problems lie and which public accounting firm has verified these numbers, so read it carefully no matter how long it is.

3. The Company/Use of Proceeds: This may appear either as a separate section or as part of the summary of offering. It will describe the use of the proceeds, showing how much of your money will go toward fees and how much will go into the investment.

4. Capitalization: This section will describe the company's current sources of capital—stocks, bonds, short-term notes or loans, or a combination of these.

5. Compensation Paid to General Partner: All fees should be broken down to show who is paid what.

6. Description of General Partner's Experience: Check carefully into the general partner's past record and experience as well as his/her employees and any other key people involved in the project.

One way to judge confidence is to find out whether the general partner has ever lent money to a troubled partnership or personally guaranteed loans to it rather than letting it go under. An honorable promoter should consider his reputation as a marketable product. Ask if any of the projects have gone bankrupt or were sold for less than purchased for. What were the financial effects on the investors?

• *Does the general partner belong to any trade affiliations?* If not, why not? Is he a novice at putting together such deals? If he is, he may be learning with *your* money!

• *Is the general partner honest?* Have any securities regulations been violated in a manner that was injurious to the investors? Ask if there have been any legal problems or complaints from investors. There is no simple way to verify a person's honesty. But if you ask around enough you will find someone who will tell you. Your state securities bureau may also have information about the integrity of the general partner.

• *Take a look at his net worth statement in the prospectus.* How old is the financial statement? If it is over six months old request a current one. (This will tell you whether there is some type of financial trouble, and whether the general partner may be tempted to dip into partnership assets.) Remember the general partner controls everything, including bank accounts. When looking over the financial statement, be sure to examine both income statement and balance sheet. Also look up the company's credit status in Dun and Bradstreet and perform a retail credit check on the general partner as an individual.

• *Is he incorporated?* Are there enough assets in the corporation for it to assume liability? Does the general partner meet I.R.S. specifications: If not, the I.R.S. could reclassify the limited partnership as a corporation, joint venture, or association for tax purposes. In such a case, the individual partners would *not* be a conduit for the tax write-offs. Whether the general partner is incorporated will not make much difference as long as he/she has financial strength and can assume liability. A rule of thumb used by financial experts is that the general partner should have a net worth of 15 percent of the sum being raised—at all times.

• *Ask for a list of investors the general partner has dealt with, both ongoing and completed.* After a few telephone calls, you should have a clear picture of the general partner. Consider calling doctors first. They will usually cooperate. The general partner's accountant and banker can also be valuable resource people. Be sure to look over the footnotes to the accounting projections in the prospectus. They will explain the assumptions on which the projections were based and any problem areas that are foreseen. Use these points for your questions.

Generally, bankers will not say anything against one of their customers. They will give you only a credit range—"Low five figures"—for example, but nothing specific. They may tell you whether the loans are being paid as agreed, whether the account is satisfactory with no overdrafts, and whether the general partner is a preferred customer, but they will not give you much quantitative information. However, even that small amount of information is helpful.

## Beware of the Prospectus!

The prospectus may contain misleading statements or even meaningless ones. For example: "Real estate we bought for $10 million ten years ago was sold today for $20 million." But how did the investors do considering the fact that those years were highly inflationary? Even if the investors made 100 percent return, it may not have been as good as it sounds, taking all else into consideration. And what about current tax laws? Will they benefit you?

Another example: "Every movie we made was a successful one." But again did the investors receive a good return on investment?

## What to Ask When Checking a General Partner's References

When checking a general partner's references, be sure to ask specific, purposeful questions. This enables you to get productive answers from the people with whom you speak. The following are some questions you should ask:

1. How long have you invested with the general partner?
2. Were the write-offs that were projected allowed by the I.R.S., and have you actually written off what was projected?
3. Is the cash flow that was projected when you invested being realized?
4. Has the project been under audit by the I.R.S.? If so, did it stand up?
5. If you have ever requested information was it answered promptly, accurately, and intelligibly?
6. Do you get regular reports, distribution checks, and information returns on a timely basis?
7. Were you asked to contribute more capital after the initial investment?
8. Has the investment ever gone through a difficult time requiring additional services or money from the general partner? Did he provide such?
9. Are you considering the investment I'm considering? If not, why not?
10. Would you recommend this general partner as a business associate? Do you believe that he is honest?

## TAX SHELTERS AND THE I.R.S.

The I.R.S. claims that it has spotted at least 25,000 dubious limited partnership deals being peddled to unwary investors. People often invest in these schemes because the promoters have an attorney's opinion that endorses their concept. In 1980, the Treasury Department began attacking opinion letters to try to curb phony shelters.

According to Roscoe L. Egger, Jr., Commissioner of Internal Revenue,[1] "Our concern with such schemes goes beyond the revenue lost to the government. Imagine how you would react as a middle- or low-income taxpayer when you read in your local paper that wealthy people are avoiding taxes by buying Bibles wholesale, then giving them to charity and deducting them at inflated retail value. This kind of story repeated often enough is bound to have an adverse impact on the attitude of many taxpayers who have complied with the law, paying their taxes in full."

Often attorneys were asked only to research certain aspects of the investment, not the entire deal. Opinions should not be given haphazardly. If there is not a better than 50-50 chance that the majority of the tax benefits that the shelter is promoting are allowable under the law, forget it. Attorneys can be bound by their opinion letters, so read them carefully to find the tax implications. The "Selected Financial Data" section will also tell which public accounting firm has reviewed the numbers stated. While a C.P.A. does not actually endorse the shelter, the name of a major accounting firm on the prospectus is a kind of imprimatur.

Do not always believe everything you read. Be sure to verify with second and third sources all the information you have collected. Remember that the prospectus and memos have been specially written to sell, not to insult the writers' bosses.

---

[1] Remarks by Commissioner of Internal Revenue Roscoe L. Egger, Jr. on "New Directions in Tax Shelters," presented at University of Chicago Law School Tax Conference in Chicago, October 30, 1981; see also *Taxation and Accounting*, No. 210 published by The Bureau of National Affairs, Inc., Washington, D.C. 20037, 10/81.

**Figure 10–1.** CHART 23: Your Personal Data.

Yourself:

1. Name ——————————————————————————— Telephone no. ———————

Address ———————————————————————————————————————

Date/place of birth ————————————————— Married (date/place) —————

Social Security no. ———————

2. Name of spouse/maiden name ———————————————————————————

Address ——————————————————————————— Telephone no. ———————

Date/place of birth ———————————————————————————————————

Social Security no. ————————————————— Married (date/place) —————

Children:

3. Name ——————————————————————————————————— Sex ————

Address ——————————————————————————— Telephone no. ———————

Date/place of birth ———————————————————————————————————

Marital status ———————————————————————————————————————

Social Security no. ————————————————————————————— Children ——

**Figure 10–1.** CHART 23: Your Personal Data (*continued*).

Children:

4. Name _____ Sex _____

Address _____ Telephone no. _____

Date/place of birth _____

Marital status _____

Social Security no. _____ Children _____

5. Name _____ Sex _____

Address _____ Telephone no. _____

Date/place of birth _____

Marital status _____

Social Security no. _____ Children _____

6. Name _____ Sex _____

Address _____ Telephone no. _____

Date/place of birth _____

Marital status _____

Social Security no. _____ Children _____

7. Mother's name/maiden name _____

Address _____ Telephone no. _____

Date/place of birth _____

Marriage (place/date) _____

8. Father's name _____

Address _____ Telephone no. _____

Date/place of birth _____

9. Spouse's mother (name/maiden name) _____

Address _____ Telephone no. _____

Date/place of birth _____

Marriage (place/date) _____

10. Spouse's father (name) _____

Address _____ Telephone no. _____

Date/place of birth _____

187

**Figure 10–2.** CHART 24: Important Papers.

| | Location | Effective date | Ownership |
|---|---|---|---|
| 1. Will | | | |
| 2. Codicils | | | |
| 3. Will | | | |
| 4. Codicils | | | |
| 5. Living trust | | | |
| 6. Testamentary trust | | | |
| 7. Marriage license | | | |
| 8. Divorce records | | | |
| 9. Birth certificates | | | |
| 10. Military discharge: | | | |

| Branch | Rank | Serial no. | Discharge |
|---|---|---|---|

11. Citizenship/passport _____

12. Safe deposit box _____

13. Employment contract _____

14. Partnership agreement _____

15. Buy-sell agreement _____

16. Retirement plan reports _____

17. Health insurance: _____

18. Others: _____

**Figure 10–3.** CHART 25: Consultants and Contacts.

| Consultant | Name and Address | Phone no. |
|---|---|---|
| 1. Attorney | | |
| 2. Accountant | | |
| 3. Life insurance agent | | |
| 4. Casualty insurance agent (disability) | | |
| 5. Medical insurance agent | | |
| 6. Real estate agent | | |
| 7. Stock broker | | |
| 8. Banker | | |
| 9. Financial advisor | | |
| 10. Pension/profit sharing trustee | | |
| 11. Retirement plan trustee | | |

190

12. Other advisors _____

13. Have you arranged a power of attorney authorizing someone to act for you in the event of a disability? ____

    Who has it? _____

14. Has your spouse arranged a power of attorney authorizing someone to act in the event of a disability? ____

    Who has it? _____

15. Miscellaneous _____

191

**Figure 10-4.** CHART 26: Professional Assets.

| Description | Date Created/ type | Approx. value/ date appraised | Trustee/ administrator |
|---|---|---|---|
| 1. Interest in trust (other than land) | | | |
| 2. Professional practice or business | (owner of corp., date of incorporation, shareholders, no. of shares) | | |
| 3. Equipment/supplies | | | |
| 4. Deferred compensation | | | |
| 5. Accounts receivable | | | |
| 6. Retirement plan: IRA | | | |
| 7. Keogh | | | |
| 8. Pension/profit sharing | | | |
| 9. Buy/sell agreement (how funded) | | | |
| 10. Method and duration of investment for business | | | |

11. One month's gross income (average) _____ Net (average) _____

_____

12. Income sources not listed above (and amount):

_____

_____

_____

_____

_____

_____

193

**Figure 10–5.** CHART 27: Tax-Deductible Expenses—Taxes.

| Check no. and date | To whom written | Total amount |
| --- | --- | --- |
| | | |
| | | |
| | | |
| | | |
| | | |
| | | |
| | | |
| | | |
| | | |
| | | |
| | | |
| | | |
| | | |
| | | |
| | | |
| | | |
| | | |
| | | |

**Figure 10–6.** CHART 28: Tax-Deductible Expenses—Donations.

| Check no. and date | To whom written | Total amount |
| --- | --- | --- |
| | | |
| | | |
| | | |
| | | |
| | | |
| | | |
| | | |
| | | |
| | | |
| | | |
| | | |
| | | |
| | | |
| | | |
| | | |
| | | |
| | | |
| | | |
| | | |

**Figure 10–7.** CHART 29: Tax-Deductible Expenses—Medical.

| Check no. and date | To whom written | Total amount |
|---|---|---|
| | | |
| | | |
| | | |
| | | |
| | | |
| | | |
| | | |
| | | |
| | | |
| | | |
| | | |
| | | |
| | | |
| | | |
| | | |
| | | |
| | | |
| | | |

**Figure 10–8.** CHART 30: Expenses for Home Improvements.

| Check no. and date | To whom written | Total amount |
|---|---|---|
| | | |
| | | |
| | | |
| | | |
| | | |
| | | |
| | | |
| | | |
| | | |
| | | |
| | | |
| | | |
| | | |
| | | |
| | | |
| | | |
| | | |

**Figure 10–9.** CHART 31: Utility Expenses.

**Home Address:** _____

| Year _____ | Electric Co. $ | Gas Co. $ | Water $ |
|---|---|---|---|
| January | | | |
| February | | | |
| March | | | |
| April | | | |
| May | | | |
| June | | | |
| July | | | |
| August | | | |
| September | | | |
| October | | | |
| November | | | |
| December | | | |
| Totals | | | |

Copyright © 1991 by Practice Management Information Corp.

**Figure 10–10.** CHART 32: Living Costs.

| | |
|---|---|
| Food: at home | _____ |
| away from home | _____ |
| Shelter | _____ |
| Utilities | _____ |
| Transportation | _____ |
| Clothing | _____ |
| Personal care | _____ |
| Medical care | _____ |
| Recreation/entertainment | _____ |
| Education | _____ |
| Tobacco, alcohol | _____ |
| Insurance, job expenses | _____ |
| Gifts, contributions/charities | _____ |
| Taxes: personal income taxes | _____ |
| Social Security, disability | _____ |
| Total Budget | _____ |
| Total Income | _____ |
| Net Available for Savings | ══════ |

**Figure 10–11.** CHART 33: Power of Attorney.

KNOW ALL MEN BY THESE PRESENTS, that I, MARY J. DOE, of the State of _____, make, constitute, and appoint, DAVID W. DOE, my true and lawful attorney-in-fact for me and in my name, place, and stead, giving and granting unto said attorney-in-fact the power to do generally and perform all and every act or acts whatsoever needful and necessary to be done for me:

To adjust, compromise, settle, or submit to arbitration, any claims, debts, demands, accounts or other matters, whether requiring the payment of money or the performing of acts by me or in my favor, so far as the same affects any matter now existing or which may arise between me and any other person or persons; conferring upon my said attorney full powers and authority to do any act that may be required for the full and complete settlement of any such claim or other matter herein specified, whether in my favor or against me.

IN WITNESS WHEREOF I have signed this instrument this _____ day of _____, 19__.

_____

MARY J. DOE
Signed, sealed, and delivered in the presence of:

_____ (Witness) and _____ (Witness).

_____ (Notary Public)

---

**Figure 10–12.** CHART 34: Cancellation of Power of Attorney.

I, MARY J. DOE, revoke any other Power of Attorneys that I have made appointing my son, DAVID W. DOE, my true and lawful attorney-in-fact, for me and in my name and on my behalf.

IN WITNESS WHEREOF I have set my hand this _____ day of _____, 19__.

_____

MARY J. DOE
Signed, sealed, and delivered in the presence of:

_____ (Witness) and _____ (Witness).

_____ (Notary Public)

# 11

# RETIREMENT: ESTATE PLANNING FOR YOUR FUTURE

Are your retirement dreams becoming a financial nightmare? If so, inflation is the major reason and it does not look as if it will cease any time soon. Your problem, then, is to design a retirement plan that takes inflation, and other factors, into consideration to ensure that you and your family will be financially secure.

The basic principle of retirement is simple: put your money away while you are working for use later in your life. You are told that you do not need as much money when you retire—that you can live comfortably on reduced budgets and reduced spending. This may be true for the first year of your retirement, but when your retirement income does not rise with the rate of inflation, how can you maintain the same standard of living?

Inflation makes retirement planning more difficult and complex. In fact, with today's rapidly climbing prices and unsettled economic conditions, it is almost impossible to determine what your retirement income needs will be. A rule of thumb widely used is that you will need about 60 to 80 percent of your pre-retirement income in order to maintain your current standard of living.

Do not count heavily on Social Security benefits to augment your retirement income. You cannot live on it, and your wife will be more vulnerable to financial disaster if left alone with only Social Security payments, which will be greatly reduced upon your death. Even if your wife is entitled to her own Social Security benefits, she will most likely receive minimum payment levels because of low earnings. The Department of Labor has studies that indicate that one-half of the women who are 65 or older live alone and receive only $3,000 annually. If you are entitled to Social Security benefits, let them be the icing on your cake!

How does your retirement nest egg shape up now? Too big? Too small? Or too lopsided?

If it is too big, you could be denying yourself and your family some pleasures that you should be enjoying right now. Too small a nest egg is far more serious and perhaps you should make some serious changes in your earning/spending pattern. A lopsided nest egg means having too many of your assets tied up in one type of investment. Your investments are not diversified.

Actually, you might say, your retirement is a trade-off. You trade off something now in order to prepare for the future. You may have to draw from your income now in order to put away enough for the future—your retirement. The fund might consist of savings, stocks, bonds, or other assets that are income-producing. You may have a retirement fund such as an I.R.A., Keogh, pension or profit-sharing plan.

Your choice of savings should be based on the amount of time in which you expect to save the money plus the value you place on such factors as safety of principal, level of interest rate, need for tax shelter, liquidity, and flexibility.

Too many planners do not remember that, unless the income with which you retire far exceeds your living costs, you will have to draw on the principal of the fund in order to meet daily living expenses. Do not forget, those withdrawals have to last for the rest of your life.

## STEPS TO A SUCCESSFUL RETIREMENT

What does retirement mean to you? Even if your retirement is many years in the future, why not think about it now? Retirement means a lot of things to people, but most of all retirement means doing what you want to do.

Cutting back in your practice is a little like retiring—whether it is working only six months a year or only one or two days or mornings a week. For whatever the reason, you too may retire one day—and you may wish that you had planned well ahead.

Retirement, like your practice, is an individual matter. Some retire *from* their specialized field; others, retire *to* a brand new career. It can be a time for change of direction, a time to do things and a time to think thoughts that are often pushed to one side during the dash and whirl of your working years.

Retirement is a milestone in your life . . . the crowning achievement of a lifetime of work. But at such a time, is your retirement plan going to represent a comfortable income for you? Millions have seen their retirement savings eroded by changing conditions. As long as inflation continues as an eroding factor, individuals retiring are simply not going to have the purchasing power that they anticipated.

Retirement experts try to claim that your expenses will be fewer: your children are usually grown and no longer a financial burden, and mortgages are finally paid off. But critics contend that even 65 to 70 percent of a lower-paid workers' salary is not enough to live on. Inflation ravages many kinds of assets, but it can be extremely destructive of savings or investment plans that allow very little flexibility. And with the pressures facing Social Security, you may have to take a more active role to ensure a comfortable retirement income for you and your spouse.

What can you do to protect yourself against rising inflation? Two things:

*First,* structure your retirement plan to allow flexibility. That is, allow yourself the freedom to be able to choose among a variety of investments and to make changes when necessary without going to great expense.

*Second,* do not wait until you are 40 or 50 years old to begin thinking about retirement because retirement planning should begin as soon as an individual begins his or her working life. You can begin by keeping an eye on the conditions that affect your plan, such as inflation.

It is crucial to have maneuverability when interest rates and prices of securities, commodities, and other assets are fluctuating greatly. Without careful planning your retirement years may be a financial disaster! Is there a way to avoid this disaster? Let's look briefly at some of the options—the so-called tax shelters or tax deferrals.

## RETIREMENT PLANS

Tax-favored retirement plans fall into several basic categories: (1) corporation plans, 401(k), annuity, or profit-sharing plans; (2) Keogh (HR-10) plans; and (3) individual retirement accounts (IRAs).

In addition to an immediate income tax deduction, all of these plans provide a current shelter for the income earned on your retirement funds.

IRAs allow employed or self-employed persons to deposit, in a separate account, funds that are deductible from current income. The taxes on the amount in your IRA are deferred until money is withdrawn. There are no withdrawals until age 59½ and there is a penalty for early withdrawals unless there is a death or disability. Not all of your contribution funds need to be put in the same investment plan, nor are you required to make contributions each and every year.

Perhaps one type of investment you might consider for your IRA, Keogh, or other type of tax-deferred pension plan is a Zero Coupon Bond (the tax-free ones, as they do come in both forms). What are Zero Coupons? They are the coupons stripped from U.S. Treasury bonds and sold separately. Each coupon is the government's promise to pay you the face value of the coupon on a specific maturity date in the future. "Zeros" are available from brokerage firms. Zeros pay no periodic interest income; they have a firm face value with a selected maturity date. They are also an ideal way to save for your child's college education. For example, 20-year zeros recently yielding 9.1% would turn $5,000 invested today into $30,000 at maturity in ten years.

*Keogh* (or HR 10) plans generally permit self-employed doctors and their employees to make tax-deductible contributions to such plans. Contributions made for your employees' benefits are deductible expenses for income tax purposes. Taxes are not due until the money is withdrawn at age 59½ years and penalties do apply for early withdrawals unless there is a death or disability.

*Pension plans* are commonly used by professional corporations. The establishment of a pension plan and its termination due to death, disability, or retirement must be approved by the I.R.S. Contributions to a pension plan as in the others, are not taxed currently. They are made with "before tax" dollars, and the tax on the interest is deferred. Contributions to this plan can be much higher than to the others, and this makes it advantageous to individuals with substantial income.

On the average, incorporated doctors tax-shelter five times as much as their unincorporated brethren. They do it by using a qualified plan.

The *profit-sharing plan* is another tax-deferred retirement plan. Investments are made by voluntary contributions to your practice's plan by the employer.

The use of *Section 401(k)* (defined contribution pension) plans have been limited in the amount you can defer and this limit is offset by contributions to IRAs. The taxes on 401(k) contributions or earnings are not paid until they are withdrawn. Employers favor this type of plan over the conventional pension plan because it reduces their corporation's pension costs by encouraging employees to save more themselves. Who is qualified to establish this type of plan? This list ranges from self-employed individuals to professional practices to the nation's largest corporations.

The SEP (Simplified Employee Pension) plan is like a qualified plan, only contributions made by the employer are made to each employee's individual retirement account, or IRA. With a traditional qualified plan, contributions are made to a trust. The employer remains responsible for investing and distributing these assets. All of these are eliminated with a SEP. Each employee sets up an IRA and the employer makes the contribution.

Qualified plans are a valuable retirement planning technique and a source of deductions that doctors and professional practices take advantage of. The disadvantages to them are that nondiscrimination rules have tightened, there are constant revisions (almost annually), interest rates vary, there are expense charges, penalties for withdrawal, and administrative fees.

## Interest Rate of Return

What kind of interest rate is the management or investment company using to handle your retirement fund? "Current" or "guaranteed" interest rate?

"Current" interest rate is the rate the company is using *now* to project effective annual yields on your accumulations. The rate varies with economic conditions and the investment experience of the company.

"Guaranteed" interest rate is the lowest rate the company will pay no matter what happens with the economy. It is not uncommon for a company to use a guaranteed rate of perhaps $6\frac{1}{2}$ percent for the first four years and then use only $3\frac{1}{2}$ percent or so thereafter.

## Expense Charges

Do you know what expenses you are charged with when someone else handles your retirement plan? There are basically three different charges as follows:

1. Front-end load expenses, which include sales commissions or other expenses applied to money paid into your plan,
2. Annual or monthly management fees and other expenses,
3. Surrender charges and transaction or service charges.

## Penalties for Early Withdrawal

The penalty for early withdrawal may be a substantial one. It may be as high as 10 percent or more, plus the income taxes that are due.

While service charges may sound modest, when you apply them to larger values after long accumulation periods, you will see that they do mount up! What happens in the case of early withdrawal because of death or disability?

## Administrative Fees

When funds are disbursed to you, what type of administrative fees will be charged? Will these fees and other expenses apply for closing out your plan if and when the time arises?

### And "Me"

When my husband Murray died (at 34), I was aware that I had been named beneficiary of his pension plan. Before the plan could be closed out, however, the closing out had to have approval from the I.R.S. The local bank that handled the qualified plan agreed to handle this tedious task shortly after I notified them. It took almost a year before we received I.R.S. approval to close out the plan—and numerous piles of paperwork. I was aware of the substantial fees that I was to be charged for all the closing paperwork. During the year of waiting there were no transactions whatsoever on the account except for the monthly balance (and accumulated interest) to be carried forward. After the I.R.S. approved closing out the plan, the funds were disbursed to me, less a rather large amount for the administrative fees. When I questioned this administrative fee (only for carrying forward a monthly balance), I was told that, as trustee, they were entitled to such a fee according to their agreement.

While service charges and administrative fees may sound modest, they do add up—substantially. Read your agreement carefully. Your understanding will help simplify any problems that may arise at a time when you least expect it. Because of the paper work and the constant changes in the laws, a good many doctors are now investing in tax-free municipal bonds as a means for retirement rather than bothering with other types of retirement plans.

Bonds issued by states, cities, or local government agencies—collectively known as *municipal bonds*—avoid federal income tax altogether. In return for the tax exemption, you will have to accept a yield that is below what you may be able to get from other investments. You can improve matters by choosing municipals issued in your state, since they are normally exempt from state and local as well as federal income taxes. Therefore, Doctor, before you invest in something with a higher rate of return, on which you will pay taxes, consider the fact that a municipal bond yield will net you the same interest as the higher percent pre-tax return on a non-sheltered investment. Municipal bonds are a great way to put away money for retirement—and you do not have to worry about all those rules and regulations in qualified plans. You can put away as much as you want each year, cash in the dividends twice annually, and eliminate all the paperwork and administrative fees. When the bonds mature, you still do not have to pay federal income taxes as you would with other plans.

## PLAN FOR YOUR RETIREMENT

The reasonably prudent person should plan well enough so as not to have to lay awake nights wondering what would happen to you if you should suddenly die, or what you will live on when you retire. At the same time you should not worry so much about your financial future that you do not take the time to wine and dine your family, and enjoy the pleasures of everyday life.

In thinking about your retirement, do not forget your patients. If you do not have an associate, you should notify them of your plans so that they will have enough time to find someone else. The letter in Chart 35 (Figure 11–1) may give you an idea of what to say to them.

### Income Analysis

Do not be surprised to find out that your retirement needs are not too much different than they are now. Take a look at the Income Analysis Work Sheet Chart 36 (Figure 11–2) and enter your figures to determine if you have an income deficit or surplus.

The only way to be certain of knowing how much you will need is to sit down with a pen and paper and Chart 37 (Figure 11–3), and look at your fixed expenses before retirement and after retirement to determine whether they will remain the same.

Let us determine whether your income will match your living expenses at retirement. First, tabulate the income you expect from your assets. Your local Social Security office will be able to provide you with the information you need regarding benefits. It is difficult to estimate your investment income, but you might consider that anywhere from 5 percent to 12 percent is a reasonable expectation. Keeping in mind our present economy, these rates of return may vary substantially. You may have to convert your present assets to income-producing ones.

After computing your monthly retirement income using Chart 38 (Figure 11–4), you may find you need to set aside additional funds to assure a financially secure retirement, or you may find your monthly income sufficient. Present monthly retirement income, less estimated monthly retirement expenses, equals your retirement needs.

Any long-range financial planning must take inflation into account or fall disastrously short of its goals. Suppose, at age 30, you set aside $1,000 each year in a tax-sheltered or tax deferral investment at 8¼ percent annual return. Use the following table to see how you would end up at age 65.

| Beginning at age | At age 65 you would have |
|---|---|
| 30 | $190,000 |
| 40 | 80,000 |
| 50 | 28,000 |
| 65 | 6,000 |

## GOLD—AN ATTRACTIVE INVESTMENT FOR THE RETIREE[1]

One way you might keep your retirement dreams from becoming a financial nightmare may be to invest in gold.

"Good as gold!" Nobody knows for sure when this phrase was first uttered in humankind's 6,000-year-old love affair with the yellow metal. Gold has been valued by man since the beginnings of civilization and dates back as far as 4000 B.C. to the ancient Egyptians. And, now as then, gold is an admired and sought-after possession. It is beautiful. Unquestionably valuable. Tantalizingly rare. Throughout history, gold has been a stalwart defense against the ravages of inflation and other financial uncertainties.

Indeed, gold fever is an incurable malady.

Only about 89,000 metric tons of gold have been mined since the beginning of history. If you were to bring all of it together in one place, there would be only enough gold to make a cube, 18 yards on a side. And there just is not much gold left in the ground. According to recent estimates, another 40,000 metric tons probably could be mined.

Gold appears to be virtually indestructible. It is immune to the effects of weather, oxygen, and water; it will not tarnish, rust, or corrode, and it withstands most acids and alkalis. Ancient civilizations have long been associated with this ageless metal with traditional beliefs that it is a symbol of immortality.

Gold is money because governments and people decide it is money. It was gold-backed currency that give rise to the banking system in the west. England, in 1923, was the first country to change to a gold-based currency that was to dominate international monetary systems. Each country's basic monetary unit was defined in terms of a fixed quantity of gold, and the amount of gold held by each government guaranteed the value of

---

[1] The Tax Reform Act of 1986 provided that certain gold and silver coins issued by the United States are not treated as collectibles. Under the Technical and Miscellaneous Revenue Act of 1988 (TAMRA), state-issued coins also are not treated as collectibles, provided that someone independent of the IRA owner holds the coins.

paper money. All paper money could be redeemed in gold from the treasury of the country in which it was issued.

In 1931, after its economic crisis, Britain abandoned the gold standard and devalued the pound. In 1933, the United States ceased the issue of gold coins during the Great Depression and Americans were forbidden to own, import, or export gold except for specified industrial uses. France followed in 1936.

The dollar was allowed to float and, in 1971, there were simply too many dollars overseas for the United States to continue its practice of redeeming dollars for gold abroad at the then official rate of $35 an ounce. It was not until December 31, 1974, after a 42-year ban, that U.S. citizens were again allowed to purchase, hold, and sell gold.

Gold purity is measured in karats. *Karat* refers to the gold content. Pure gold is 24 karats. *Fine* is a metallurgical term indicating the purity of the metal. Thus, 24 karats is 1.000 fine, 18 karats is .750 fine, etc. Gold bullion is gold refined to a purity of .9995 or higher and is usually the medium employed by investors. Bullion comes in various sizes, measured by the troy ounce. The troy system is the worldwide system used to measure the weight of precious metals and is based on a 12-ounce pound. A troy ounce is 31.1 grams and is a little heavier than a regular, or avoirdupois, ounce. For investment purposes, only the following weights are relevant: 400-ounce "delivery bars," used in domestic transactions, smaller bars of 50 ounces, one kilo (32.15 ounces), 25 ounces, one-half kilo (16.075 ounces), 10 ounces, and wafers of five ounces, one ounce, and one-half ounce. All gold bullion is marked with a registered number and the degree of purity, including the name of the prescribed refinery or assay office responsible for certifying its purity.

## The London Fix

For five days a week, twice a day, in London, the representatives of five venerable precious metal dealers gather to "fix" the gold price, which has the effect of establishing an equilibrium price that balances supply and demand. The London "fix" is a benchmark for most commercial and investment transactions in the industrial world, but it may vary because of commissions, delivery, assay, and storage and insurance fees. Members of the London Gold Market are: Mocatta and Goldsmid Limited; Sharps, Pixley Limited; N.M. Rothschild and Sons Limited; Johnson Matthey Bankers, and Samuel Montagu and Company Limited.

As it is commonly said, as the earth turns, the gold price follows the sun. As the London market closes, the New York market opens, followed again by the Hong Kong market.

It has been brought out by *Business Week*,[2] in its supplement, "Investing

---

[2] February 5, 1979.

in Gold," that ". . . always less discussed are the tax advantages to owning gold. Simply put, it is easy to cheat the government out of its tax bite by paying cash for gold and storing it privately." The supplement further stated that "No one wants to be quoted on this factor, but it is a crucial one for many purchasers of the metal."

## Types of Coins

Newly minted coins, valued primarily for their gold content, are called "bullion coins," even though some are worn as jewelry. These coins are readily recognized, convenient, portable, and easily traded. The weight and purity of bullion coins are widely accepted; unlike gold bars and wafers, there is no need to have them assayed upon purchase or resale. Their value can be determined daily according to the price offered for an ounce of gold. Dealers in bullion coins demand a modest premium over a particular coin's bullion value, usually 5 to 10 percent, to cover minting and distribution.

Numismatic coins are priced higher than their intrinsic value (the actual current value of gold content) because of their rarity. These are not readily marketable at a particular time and place and, the higher the premium over bullion content, the greater the risk as an investment. The U.S. $20 St. Gauden's coin is considered to have numismatic value, owing in large part, to its beauty and design.

Because pure gold is too soft to resist the wear and tear of circulation, most gold coins are alloys—gold and copper—producing strong, durable coins that resist marring. An exception is the Canadian Maple Leaf, which contains exactly one troy ounce of pure unalloyed gold.

One of the least expensive ways of getting gold is by buying stock of gold mining companies. American Depository Receipts (ADRs) are traded over the counter much like any other security. Here there is a possibility of regular dividends paid from a large portion of the mines' annual after-tax earnings.

The riskiest gold investment is gold futures. Gold futures contracts represent commitments to buy or sell a specified amount of gold at a specified time period in the future at a previously agreed-upon price. Open bidding determines the price of such contracts, which may be purchased on margin. Trading gold futures is similar to trading most other commodities. And, just as with most commodities trading, more people are going to lose money than make it.

If you are interested in becoming a participant in the gold futures market, you can open an account with any brokerage firm that is, or deals with, a member of a commodity exchange that provides the services suitable to your needs. There are five exchanges in the United States where gold futures are traded. They are the Chicago Board of Trade, the Commodity Exchange of New York, the International Monetary Market of Chicago

Mercantile Exchange, the New York Mercantile Exchange, and the Mid-American Commodity Exchange.

Doctor, if you are buying gold as an investment, it is important to deal only with known and reputable brokers, banks, and dealers. Be sure that the party effecting the sale will guarantee what is sold and will be ready to repurchase if you so desire. The trading of gold is widespread, and, as a trading object, provides for a liquid market. As an investor, you should remember that there is always the possibility that the U.S. Treasury Department or the International Monetary fund might unload more of their hoards of gold at any time, and this action could depress prices. Both have done so in the past.

As with any security investment, you must weigh the risk/reward ratio carefully. The past is no guarantee of the future, but be aware of all aspects before investing in gold, since gold does not provide a current income.

## Gold Used in Dental Offices

In addition to investments and jewelry, gold is used in electronics and dentistry. Many companies offer dental programs through which dentists can purchase their casting gold alloy. For example, one firm offers dental casting units through a Wats line quote system, and each unit includes one troy ounce of pure gold (such as a Canadian Maple Leaf coin), along with two .900 fine silver dimes. Their metallic constituents meet American Dental Association composition requirements for Type III alloys and casting may be hardened at 400 degrees Fahrenheit for 10 minutes. However, a word of caution is needed for the dental practitioner who would purchase gold and silver coins on the pretense of using them in the dental office, when, in fact, the coins were going into a safe deposit box. The I.R.S. is very much aware that dentists use gold and silver alloys, and they are being quite thorough in their audit investigations.

## HI, HO SILVER! ANOTHER INVESTMENT ON THE GALLOP!

Do you remember when a dime bought you a cup of coffee? It still might, providing your dime was minted prior to 1965. Pre-1965 dimes contain 90 percent silver. Today, the dime contains none! In fact, prior to 1965 all U.S. dimes, quarters, half-dollars, and dollars contained 90 percent silver. Now they are all devoid of silver.

Rare coins are considered hard asset commodities. They are tangibles. Generally, the existence of rare coins is a matter of worldwide record. A coin becomes rare when the supply is limited and that same coin cannot be minted again. Unlike the instability of the values of most other commodities, the rare coin supply cannot change and does not fluctuate much to any appreciable degree. Nevertheless, the demand for rare coins has been and still is increasing throughout the world.

The rising trend of prices of collectors' items in the coin world far outpaces those usually obtainable in the more traditional investment areas. This gives us the classic examples of the effect inevitably produced in any market by a growing demand upon a finite and even dwindling supply.

## Evaluating Silver

Grading a coin is of the utmost importance if you are considering such a purchase. The grade of a coin is determined by the condition of that coin. Two coins of identical mintage may be thousands of dollars apart in price just because one is a perfect uncirculated coin while the other is slightly worn or scratched.

Since before 700 B.C. rare coins have been collected by the wealthy and the professional investor/collector. They have made it their business to know all the intricate ways to profit from their investments.

## King of Coins

The silver dollar has been called the "King of Coins" because it represents strength and is a symbol of days gone by when U.S. coins were still made of 90 percent silver and were "real" money. Silver dollars have often been used for gifts to friends and relatives. In addition, not many other coins claim to graphically reflect our American history as does the silver dollar. From its inception with the Morgan design in 1878 (the result of strong mining interests) to the conclusion of the Peace series in 1935, design changes, die varieties, high, low, or nonexistent mintage—all reflect the economic and social history of our country.

## Modern Silver Rush

The death knell for the traditional silver coin was sounded in 1965, and a modern-day silver rush began. People began pulling from circulation every pre-1965 coin they could lay their hands on. Silver dollars were not readily available in circulation, and, therefore, were more difficult to obtain since nearly half of the total silver dollar mintage had been previously melted for its silver content.

In 1971, the Eisenhower dollar series was instituted partially because of the needs of the Nevada gaming industry and for the future vending industry needs. These coins were intended for general circulation, and contained *no* silver.

# SILVER INVESTING

Traditional investments (real estate, stocks, commodities, and the like) just have not performed well with double-digit inflation. Silver, however, has an unbelievable track record. For example, an uncirculated silver dollar dated 1892S was valued in 1960 at $75 and in the 1980s at $27,500; and a 1928S silver dollar was valued in 1960 at $5 and in the 1980s at $2,200.

## Silver Investments As Compared to Gold

In the minds of many people, silver is still very inexpensive for a precious metal. People do not want to wait to see what develops with silver the way prospective buyers do with gold. Silver remains affordable for many people, however, they are beginning to realize that choice coins disappear from the marketplace almost as quickly as they are offered, and frequently these coins do not reappear until their values have increased significantly.

Rare coins are considered by many to be less of a speculation than the gold bullion that fluctuates almost daily. Rare silver coins hold their value not only because they are silver, but also because they are scarce or rare items for collectors and investors. There is no such thing as a certainty. Everything involves some degree of risk. But rare coins have always given people a feeling of a secure investment.

When people purchase a coin for the first time, they often do not consider having a proper outlet for selling that coin at a fair-market price. This also should be considered. There are national teletype networks that will offer your coins an exposure to hundreds of dealers across the country. Generally a small commission is charged. You might also find buyers with reputable rare coin dealers in your home town. You will find that knowing who to contact when a death occurs is a comfort since coin collections are included in the estate tax if they are valued (either as a whole or individually) at over $3,000.

## Silver Content

Silver is harder than gold, but softer than copper. Since pure silver is too soft to stand up under constant wear, it is alloyed with copper before it is made into commercial articles. Silver coins in the United States were made of 900 parts silver and 100 parts copper. In Great Britain, coins contained 925 parts silver and only 75 parts copper.

## Silver Semantics

The word *sterling* has been used to mean high quality silver since the fourteenth century. At that time, the coins of England had decreased in value and the only coins that contained large proportions of silver were those coined by the merchants of the Hanseatic League in northern Germany. These coins were called Easterlings to distinguish them from the low-silver alloy coins of England. English speech quickly turned *Easterling* to *sterling*.

## Silver and Film

Many methods are employed for the extraction of silver or silver and gold ores, scrap, alloys, and the recovery of used photographic materials. Silver is recovered from photographic processing solutions by replacing the silver with another metal, such as zinc, by electrolysis or by precipitation with chemicals such as sodium hydroxide or sodium sulfide.

Silver is also recovered from used photographic film by burning it and dissolving the silver in the ashes with nitric acid. (If you sweep the residue for its silver content after the ashes burn down, you may be paid $10 or more for each pound of x-ray film.) The emulsion on unexposed film contains silver salts from which metallic silver may be recovered. New x-ray film contains about three times as much silver as processed film. The silver contained in each box of 100 x-ray film 14″ × 17″ could be valued as high as $175. Doctors who use x-rays should consider keeping unused x-ray film in a locked storeroom or closet rather than on open supply shelves.

Today silver is an industrial commodity. It is also considered to be a precious-metal because of its scarcity and price. And to the coin collector-investor, silver coins can be a profitable nest egg.

## TRADING DIFFERENCES BETWEEN SILVER AND GOLD

The main difference between trading silver and gold is the difference in the bulk of the two metals. For instance, silver coins are sold in 50-pound sacks, and, since silver costs much less than gold, you can speculate and lose as much and possibly more in the silver market.

When you buy silver or gold there are the wholesale and retail markups and commissions. The number of publicly traded silver companies is much fewer than the number of gold mining stocks. But there are a few, two of which are the Sunshine Mining Company and the Hecla Mining Company.

**Figure 11–1.** Chart 35: Sample Retirement Letter to Patients.

Dear (patient):

It's been a pleasure for me to have been of service to you. Now, with mixed emotions, I announce my impending retirement from practice on (date).

I will miss all of you, but I am looking forward to living a more relaxed life doing things I will now have time to do.

I would suggest that you select a new doctor. Please advise my office of your selection (in writing), not later than by the end of the month, so we can transfer your records.

However, I feel certain that you will be in good hands with Doctor _____ with whom I have worked closely for the past several months. If our office does not hear otherwise, we will turn over your records to him. Dr. _____ will be taking over my office and equipment when I depart. I know he has excellent training and skills, and would be pleased if you confirmed my judgment of him by selecting him as your doctor. He will give you excellent care.

I will continue seeing patients at regular office hours until the end of the month. If you do not have an appointment between now and then and want to stop by, I would be pleased to see you between 1:00 and 4:00 Thursday afternoons (when I am not seeing regularly scheduled patients).

Sincerely,

_____

(YOUR NAME)

Copyright © 1991 by Practice Management Information Corp.

**Figure 11–2** CHART 36: Income Analysis.

| | |
|---|---|
| Husband's annual net income | $_____ |
| Wife's annual salary | _____ |
| Retirement plan fund | _____ |
| Savings | _____ |
| Other income-producing assets | _____ |
| TOTAL | $_____ |

**If the husband died today**

| | |
|---|---|
| Wife's salary | $_____ |
| 9% interest from assets | _____ |
| 5% interest from life insurance | _____ |
| TOTAL | $_____ |

**Capital analysis**

$_____ Two-thirds of husband's and wife's combined earnings is what the surviving spouse needs.

– _____ Subtract total from "Income Analysis" (above) if husband died today

$_____ Income deficit or surplus

Copyright © 1991 by Practice Management Information Corp.

**Figure 11–3.** CHART 37: Fixed Expenses Before Retirement/After Retirement.

| Description | Present cost | After-retirement cost |
|---|---|---|
| Insurance Premiums: | | |
| Homeowners | | |
| Auto #1 | | |
| Auto #2 | | |
| Boat | | |
| Jewelry | | |
| Life _____ | | |
| _____ | | |
| Major Medical | | |
| Disability | | |
| Hospitalization | | |
| Taxes: | | |
| Property Taxes (city) | | |
| Property Taxes (county) | | |
| License for car(s) | | |
| Misc. | | |
| State Income Tax | | |
| Federal Income Tax | | |
| Religious dues, etc. | | |
| Mortgages or Loans due | | |
| TOTAL EXPENSES | $_____ | $_____ |

**Figure 11–4.** CHART 38: Your Monthly Retirement Income.

| Description | Present $ | After-retirement $ |
|---|---|---|
| Salary | | |
| Investment income | | |
| Income producing property (rental) | | |
| Dividends from stocks and bonds | | |
| Other | | |
| Social Security benefits | | |
| Retirement plan: IRA | | |
| Keogh | | |
| Pension | | |
| Profit sharing | | |
| Annuities | | |
| Total monthly income | $_____ | $_____ |

Copyright © 1991 by Practice Management Information Corp.

# 12

---

# WHAT TO DO WHEN YOUR SPOUSE OR LOVED ONE DIES

A major part of a family's finances concerns their needs after the death of one of the spouses as well as while both spouses are alive. The best and usually the only way to insure that desired plans are carried out is through a will. However, I'd like to share a letter with you, one that might also suggest other actions a caring partner can take. Then the rest of this chapter is addressed to the surviving spouse and his or her immediate concerns after the death of the loved one.

THE LAST LOVE LETTER

November 17, 1976

Dear Linda:

It's a beautiful spring day as I write this, and I'm feeling more at peace with myself than I have in a long time. Most of the early struggles are behind us now; the practice is thriving; our children show every sign of fulfilling the bright hopes we have for them. And this afternoon I took that long-delayed step. I wrote my Will.

It tells everything there is to say about disposing of my

"worldly assets"—just the way we discussed it. But after I put my signature to the Will, our attorney, said to me: "Isn't there anything else you want to put down on paper, to be read after you die?"

He explained that a Will is a formal, legal document. It has to be signed in a certain way and witnessed in a certain way. After a man dies, this legal document must be presented before a court and probated. All the directions in it, unless they violate some law or are against public policy, must be carried out.

"I'm sure," our attorney said, "that there are other things you'd like to tell your family—information, advice, suggestions— which are completely private and which they can either accept or reject."

Indeed there are, which is why I'm sitting in the bright sunlight right now, passing up an afternoon of boating, and writing this letter to you.

Let's begin with our attorney, himself, since this letter is his idea. He is bright, and I trust him implicitly. He knows all my plans for the family, and you'll get sympathetic and expert advice from him. I've listed you as executrix of my estate, but you'll surely need legal advice in carrying out the terms. Unless you have a special reason for choosing someone else, our current attorney is my recommended choice. He can also pick any appraiser who might be needed in settling the estate.

You'll need help from other people as well. Steve Karlin is the man to contact about my life insurance. If you phone him, he could get you the face value of my life insurance in a week. But don't rush to do that; sit down and talk with him first. It may be that one of the other options, such as installment payments, would serve you better. I deliberately left you the option to pick any one of several settlement methods. Steve can explain them all to you and, in light of the financial picture at the time, recommend which one you should pick.

Of course, you'll need some ready cash to meet immediate expenses. Our joint savings and checking accounts and the safe deposit box will be frozen until the contents are inventoried after a court order. That's why I set up that savings account in your name alone. That should tide you over until the other accounts are released, or until Steve can get you some life insurance money.

There's no way I can predict what other money problems we may have when you finally read this letter. None, I hope. Still, you should remember the name of Donald Lynch over at the Security National Bank. He handled the loan for my equipment, and I've always financed our cars through him. He'll help you with financing problems in any way possible. If you need other banking services, Donald can refer you to the proper people in his place.

Our broker, Joe Van Dyke, at Dean Witter Reynold, has been our principal investment adviser. He can give you an up-to-date accounting of our investment holdings: what we paid for them, and what they're worth now.

Investing in the stock market was one thing when I was alive and well, earning a good living and could afford to take a few risks. It's quite another thing now when you must conserve what you have. You'll want to make some drastic changes in how our money is invested.

I recommend you switch out of any speculative issues, and into solid, income-earning securities and tax-free municipal bonds. Make sure if you reinvest any assets that you reinvest in things with a good, long-term record. Joe can make specific recommendations.

You'll have some other new problems, too. There's a little matter of estate taxes. The Will I've drawn does leave everything to you and there will be no taxes due when I die as there is an unlimited marital deduction. However, everything I have left to you will be included in your estate when you die since the marital deduction isn't a true deduction, but a tax deferral. All expenses you incur in settling the estate are legitimate estate tax deductions, so keep careful record of them by opening up a separate estate checking account. Our accountant, Herb O'Keefe, can supply the answers to any tax questions you have.

The most difficult problem, by far, will be disposing of the practice. First thing, have an appraisal done by those reputable and known professional practices, like American Practice Appraisers, Inc. It may be a really tough job disposing of the practice itself. Have the appraisal company value the equipment at its liquidation or scrap value. That's the bottom line if the practice cannot be sold.

Send a letter of announcement to everyone, asking those with unpaid accounts to settle up. Miss Smith in my office can handle that. She should follow up the unpaid bills with two more letters at monthly intervals. After that, turn them over for collection. Don't be surprised or dismayed if a quarter or a half of my accounts never are collected; it happens often.

Check the office and see if there are any unopened cartons. They can usually be returned to the supply house for a credit. Used equipment and supplies, of course, you'll offer for sale with the practice. If you cannot sell the equipment or supplies consider donating them to an underdeveloped country through a qualified charity so you can get a charitable deduction for the contribution.

As for the office records, you should hold on to them for the present. You'll turn them over to someone buying the practice, or to any other doctor the patient requests. If the practice never is bought, you can store the records. And, you might consider donating the equipment and supplies to an underdeveloped country (through a charitable organization) where it will be needed and appreciated.

The study club (you know who to contact) can help you

locate a buyer. We do have an "Emergency Care Office Agreement" in effect and there is a committee who'll know where and how to advertise the practice for sale. The study group should pitch in and help you, just as I would help Jill, Eileen, or Rachelle, if the situation were reversed.

That's enough advice and advisers for now. Here are a few vital statistics which you'll need to know and might not have at your fingertips.

I was born in Chatham County on January 1, 1942. Father, Jacob; Mother, Florence. I graduated from Emory University in 1965. From there I attended New York University's postgraduate school and graduated in 1967. I served in the Navy from August, 1967, through May, 1969, entered lieutenant, discharged as a captain. My honorable discharge papers are located in the safe at the office.

I don't belong to any lodge or fraternal order which offers burial benefits. I do have a cemetery plot deeded to me by my father. The deed is located in the attic; you'll need it for the funeral.

One of the first stops afterward should be the local Social Security office. You're entitled to a cash benefit of $255 toward funeral expenses, and you may also be entitled to a widow's allowance, depending on the ages of the children. I'm sure the people at Social Security can tell you exactly what it amounts to. You're also entitled to a cash benefit of $250 toward funeral expenses from V.A. since I was in the military. But those benefits are not automatic, you must file a claim.

On a separate sheet I'm attaching a complete inventory of our assets. It lists every item of real estate, bank account, every security, and every life insurance policy I own—and where they're located. I've listed our debts: the mortgage on the house, the car loan, and the mortgage on the office building. There's also an inventory of everything in my safe at the office (you have the combination). You'll also find the Will in the safe, so it will be immediately available when needed.

I have to rush off now; there's just time to go sailing before it gets too late. I've said everything there is to say except thank you . . . for the gift of "you," all these happy days.

Love,
Murray

## WHEN SOMEONE CLOSE DIES

How well you plan for the uncertainty of the future determines how well you will be able to handle the numerous problems that can arise.

There is an enormous sense of grief and loss when someone close to us dies. In the midst of all these feelings, you are thrown into complex business arrangements often involving large sums of money. If you are too emotionally upset to exercise good judgment, you might find that you make costly mistakes that cannot be corrected.

Death is a crisis-precipitating event that can be even more difficult when you try to find important documents and records and cannot; or when you find that you have to sell some of your assets, maybe even your home, to pay taxes; or when you find that your spouse died without a will. A good many people, otherwise knowledgeable and competent, have not taken the time to make these arrangements, or maybe they believe that they will be here forever.

It is essential that you have complete information about all your family facts. Organizing these facts now will help you later. Charts 39 and 40 (Figures 12–1 and 12–2) at the end of the chapter will help you. See also Table 12–1.

## FUNERAL ARRANGEMENTS

It seems that when people are particularly vulnerable, because of emotional trauma, the lack of information, and pressures around them, they are easily exploited and sometimes deceived by some undertakers. Undertakers some-times refuse to quote prices of their services and products over the tele-

---

**Table 12–1.** Checklist of things to do when your spouse or loved one dies.

1. Call your rabbi, minister, or priest to make arrangements for the funeral.
2. Check the location of the burial plot.
3. Inform friends and relatives of the time, date, and place of the funeral.
4. Notify your attorney and the executor to begin probate proceedings as soon as possible.
5. Collect the necessary papers so that you can file for Social Security and VA benefits.
6. Notify your insurance agents to obtain the necessary forms to begin the paper work.
7. Notify your CPA to begin compiling a list of your assets. Federal Estate Taxes are due nine months from date of death.
8. Notify the funeral director as to the number of Certified Death Certificates you will need.
9. No longer needed medical/dental books could be donated to such places as: American Service Archives, 1847 Texas Ave., Shreveport, La. 71103, giving you a tax deduction. On receipt, the organization will forward an appraisal for you to use as a charitable income tax deduction. Donations of medical and dental equipment: Dental Health International, Athens, Georgia (a nonprofit organization that sets up medical and dental clinics in less-developed countries.)

---

phone, and a good many will give you only a lump-sum figure, not itemized prices for such things as caskets, vaults, grave liners, and their other services. There will also be the cost of transporting the body, the interment receptacle used for each burial, clothing, newspaper notices, and honoraria for the clergy or rabbi who performs the ceremony. You might even find that your city has a tax for entrance into the burial grounds.

Both Social Security and the Veterans Administration (V.A.) do have burial benefits for those who qualify. Obtain the necessary forms and fill them out if you hope to claim these benefits.

Shortly after Murray died I submitted the necessary forms to the funeral home. I received a phone call from the funeral director telling me that I had not filled out the V.A. form properly and they would retype it for me so that I might sign the corrected form. I asked them to please mail the form to me. Since we had rented chairs from them to put in our home to accommodate people, they explained that it was no trouble to bring this form with them when they came to pick up the chairs. This sounded logical to me. Although I didn't think I had made a mistake, I knew that, being under emotional trauma and pressures, I might have filled the V.A. form out incorrectly.

When the funeral director arrived at my house to pick up the chairs, he carried a clipboard with him. He asked me to please sign the corrected V.A. form which I did after I quickly looked it over. Then, very casually he flipped the page on his clipboard and said to me, "If you will just sign this form, we will have a headstone prepared according to your religion and set on the grave. . . ." The price at the bottom of the form was quite a large amount.

As difficult as it was, Murray did discuss with me certain aspects of his funeral before he died. I tried to remain calm as he discussed whom he wanted for pallbearers, that he felt that life was for the living, that I should not spend a lot on unnecessary frills, and that I should be more concerned about living and our three children.

If it had not been for that conversation, I probably would not have had enough nerve to say what came out next. I asked the funeral director, "Is this the cheapest headstone that you have?" He must have been quite shocked at that remark because all he could do was stumble over a few words and say, "No, it isn't. I didn't bring the other prices with me. I'll have to let you know."

I never heard from him! It was several months before I got up enough nerve to call several other marble companies to get prices on headstones. For less than half that quoted price I found one that was not only reasonable, but said exactly what I wanted. It was not elaborate, but I felt it was very dignified and in good taste.

## Do Not Leave Your Home Unattended

One more thing worth mentioning: Do not leave your home unattended when you attend a funeral. There are those who read obituaries just for the purpose of robbing a home when no one is there. You might ask your rabbi, minister, or priest for advice about finding someone to stay at your home. You might also keep in mind that funeral expenses must be paid by the estate—before taxes—and generally take priority over most other debts.

## YOUR CASH NEEDS

It may take as many as nine months (and sometimes more) to settle the estate. During that time, the family will still have rent or a mortgage payments, and all the other usual living costs. There will be the expenses of administering and settling the estate, legal and accounting fees, as well as federal estate taxes to pay.

Will your estate have the ready cash to meet these demands? What if your liquid assets are not nearly large enough to meet the cash needs of your estate for at least the first year? Perhaps you should consider purchasing more life insurance or putting some of your assets in more liquid form. For example, you might consider selling off some real estate and putting the cash into treasury bills or tax-free municipal bonds. Without enough ready cash, your family could be forced to sell some property at distress prices to meet the taxes, bills, and other costs of estate administration. Chart 41 (Figure 12–3) will help you determine your cash needs and identify your liquid assets.

You should set up an estate checking account. Your bank will provide you with the necessary estate checks, maybe even as a courtesy (if you ask) but without your name printed on them (which really is not necessary). Funeral, medical expenses incurred during the final illness, and administrative costs should be paid from this account as well as state and federal estate taxes. As soon as you have settled the estate, this account may be closed.

## LEGAL MATTERS

You may find that there are complications involved when you are required to accumulate the assets of the estate and distribute them, especially if you are acting as executor (or executrix) of your spouse's estate. You may find it advisable to consult an attorney, especially if there are such matters as the recording of deeds to real property, the disposition of stocks, bonds, or savings accounts, the disposition of business or practice assets, or the dispersal of any estate asset.

A will is merely a piece of paper telling what you want done with whatever property you possess at the time of your death. Whether you die with a will or without one, the fact of your death must be established with the appropriate court in your state before your property and belongings can be distributed. This legal procedure is known as *probate*. Under this arrangement, many courts supervise the collection and protection of the property, payment of the decedent's debts and taxes, and the transfer of the title of property to the appropriate heir.

The executor (or personal representative) ordinarily has the power to select an attorney who will file a petition for probate. The clerk of the probate court fixes a time for a hearing of the petition and the executor is required to notify all those who are named in the will as beneficiaries or all those persons who would have inherited if there had been no will, to appear at the hearing. Your attorney usually helps out in this matter by giving such notice by registered mail or by personally delivering a copy of the citation regarding the hearing to the interested parties. In addition, most states require newspaper publication of the proposed hearing.

Normally, the executor, your attorney, and the witnesses to the will appear before the probate court and affirm that this is the testator's signature, that they recognize the document as the testator's will, that the testator had told them it was his/her will, that the testator had signed the will in their presence and in the presence of the other witnesses. Some states have omitted having witnesses appear at the hearing when there is a Self-Proving Declaration (usually the very last page after the will is signed) in which the witnesses, the testator, and a Notary Public have signed in the presence of each other.

On the day of the hearing, if no one objects to the validity of the will, the court issues an order admitting the will to probate and authorizes Letters Testamentary to be issued to the legal representative (executor). If there is no will and no one objects, the court authorizes Letters of Administration to be issued to the legal representative (administrator). The court then fixes the amount of the legal representative's bond, if one is required, and administers the oath of office to him or her.

Before any bank, savings and loan institution, or brokerage firm will allow withdrawal or transfer of assets, proof must be shown that the person has authority to do so. This is done by showing the Letters Testamentary or Letters of Administration that the court had issued.

If you own real estate in states other than the one in which you reside, you need to make sure that your will complies with the laws of the state where the real estate is located, because it also needs to be probated in each of those states in order to transfer title. Once your will is probated in the state where you are domiciled, your attorney will then have a certified copy of it sent to the other states.

## APPLYING FOR SOCIAL SECURITY
## AND VETERAN'S BENEFITS

The Social Security Administration keeps an individual account of your earnings. This account determines what amount you are entitled to receive if you are retired and/or disabled and to what benefits your survivors are entitled. You must apply for these benefits if you are to obtain them.

If you do not have the necessary papers listed in Table 12–2 you may find out, as I did, the inconvenience of poor recordkeeping. When I walked into the Social Security office, I was first told to take a number and fill out preliminary forms. No questions can be answered until your number is called.

After waiting an hour, I found that I had to come back because I did not have all the needed information. This meant I would have to take another number and wait again to be called. Save yourself this annoyance. Put the important papers where you can find them. If you do not have such things as your marriage license or birth certificates, write and get them. Some benefits may be lost if you have to delay your application.

Everything takes time! It usually takes from two to three months, and sometimes longer, before you will begin receiving benefits. There is paperwork involved when you file for either Social Security or V.A. benefits. Do not put it off!

If your spouse was a member of the armed forces at any time during a war, even if not directly involved in it, you might find you are eligible to receive burial benefits from the V.A. of up to $250. This plus the $255 burial benefits from Social Security will help. If you have minor children, you might even find that V.A. and Social Security will give you a monthly allowance. Notify your local V.A. office, and they will send you the necessary forms to fill out. Figure 12–4 (Chart 42) is a sample letter that will help you with this task.

Remember, benefits do not just come to you, you must apply for them

---

**Table 12–2.** Necessary papers.

---

Papers needed when you file for Social Security and/or V.A. benefits:

1. Your marriage license

2. Birth certificates for you, your spouse, your minor children

3. Social Security number for each person in item 2

4. U.S. Military Release Forms with dates of release

5. Certified copy of death certificates

6. W-2 Withholding Tax Form for previous year

---

**Table 12–3.** Death certificates needed.

You will need a *certified* copy of the death certificate for the following agencies and purposes.

1. Social Security
2. Veterans Administration
3. Probate of will
4. Federal Estate Taxes
5. State Inheritance Taxes
6. For each bank or savings institutions in which the decedent had accounts: checking, savings, C.D., etc.
7. One for *each* stock or bond to be transferred
8. One for each insurance policy claim
9. Retirement plan benefits

at your local Social Security office, your local V.A. office, and those insurance companies that insured the deceased. Sample letters are provided in Figures 12–5 and 12–6, Charts 43 and 44.

In order to obtain benefits, you must have proof of your eligibility. This is done by way of a certified copy of the death certificate. Certified copies of the death certificate (*not* photocopies) may usually be obtained for a nominal fee from either the funeral home, from the health department, or from the Office of Vital Statistics in your city. See Table 12–3, "Death Certificates Needed," for those agencies that will need a copy of the death certificate.

## CLOSING A PROFESSIONAL PRACTICE OR OFFICE

Naturally, the best solution to the problem of closing a professional practice or office is to arrange for the sale of the practice beforehand. If that is not possible, your executor will have to do it. The local Study Club or state association may be able to help in locating a buyer.

You might suggest appropriate severance-pay arrangements for your office staff, and advise your executor whether any personnel should be kept on to help close the office affairs.

If the practice cannot be sold you may consider making a donation of the equipment and instruments to a nonprofit organization. When I could not sell Murray's practice, I donated the equipment and instruments to Dental Health International who in turn made arrangements for them to be sent to an underdeveloped country. The following excerpt from a letter written to me by the director of the hospital that received the equipment made me feel I had made the right decision.

> When I arrived in Cameroon last August I was pleased to find the dental equipment had changed drastically since I was here four years ago. At that time the Banso dental clinic consisted of an antiquated, malfunctioning belt driven unit and a set of forceps. The modern equipment you donated has made a tremendous difference in the quality of dentistry here. The electric reclining chairs, Pelton Crane light and x-ray unit arrived in excellent condition and are working beautifully. The x-ray machine has made root canal therapy possible and we are able to restore many teeth that would otherwise have been extracted.
>
> Modern, dependable equipment is a rarity in this part of Africa. I believe we have the only dental clinic with air driven handpieces in the northwest province. Patients are coming to us even from the larger cities because they have heard about our clinic.

If you have medical textbooks and the hospital library does not need them, you might consider donating them to the following nonprofit organization: American Service Archives, 1847 Texas Avenue, Shreveport, LA 71103.

A letter should be sent to patients to properly notify them. Should you mention collections in this letter? Yes, but simply suggest that accounts be settled as soon as possible. As a last resort, turn outstanding accounts over to a collection agency that will bill the patients.

When a doctor dies, there are certain agencies that must be notified as soon as possible. Some notifications are required by law, some are good public relations, and others just make good sense.

State boards of dental and medical examiners want to know where their licensed dentists and physicians are living or if they have died. The Drug Enforcement Agency (DEA), an agency of the U.S. Department of Justice, needs to be notified when a doctor dies, retires, or moves to a different city. The Certificate of Registration must be sent to your local DEA field office, where it will be kept on file.

Records containing an inventory of all controlled substances on hand when the practice terminates should be kept for at least two years. Copies of official order forms used and any unused order forms should be returned to the local DEA field office.

Controlled substances on hand should be returned to the supplier or to the DEA field officer. Prescription blank forms should be destroyed.

Specialty societies, county medical and dental societies, state medical and dental associations, and either the American Medical Association or the American Dental Association should be notified as soon as possible if a doctor dies, retires, or moves. Both the A.M.A. and the A.D.A. maintain a national registry of all doctors. Addresses for most medical and dental specialty organizations are available through the national associations.

## HOW LONG SHOULD PATIENT RECORDS BE KEPT?

Whenever it becomes necessary to close a doctor's office, one of the most perplexing problems is, "What should be done with the patient records?" The doctor's estate (or the doctor to whom the practice is sold) should preserve patient records. Your state statute of limitations on malpractice claims or torts should provide you with some guidance as to how long you should keep your patient records. Consult your attorney to be sure, because there are often exceptions to the rule. Most statutes no longer expire within two to six years from the last date of treatment, unless the patient is a minor, in which case the statute of limitations does not begin to run until majority has been reached. Many statutes on malpractice or torts do not begin to run until the date the patient *discovers* the injury and its negligent origin. This could be many years after the last date of treatment. Where abandonment is concerned, some states apply the statute of limitations relative to contracts, which is often as much as six years or longer.

A doctor's current patients should be notified when an office closes and should be provided an opportunity to have their records forwarded.

What do you do in case of severe space limitations? You should microfilm records and store them in an office basement, residence attic, or anywhere that security can be assured and moisture controlled. In any case, the state association and county society should be advised of the location of remaining records.

## INFORMATION THAT SHOULD BE SAVED

Knowing what information should be saved and for how long has often been a concern for doctors. Those items that should be retained permanently are:

- Articles of incorporation (and by-laws)
- Corporate minutes
- Deeds and titles
- Patent, copyright, and trademark records
- Income, gift, and estate tax returns
- General ledger and journal reports
- Annual financial statements and audit reports

You should keep supporting documents for information on a tax return for the statute of limitations period (or seven years). These would include such things as bank statements, canceled checks, employee earnings and service records.

## NOTIFYING AN EMPLOYER AND ASSOCIATES

While most employers and associates are willing to assist, it is reasonable for you to contact them regarding matters that might be overlooked or delayed. Such matters might be group life insurance coverage, pension fund contributions, profit sharing plans, Keogh, IRA, accrued vacation and sick pay, terminal pay allowances, unpaid commissions, death benefits from the corporation, disability income, and the like. Are you as widow or widower eligible for dependency benefits from medical or disability insurance and for how long? Figure 12–7 (Chart 45) is a sample letter to an employer.

## THE FINAL STEP IN ESTATE SETTLEMENT

Determining and handling the estate and personal tax liabilities of the decedent is the final step in estate settlement. You may find that an accountant can best handle this with the information that you provide. It is the duty of the executor (or executrix) to see that the proper tax returns are filed within nine months from the date of death. The return must be received by the I.R.S. for them to consider it filed (not simply postmarked and mailed as required for your 1040 income tax return).

You have a choice of establishing the value of the property of the decedent at the date of death or using the value six months after death. If you decide to use the value of property six months after death, you cannot later change even if inflation has caused that property's value to increase.

A joint income tax return may also be filed by the surviving spouse for two years after the date of death, provided that the spouse does not remarry before the close of the year in which the return was filed.

Payment of the taxes is due at the time the return is filed. The I.R.S. may give you an extension but they may take a lien on the property and will charge interest on any unpaid balance.

State inheritance taxes and federal estate taxes, as well as other costs necessary to settle an estate, must be considered. There must be cash available to pay these costs, otherwise, the money will have to be raised by selling part of the valuable property that you want the heirs to receive. Table 12–4 outlines the procedure for settling estate taxes.

**Table 12–4.** Checklist for estate taxes.

(Partial list of things to do)

1. Obtain a certified copy of the will.

2. Obtain a certified copy of Letters Testamentary.

3. Assist with inventory of safe deposit box, safe, or other place for keeping valuables. If inventory has already been made, obtain a copy.

4. Obtain insurance policy numbers and other information for any life insurance on life of decedent. Write to insurance company for Form 712. (This form lists beneficiaries and owner of policy.)

5. Apply for a tax identification number for the estate, or determine if application has already been filed.

6. Determine that real estate appraisal or other means of valuing real estate has been arranged.

7. Determine that practice appraisal for valuing practice has been arranged.

8. See that a separate bank account is set up for the estate. All receipts and disbursements pertaining to the estate *must* go through this account. Talk with your accountant for more details.

9. Make a record of all checking accounts of decedent.

10. Compile a record of any other assets and liabilities of the estate not covered previously.

**Figure 12–1.** CHART 39: The Facts You Need for Burial Decisions.

Cemetery plot location _____

Deed to plot location _____

Church/synagogue to notify _____

Who will officiate? _____ Phone no. _____

Funeral director_____ Phone no. _____

Casket:         Yes _____ No _____ Purchase at _____ Cost _____

Vault:          Yes _____ No _____ Purchase at _____ Cost _____

Stone marker:  Yes _____ No _____ Purchase at _____ Cost _____

Other _____

I have donated my _____ to _____
                    (eyes, etc.)

_____

Location of agreement for donation _____

**Figure 12–2.** CHART 40: Obituary.

_____ died at the age of _____

due to _____ at _____ on

_____, 19_____.

Services will be held at _____ on _____ at _____ o'clock.

Burial will be at _____ on _____, 19_____.

The deceased will be best remembered for the following

activities and contributions: _____

_____

_____

_____ is survived by _____

_____

_____

Remembrances may be sent to _____

_____

**Figure 12–3.** CHART 41: Your Cash Needs and Liquid Assets.

## Cash Needs

1. Final estate settlement costs         $ _____

2. Federal estate taxes         _____

3. State inheritance taxes         _____

4. Cash bequests         _____

5. One-year living costs         _____

6. Total one-year cash needs         _____
   (add lines 1–5)

## Liquid Assets

7. Bank accounts and other ready cash         _____

8. Life insurance proceeds         _____

9. Lump sums from retirement programs         _____

10. Stocks and bonds         _____

11. Other readily marketable assets         _____

12. Total ready cash         _____
    (add lines 7–11)

13. Additional cash needs         _____
    (line 6 minus line 12)

**Figure 12–4.** CHART 42: Sample Letter to the Veterans Administration.

For Eastern U.S.:
V.A. Center
500 Wissahickon Avenue
Philadelphia, PA 19010


For Western U.S.:
V.A. Center
Ft. Snelling
St. Paul, MN 55111

Dear Sir:

Re: _____full name_____, government life insurance policy number _____, V.A. "c" (claim) number _____; deceased's serial number _____, who served in the U.S. (branch) _____from _____to _____19___. Date of honorable discharge was _____.

Please send me the necessary information and forms for funeral benefits, educational assistance, and medical assistance.

I have (number) _____minor children who are _____years, _____ years, and _____years old.

If you have any additional information I may need, please let me know.

Thank you,

Sincerely,


_____ (your name)
_____ (your address)
_____

**Figure 12–5.** CHART 43: Sample Letter Requesting Life Insurance Policy Proceeds.

Name of Insurance Company
Address
City, State, Zip Code

Dear Sir:

Re: Policy no. _____ in the name of _____ ,
now deceased as of _____ (date).

Please send me whatever information or forms you will require to make claim to proceeds of the above policy.

The last premium paid was on _____ , 19___ , in the amount of
$_____. Please send me any accrued interest from date of death until such time as proceeds are sent.

Please search your file for any other coverages that (name of deceased) may have had.

Please also send me Form 712 for filing with the Estate Tax forms as soon as possible.

Thank you.

Sincerely,

_____ (your name)
_____ (your address)
_____

**Figure 12–6.** CHART 44: Sample Letter Regarding Insurance Settlement Options.

Name of Insurance Company
Address
City, State, Zip Code

Gentlemen:

Re: Policy no. _____ in the name of _____
(full name), now deceased as of _____ date.

I wish to exercise my right as beneficiary to elect settlement options. Please send me any information or forms necessary advising me of the types of settlement options you offer.

Please search your files for any other coverage that the deceased may have had.

Sincerely

_____ (your name)
_____ (your address)
_____

**Figure 12–7.** CHART 45: Sample Letter to an Employer.

Dear _____ :

This is to advise you officially that my <u>(husband's/wife's full name)</u> died on _____ (date). I would appreciate your sending me any information on fringe benefits, such as group life insurance coverage, pension or profit funds, accrued vacation or sick pay, terminal pay allowances, unpaid commissions, or disability benefits.

Please send me a list of whatever documents you will require and the necessary forms to be completed by me as beneficiary.

Thank you,

Sincerely,

_____ (your name)

_____ (your address)

_____

Copyright © 1991 by Practice Management Information Corp.

# EPILOGUE

## A FINAL WORD OF ADVICE: FINANCIAL SURVIVAL IS UP TO YOU

There is no magic formula to suit all situations. Yet there is information about your family's affairs that you must be familiar with in order to handle any situation that may arise. How well you handle the uncertainty of life is determined to some extent by how knowledgeable you are in your own financial affairs.

Your top priority should be an appraisal of how well you and your family are meeting needs now and in the future—while you are living, when you retire, if you become disabled and after you are dead. Consider everyone close to you: your spouse, your children, your parents, and maybe even your grandchildren. Now is the time to end the prudish silence about death and begin planning for your family's financial survival. After all, the basic work is yours! The idea is to leave most of what you have worked so hard for to your loved ones. If you die, you cannot explain and counsel what you think is best.

I have known joy as well as sadness about things in life that really count, and, from the tragic experience of the death of my husband—someone who was extremely close to me (my best friend)—I have grown, and have not been destroyed. This is why I hope to have a role in helping you prepare for the future and avoid the negative and defeatist approach that is so often common in a situation such as this. The impact of cancer on our family life was devastating; however, we both felt that we had the kind of happiness that life gives to just a few. I am grateful to have shared a small portion of my life with someone like Murray.

A wise man once said: "If you give a man a fish, he'll have a meal. If you teach him how to fish, he'll have food for the rest of his life." I hope that what I have taught you here is food for the rest of your life.

## LIFE'S WINDING PATH

*Linda Gartner Ginsberg*

The man sat on his deck looking up at the moon,
And knew the sun would come up, much too soon;

As he sat and pondered of days gone by,
Of family, friends, . . . he gave a sigh;

The summer of his life had disappeared,
With spring almost over, winter neared;

The accomplishments of his life showed in his tired face,
Lines drawn and wrinkled that had kept tune to life's pace;

The night was still as the moon's shadow was seen through the trees,
The old man wanted to pray as he bent down on his knees;

He was thankful for a taste of life's fruitful drink,
Life had been good to him but at times it did seem dark and bleak;

As the moon began to fade, the sun crept up from the East,
Where did the winter go, would the old man's world now cease?

# GLOSSARY

**Administration**   The management of a decedent's estate, including the marshaling of assets, the payment of expenses and debts, the payment or the delivery of bequests, and the rendition of an account.

**Administrative expenses**   Fiduciary commissions, attorney's and accountant's fees, appraisal fees, probate costs, and other expenses of administering an estate or trust.

**Administrator**   A fiduciary, appointed by the probate court to administer the estate of a decedent, generally in accordance with the intestate laws of the state.

**Agent**   One empowered by another to act for him or her; *see* **power of attorney.**

**Annuity**   A contract that will provide one with periodic income payments for a specified length of time.

**Attestation**   Act of authenticating by signing as a witness.

**Attorney-in-fact**   One qualified to act as a legal agent.

**Basis**   In simplified terms, the tax recognition of the original purchase price of a piece of property. *See also* **Stepped-up basis.**

**Bearer bond**   A bond that provides for interest and principal to be paid to the holder (bearer); an unregistered bond.

**Beneficiary**   One who inherits a share or part of a decedent's estate, or one who takes the beneficial interest under a trust.

**Bequest**   A gift by will; (often synonymous with legacy).

**Bond**   A binding agreement, or writing by which a person binds himself or herself, usually to pay a certain sum on or before a future date.

**Clifford trust**   A reversionary or short-term trust that lasts ten years and a day named after George B. Clifford who pioneered this legal device for shifting income in a landmark U.S. Supreme Court case in 1940.

**Codicil** An instrument made subsequent to a will and modifying it in some respect. It may explain, modify, add to, subtract from, qualify, alter, restrain, or revoke provisions in the original will.

**Commission** Compensation.

**Common law** That body of law and juristic theory that originated, developed, and formulated, and is administered in England and obtains among most of the states here.

**Community property** Property owned equally by a husband and wife in those eight states recognized as community property states.

**Competent** Legally qualified or capable.

**Consideration** For legal purposes, an exchange; quid pro quo (this for that).

**Consideration** For tax purposes, money or money's worth.

**Convey** To transfer or deliver to another, as the title to property.

**Corpus** Principal assets of a trust.

**Crown loans** No-interest loans named after the Lester Crown case, 67 T.C.1066, 585 F.2d 234 (1978).

**Custodial account** An account through which assets are held by a custodian for the benefit of the owner.

**Decedent** A deceased person.

**Deed** An instrument in writing conveying some asset(s) that has been duly executed and delivered.

**Devise** A gift under a will.

**Disclaimer** A repudiation or renunciation. A *qualified* disclaimer with respect to any interest in property is a statement that a person rejects or does not accept any interest in the property and that property is then treated as if it had never been transferred to that person.

**Domicile** That place that is a person's permanent home and to which, whenever he or she is absent, that person has the intention of returning.

**Donee** The recipient of a gift.

**Donor** The person who makes a gift.

**Escheat** Reversion of property to the state because there are no persons legally entitled to hold it.

**Estate tax** An excise tax on the privilege of transferring property at death.

**Excise tax** A tax on the privilege of transferring property without consideration (money).

**Executor, executrix** The person named in a will to carry out the provisions of the will and to administer the estate; the person responsible for filing estate taxes.

**Fee simple**   Absolute ownership.

**Fiduciary**   One occupying a position of trust and confidence such as an executor, administrator, or trustee.

**Financial survival**   Deliberate planning.

**General power of appointment**   A power to determine who will own or enjoy the property that is subject to the power of appointment in the trust instrument. (A special power of appointment is a limited power.)

**Gift**   Something given from affection, admiration, or like qualities, expecting nothing in return.

**Gift splitting**   A gift made by a husband and wife to someone else to which both spouses indicate their consent on the gift tax return of the other. To split the gift the spouses must be legally married to each other at the time of the gift. Generally, in community property states the election is not available to spouses who make gifts of community property, because both spouses are already considered to own the gift property equally.

**Gift tax**   An excise tax payable on the privilege of transferring property with no consideration (for no money).

**Grantor**   A person who establishes a trust.

**Heir**   One who inherits or is entitled to inherit.

**Incidents of ownership**   Any of the following: Any rights to economic benefit; the power to change a beneficiary; the power to surrender or cancel; the power to assign or revoke; the power to pledge the asset for a loan; the power to obtain the surrender value; any reversionary rights or interest of more than 5% of the value of the asset.

**Inherit**   To take by descent.

**Inter vivos**   While living. An inter vivos trust is a trust established during the lifetime of the person creating the trust, rather than under his or her will. Also, a *living trust.*

**Intestate**   Without a will.

**Issue**   Child or children.

**Lapsed**   To go without a taker.

**Legacy**   A gift by will.

**Legatee**   One to whom a gift is given by will.

**Letters testamentary**   A written document granted by the probate judge to an executor named in a will, authorizing him to act as such.

**Marital deduction**   A deduction from the gross estate of the value of property that is included in the gross estate but that passes, or has passed, to the surviving spouse; a tax deferral of this property being taxed to the surviving spouse's estate.

**Net worth**   Assets minus liabilities.

**Palimony**   An award or settlement given to an unmarried person if that person can show that there was an agreement to share property and earnings while that person and another lived together.

**Par value** The monetary value assigned to each share of stock at time of issue.

**Per capital** As an individual; equally.

**Per stirpes** By the right to represent a deceased ancestor.

**Probate** To offer official proof; transferring assets from their current, indefinite state of ownership, to a secure status of ownership by whomever the law regards as the rightful (new) owner.

**Probate estate** Property left to beneficiaries under a will.

**Qualified Terminable Interest Property (QTIP)** Property that passes from the decedent in which the surviving spouse has a qualifying income interest for life. Generally, a marital deduction is not allowed for property passing from a decedent to a surviving spouse that is *terminable,* because such interests terminate or fail after the passage of time, or upon the occurrence or nonoccurrence of some contingency. However, one may elect the marital deduction for all or part of this interest if it meets the requirements of qualified terminable interest property as defined by the Internal Revenue Code.

**Registered bond** A bond that provides for the owner's name to be recorded on the books of the issuer.

**Remainder** An estate in expectancy, which becomes an estate in possession on the determination of a prior estate created at the same time and by the same instrument.

**Remainderman** The person who is entitled to receive the principal of an estate upon the termination of the intervening life estate or estates.

**Residual estate (residue)** The remaining estate of a decedent after the payment of all expenses, charges, and bequests.

**Reversion** Rights of future possession or enjoyment.

**Revocable trust** A living (or inter vivos) trust that may be amended or revoked by the creator of the trust.

**Settlor** One who creates a trust (makes the gift).

**Situs** The location (where real estate is located).

**Stepped-up basis** The re-evaluation of the basis (the original purchase price) giving effect to the tax law's recognition of the fair market value of a piece of property on the date of death. *See also* **Basis.**

**Taxable estate** Property that comes back into an estate for tax purposes because of some type of incidence of ownership.

**Tenant** One who holds or possesses property.

**Testament** An act by which a person determines the disposition of property after death, usually in a will.

**Testate**   Having made a valid will.

**Testator, testatrix**   The person who makes a will.

**Trust**   A legal arrangement under which one party (the grantor or settlor) transfers assets to a second party (the trustee) to be held and invested for the benefit of one or more beneficiaries.

**Trustee**   An individual or institution that is named to hold, manage, and distribute the assets of a trust.

**Unified credit**   A deduction from the gross estate; an exemption equivalent.

**Vest**   To fix the right of present or future enjoyment.

**Will**   The legal declaration of a person's mind as to the disposition of property after death.

# APPENDICES

(*Author's Note:* Neither the author nor the publisher is responsible for the applicability, accuracy, validity, or the tax consequences of any of the forms contained in the appendices. These are provided for informational purposes only.)

247

# APPENDIX A

## I.R.S. FORM 706
## UNITED STATES ESTATE
## (AND GENERATION-SKIPPING
## TRANSFER) TAX RETURN

The first three pages of Form 706, along with the general instructions for its preparation, are presented in this Appendix as a sample of the estate tax form that must be prepared and submitted. Be aware, however, that the complete form is 35 pages long and consists additionally of Schedules A through R. Each schedule includes its own specific instructions for completion. Those who live in community property states have a slightly different form as property is owned jointly between spouses.

General instructions for preparing the form, and a sample of the form, follow.

### PURPOSE OF FORM

The executor of a decedent's estate uses Form 706 to figure the estate tax imposed by Chapter 11 of the Internal Revenue Code. This tax is levied on the entire taxable estate, not just on the share received by a particular beneficiary. Form 706 is also used to compute the Generation-Skipping Transfer (GST) tax imposed by Chapter 13 on direct skips (transfers to skip persons of interests in property included in the decedent's gross estate).

### WHICH ESTATES MUST FILE

Form 706 must be filed by the executor for the estate of every U.S. citizen or resident whose gross estate, plus adjusted taxable gifts and specific exemption, is more than certain limitations.

To determine whether you must file a return for the estate add:

(1) The adjusted taxable gifts (under section 2001(b)) made by the decedent after December 31, 1976; and

(2) The total specific exemption allowed under section 2521 (as in effect before its repeal by the Tax Reform Act of 1976) with respect to gifts made by the decedent after September 8, 1976; and

(3) The decedent's gross estate valued at the date of death.

You must file a return for the estate if the total of (1), (2) and (3) above is more than $500,000 for decedents dying in 1986, or $600,000 for decedents dying after 1986. For filing requirements for decedents dying after 1981 and before 1986, see the November 1987 Revision of Form 706.

**Gross estate.**—The gross estate includes all property in which the decedent had an interest (including real property outside the United States). It also includes:

- Certain transfers made during the decedent's life without an adequate and full consideration in money or money's worth;

- Annuities;

- Joint estates with right of survivorship;

- Tenancies by the entirety;

- Life insurance proceeds (even though payable to beneficiaries other than the estate);

- Property over which the decedent possessed a general power of appointment;

- Dower or curtesy (or statutory estate) of the surviving spouse;

- Community property to the extent of the decedent's interest as defined by applicable law.

For more specific information, see the instructions to Schedules A through I.

## U.S. CITIZENS OR RESIDENTS; NONRESIDENT NONCITIZENS

File Form 706 for the estates of decedents who were either U.S. citizens or U.S. residents at the time of death. File **Form 706NA,** United States Estate (and Generation-Skipping Transfer) Tax Return, Estate of nonresident not a citizen of the United States, for the estates of nonresident alien decedents (decedents who were neither U.S. citizens nor residents at the time of death).

**Residents of U.S. possessions.**—All references to citizens of the United States are subject to the provisions of sections 2208 and 2209, relating to decedents who were U.S. citizens and residents of a U.S. possession on the date of death. If such a decedent became a U.S. citizen only because of his or her connection with a possession, then the decedent is considered a nonresident alien decedent for estate tax purposes, and you should file Form 706NA. If such a decedent became a U.S. citizen wholly independently of his or her connection with a possession, then the decedent is considered a U.S. citizen for estate tax purposes, and you should file Form 706.

**Executor.**—"Executor" means the executor, personal representative, or administrator of the decedent's estate. If none of these is appointed, qualified, and acting in the United States, every person in actual or constructive possession of any property of the decedent is considered an executor and must file a return.

## WHEN TO FILE

You must file Form 706 to report estate and or Generation-Skipping Transfer tax within 9 months after the date of the decedent's death unless you receive an extension of time for filing. Use **Form 4768,** Application for Extension of Time to File, to apply for an extension of time. If you received an extension, attach a copy of it to Form 706.

Form **706**
(Rev. October 1988)
Department of the Treasury
Internal Revenue Service

# United States Estate (and Generation-Skipping Transfer) Tax Return

Estate of a citizen or resident of the United States (see separate instructions). To be filed for decedents dying after October 22, 1986, and before January 1, 1990.
For Paperwork Reduction Act Notice, see page 1 of the instructions.

OMB No. 1545-0015
Expires  8-30-91

**Part 1.—Decedent and Executor**

| 1a Decedent's first name and middle initial (and maiden name, if any) | 1b Decedent's last name | 2 Decedent's social security no. |
|---|---|---|

| 3a Domicile at time of death | 3b Year domicile established | 4 Date of birth | 5 Date of death |
|---|---|---|---|

| 6a Name of executor (see instructions) | 6b Executor's address (number and street including apartment number or rural route; city, town, or post office; state; and ZIP code) |
|---|---|

| 6c Executor's social security number (see instructions) | |
|---|---|

| 7a Name and location of court where will was probated or estate administered | 7b Case number |
|---|---|

8  If decedent died testate, check here ▶ ☐  and attach a certified copy of the will.    9  If Form 4768 is attached, check here ▶ ☐

10  If Schedule R-1 is attached, check here ▶ ☐    See page 2 for representative's authorization.

| | | |
|---|---|---|
| 1 Total gross estate (from Part 5, Recapitulation, page 3, item 10). . . . . . . . . . | **1** | |
| 2 Total allowable deductions (from Part 5, Recapitulation, page 3, item 25) . . . . | **2** | |
| 3 Taxable estate (subtract line 2 from line 1) . . . . . . . . . . . . . . . . | **3** | |
| 4 Adjusted taxable gifts (total taxable gifts (within the meaning of section 2503) made by the decedent after December 31, 1976, other than gifts that are includible in decedent's gross estate (section 2001(b))). . | **4** | |
| 5 Add lines 3 and 4 . . . . . . . . . . . . . . . . . . . . . . . . | **5** | |
| 6 Tentative tax on the amount on line 5 from Table A in the instructions . . . . . . | **6** | |
| **Note:** If decedent died before January 1, 1988, skip lines 7a-c and enter the amount from line 6 on line 8. | | |
| 7a If line 5 exceeds $10,000,000, enter the lesser of line 5 or $21,040,000. If line 5 is $10,000,000 or less, skip lines 7a and 7b and enter zero on line 7c | **7a** | |
| b Subtract $10,000,000 from line 7a . . . . . . . . . . . . . . | **7b** | |
| c Enter 5% (.05) of line 7b . . . . . . . . . . . . . . . . . . . . | **7c** | |
| 8 Total tentative tax (add lines 6 and 7c) . . . . . . . . . . . . . . . . | **8** | |

**Part 2.—Tax Computation**

| | | | |
|---|---|---|---|
| 9 | Total gift tax payable with respect to gifts made by the decedent after December 31, 1976. Include gift taxes paid by the decedent's spouse for split gifts (section 2513) only if the decedent was the donor of these gifts and they are includible in the decedent's gross estate (see instructions) | | 9 |
| 10 | Gross estate tax (subtract line 9 from line 8) | | 10 |
| 11 | Unified credit against estate tax from Table B in the instructions | 11 | |
| 12 | Adjustment to unified credit. (This adjustment may not exceed $6,000. See instructions.) | 12 | |
| 13 | Allowable unified credit (subtract line 12 from line 11) | | 13 |
| 14 | Subtract line 13 from line 10 (but do not enter less than zero) | | 14 |
| 15 | Credit for state death taxes. Do not enter more than line 14. Compute credit by using amount on line 3 less $60,000. See Table C in the instructions and **attach credit evidence** (see instructions) | | 15 |
| 16 | Subtract line 15 from line 14 | | 16 |
| 17 | Credit for Federal gift taxes on pre-1977 gifts (section 2012)(attach computation) | 17 | |
| 18 | Credit for foreign death taxes (from Schedule(s) P). (Attach Form(s) 706CE) | 18 | |
| 19 | Credit for tax on prior transfers (from Schedule Q) | 19 | |
| 20 | Total (add lines 17, 18, and 19) | | 20 |
| 21 | Net estate tax (subtract line 20 from line 16) | | 21 |
| 22 | Generation-skipping transfer taxes (from Schedule R, Part 2, line 12) | | 22 |
| 23 | Section 4980A increased estate tax (attach Schedule S (Form 706)) (see instructions) | | 23 |
| 24 | Total transfer taxes (add lines 21, 22, and 23) | | 24 |
| 25 | Prior payments. Explain in an attached statement | 25 | |
| 26 | United States Treasury bonds redeemed in payment of estate tax | 26 | |
| 27 | Total (add lines 25 and 26) | | 27 |
| 28 | Balance due (subtract line 27 from line 24) | | 28 |

Under penalties of perjury, I declare that I have examined this return, including accompanying schedules and statements, and to the best of my knowledge and belief, it is true, correct, and complete. Declaration of preparer other than the executor is based on all information of which preparer has any knowledge.

_____     _____
Signature(s) of executor(s)                                                 Date

_____     _____     _____
Signature of preparer other than executor          Address (and ZIP code)                          Date

Form 706 (Rev. 10-88)

## Estate of:

## Part 3.—Elections by the Executor

*Please check the "Yes" or "No" box for each question.*

| | Yes | No |
|---|---|---|
| 1 Do you elect alternate valuation? . . . . . . . . . . . . . . . . . . . . | | |
| 2 Do you elect special use valuation? . . . . . . . . . . . . . . . . . . . | | |
|   If "Yes," you must complete and attach Schedule A–1 | | |
| 3 Do you elect to pay the taxes in installments as described in section 6166? . . . . . | | |
|   If "Yes," you must attach the additional information described in the instructions. | | |
| 4 Do you elect to postpone the part of the taxes attributable to a reversionary or remainder interest as described in section 6163? | | |
| 5 Do you elect to have part or all of the estate tax liability assumed by an Employee Stock Ownership Plan (ESOP) as described in section 2210? | | |
|   If "Yes," enter the amount of tax assumed by the ESOP here ▶ $ _____ and attach the supplemental statements described in the instructions. | | |

## Part 4.—General Information Note: *Please attach the necessary supplemental documents.* **You must attach the death certificate.**

Authorization to receive confidential tax information under Regulations section 601.502(c)(3)(ii), to act as the estate's representative before the Internal Revenue Service, and to make written or oral presentations on behalf of the estate if return prepared by an attorney, accountant, or enrolled agent for the executor:

| Name of representative (print or type) | State | Address (number and street, city, state, and ZIP code) |
|---|---|---|
| | | |

I declare that I am the attorney/accountant/enrolled agent (strike out the words that do not apply) for the executor and prepared this return for the executor. I am not under suspension or disbarment from practice before the Internal Revenue Service and am qualified to practice in the state shown above.

| Signature | CAF Number | Date | Telephone Number |
|---|---|---|---|
| | | | |

1 Death certificate number and issuing authority (attach a copy of the death certificate to this return).

2 Decedent's business or occupation. If retired, check here ▶ ☐ and state decedent's former business or occupation.

**3** Marital status of the decedent at time of death:

☐ Married

☐ Widow or widower—Name, SSN and date of death of deceased spouse ▶ --------------------------

☐ Single

☐ Legally separated

☐ Divorced—Date divorce decree became final ▶

| 4a Surviving spouse's name | 4b Social security number | 4c Amount received (see instructions) |
|---|---|---|
| | | |

**5** Individuals (other than the surviving spouse), trusts, or other estates who receive benefits from the estate (do not include charitable beneficiaries shown in Schedule O) (see instructions). For Privacy Act Notice (applicable to individual beneficiaries only), see the Instructions for Form 1040.

| Name of individual, trust or estate receiving $5,000 or more | Identifying number | Relationship to decedent | Amount (see instructions) |
|---|---|---|---|
| | | | |

All unascertainable beneficiaries and those who receive less than $5,000

Total . . . . . . . . . . . . . . . . . . . . . . . . . . . . . . . . . . . . . . . . . . . .

*(Continued on next page)*

**Page 2**

## Part 4.—General Information (continued)

**Please check the "Yes" or "No" box for each question.**

| | | Yes | No |
|---|---|---|---|
| 6 | Does the gross estate contain any section 2044 property (see instructions)? . . . . . . . | ▨ | ▨ |
| 7a | Have Federal gift tax returns ever been filed?. . . . . . . . . . . . . . . | ▨ | ▨ |
| | If "Yes," please attach copies of the returns, if available, and furnish the following information: | | |
| 7b | Period(s) covered | 7c | Internal Revenue office(s) where filed | | |
| | **If you answer "Yes" to any of questions 8–16, you must attach additional information as described in the instructions.** | | |
| 8a | Was there any insurance on the decedent's life that is not included on the return as part of the gross estate? . . . . | | |
| b | Did the decedent own any insurance on the life of another that is not included in the gross estate? | | |
| 9 | Did the decedent at the time of death own any property as a joint tenant with right of survivorship in which (1) one or more of the other joint tenants was someone other than the decedent's spouse, and (2) less than the full value of the property is included on the return as part of the gross estate? If "Yes," you must complete and attach Schedule E. . . . . | | |
| 10 | Did the decedent, at the time of death, own any interest in a partnership or unincorporated business or any stock in an inactive or closely held corporation? . . . . . . . . . . . . . . . . . | | |
| 11a | Did the decedent make any transfer described in section 2035, 2036, 2037 or 2038 (see the instructions for Schedule G)? If "Yes," you must complete and attach Schedule G . . . . . . . . . . . . . | | |
| b | If "Yes," was it a valuation freeze subject to section 2036(c)? . . . . . . . . . | | |
| 12 | Were there in existence at the time of the decedent's death: | | |
| a | Any trusts created by the decedent during his or her lifetime? . . . . . . . . . | ▨ | ▨ |
| b | Any trusts not created by the decedent under which the decedent possessed any power, beneficial interest, or trusteeship? . . . | | |
| 13 | Did the decedent ever possess, exercise, or release any general power of appointment? If "Yes," you must complete and attach Schedule H. | | |
| 14 | Was the marital deduction computed under the transitional rule of Public Law 97-34, section 403(e)(3) (Economic Recovery Tax Act of 1981)? If "Yes," attach a separate computation of the marital deduction, and note on item 18 of the Recapitulation, and note on item 18 "computation attached." | ▨ | ▨ |
| 15 | Was the decedent, immediately before death, receiving an annuity described in the "General" paragraph of the instructions for Schedule I? If "Yes," you must complete and attach Schedule I. . . . . . . . . . . | | |
| 16 | Did the decedent have a total "excess retirement accumulation" (as defined in section 4980A(d)) in qualified employer plan(s) and individual retirement plan(s)? If "Yes," you must attach Schedule S (Form 706) (see instructions) | | |

## Part 5.—Recapitulation

| Item number | Gross estate | Alternate value | Value at date of death |
|---|---|---|---|
| 1 | Schedule A—Real Estate . . . . . . . . . . . . . | | |
| 2 | Schedule B—Stocks and Bonds . . . . . . . . . . | | |
| 3 | Schedule C—Mortgages, Notes, and Cash . . . . . . | | |
| 4 | Schedule D—Insurance on the Decedent's Life (attach Form(s) 712) . | | |
| 5 | Schedule E—Jointly Owned Property (attach Form(s) 712 for life insurance) . | | |
| 6 | Schedule F—Other Miscellaneous Property (attach Form(s) 712 for life insurance) . | | |
| 7 | Schedule G—Transfers During Decedent's Life (attach Form(s) 712 for life insurance) . | | |
| 8 | Schedule H—Powers of Appointment. . . . . . . . | | |
| 9 | Schedule I—Annuities . . . . . . . . . . . . . | | |
| 10 | Total gross estate (add items 1 through 9). Enter here and on line 1 of the Tax Computation. | | |

| Item number | Deductions | Amount |
|---|---|---|
| 11 | Schedule J—Funeral Expenses and Expenses Incurred in Administering Property Subject to Claims . | |
| 12 | Schedule K—Debts of the Decedent . . . . . . . . | |
| 13 | Schedule K—Mortgages and Liens . . . . . . . . | |
| 14 | Total of items 11 through 13 . . . . . . . . . . | |
| 15 | Allowable amount of deductions from item 14 (see the instructions for item 15 of the Recapitulation) | |
| 16 | Schedule L—Net Losses During Administration . . . . . | |
| 17 | Schedule L—Expenses Incurred in Administering Property Not Subject to Claims . | |
| 18 | Schedule M—Bequests, etc., to Surviving Spouse . . . . | |
| 19 | Schedule O—Charitable, Public, and Similar Gifts and Bequests . . | |
| 20 | Total of items 15 through 19—If you did not complete Schedule N, skip lines 21-24 and enter the line 20 amount on line 25 . | |
| 21 | Intermediate taxable estate (subtract item 20 from item 10) . | |
| 22 | Maximum ESOP deduction (from Table D in the Instructions) . | |
| 23 | Enter the amount from Schedule N, line 8. . . . . . | |
| 24 | Allowable ESOP deduction—enter the lesser of item 22 or 23 . | |
| 25 | Total allowable deductions (add items 20 and 24). Enter here and on line 2 of the Tax Computation . | |

# APPENDIX B

# INSTALLMENT INDEBTEDNESS PROVISIONS OF SECTION 453C OF THE INTERNAL REVENUE CODE

## Rulings and Decisions Under the Internal Revenue Code of 1986

**Section 453C.—Certain Indebtedness Treated as Payment on Installment Obligations**

26 CFR 1.453C-OT: Table of contents (temporary).

**T.D. 8224**

**TITLE 26—INTERNAL REVENUE.—CHAPTER 1, SUBCHAPTER A, PART 1—INCOME TAX; TAXABLE YEARS BEGINNING AFTER DECEMBER 31, 1953**

**Certain Indebtedness Treated as Payments on Installment Obligations**

AGENCY: Internal Revenue Service, Treasury.

ACTION: Temporary regulations.

SUMMARY: This document contains temporary regulations relating to the treatment of indebtedness as payments on installment obligations. The text of the temporary regulations set forth in this document also serves as the text of the proposed regulations for the notice of proposed rulemaking in the Proposed Rules section of * * * [LR-82-88, page 56, this Bulletin]. The Tax Reform Act of 1986 and the Revenue Act of 1987 made changes to the law. The regulations affect taxpayers who use the installment method to report sales of real or personal property made in the ordinary course of their business, or sales of real property used in a trade or business or held for the production of rental income, and provide them with guidance needed to comply with the law.

EFFECTIVE DATE: The regulations are effective on September 8, 1988, and are applicable to taxable years ending after December 31, 1986.

FOR FURTHER INFORMATION CONTACT: William L. Blagg of the Legislation and Regulations Division, Office of Chief Counsel, Internal Revenue Service, 1111 Constitution Avenue, N.W., Washington, D.C. 20224 (Attention: CC:LR:T), (202) 566-3238 (not a toll-free call).

## SUPPLEMENTARY INFORMATION:

### BACKGROUND

This document contains amendments to the Income Tax Regulations (26 CFR Part 1) under section 453C of the Internal Revenue Code of 1986. These amendments conform the regulations to the provisions of section 811 of the Tax Reform Act of 1986 (Pub. L. 99514, 100 Stat. 2085) (the 1986 Act) [1986–3 (Vol. 1) C.B. 1, 282] and section 10202(a) of the Revenue Act of 1987 (Pub. L. 100–203, 101 Stat. 1330-338) (the 1987 Act).

### EXPLANATION OF PROVISIONS IN GENERAL

Section 453C limits the use of the installment method of reporting. The limitation applies to applicable installment obligations that are outstanding as of the close of the taxable year. Under the limitation, a taxpayer's allocable installment indebtedness for the taxable year is allocated to such applicable installment obligations and is deemed a payment (deemed payment) received on the obligations as of the close of the taxable year. The deemed payment is subject to the general rules of the installment method for determining gain and recovery of basis.

Actual payments received on an obligation subsequent to a deemed payment on the obligation are treated as the receipt of tax paid amounts up to the amount of the deemed payment on the obligation and are not taken into account under the installment method under sections 453 and 453A (as in effect prior to their amendment by section 10202 of the 1987 Act, discussed more fully below). Only actual payments in excess of prior deemed payments are taken into account under pre-1987 Act sections 453 and 453A.

For any taxable year, the amount of a deemed payment on an applicable installment obligation cannot exceed the remaining contract price of the obligation. For this purpose, the remaining contract price is the excess, if any, of the total contract price for the disposition over deemed and actual payments received on the obligation. Actual payments that are not taken into account under pre-1987 Act sections 453 and 453A because they do not exceed previous amounts of deemed payments, as discussed above, are not treated as the partial receipt of the contract price. If, in any taxable year, allocable installment indebtedness exceeds the amount that may be deemed a payment on the obligations arising in that taxable year and outstanding as of the close of that taxable year, the excess is allocated to outstanding obligations arising in the immediately preceding taxable year and then to such obligations arising in the second immediately preceding taxable year.

## APPLICABLE INSTALLMENT OBLIGATIONS

The term "applicable installment obligation" includes any obligation arising from a disposition occurring after February 28, 1986, on the installment method, of personal property by a person who regularly sells or otherwise disposes of such property on the installment plan or real property held for sale to customers in the ordinary course of a trade or business. The term also includes any obligation arising from a disposition occurring after August 16, 1986, on the installment method, of real property used in a trade or business or held for the production of rental income, provided the sales price of such real property is more than $150,000. However, the term includes only those obligations of the type described above that are held by the person that sold the property for which the obligation was received (or a member of the same affiliated group as such a person) or that are transferred in a transaction in which the transferee takes the transferor's basis in the obligation.

Due to the limited future application of section 453C, the temporary regulations provide that the term "applicable installment obligation" includes an obligation arising from the disposition of an interest in an entity only if the disposition of the interest in the entity was for a principal purpose of avoiding section 453C. No inference is intended with respect to the treatment of a disposition of an interest in an entity for purposes of any other section of the Code, including section 453A.

Finally, the term "applicable installment obligation" does not include obligations arising from the disposition of personal use property or the disposition of property produced or used by a taxpayer in the trade or business of farming. These rules are discussed more fully below.

## ALLOCABLE INSTALLMENT INDEBTEDNESS

A taxpayer's allocable installment indebtedness for a taxable year is generally the excess (if any) of the installment percentage of the taxpayer's average quarterly indebtedness, over the aggregate amount treated as allocable installment indebtedness with respect to outstanding obligations arising in a prior year. However, this prior year allocable installment indebtedness must first be reduced by the amount of actual payments on applicable installment obligations that are not taken into account for purposes of pre-1987 Act sections 453 and 453A.

The installment percentage is the percentage that results from dividing the outstanding face amount of applicable installment obligations outstanding as of the close of the taxable year by the sum of the outstanding face amounts of all installment obligations and the adjusted bases of all assets held by the taxpayer as of the close of the taxable year. In determining the taxpayer's average quarterly indebtedness, payments made with a principal purpose of reducing or eliminating the indebtedness determination will be ignored. Thus, indebtedness decreases near the end of a quarter followed by indebtedness increases soon after the start of the next quarter may be ignored in computing average quarterly indebtedness.

If a taxpayer has no obligations arising from dealer dispositions of real or personal property outstanding at any time during a taxable year, the taxpayer does not compute average quarterly indebtedness for that taxable year. Instead, the taxpayer uses its indebtedness outstanding as of the close of the taxable year. If a taxpayer has obligations arising from dealer dispositions of real or personal property during the taxable year, but none of these obligations are outstanding as of the close of the taxable year, the taxpayer may compute allocable installment indebtedness using either average quarterly indebtedness or indebtedness outstanding as of the close of the taxable year.

In determining the adjusted bases of a taxpayer's assets, the taxpayer may use the deduction for depreciation which is used in computing earnings and profits under section 312(k), regardless of whether the taxpayer is required to compute earnings and profits. In addition, personal use property is not taken into account as an asset.

The temporary regulations provide that the outstanding face amount of an obligation is the total of all remaining payments due under the obligation, including the fair market value of any contingent payments.

## INDEBTEDNESS

The temporary regulations adopt a broad definition of indebtedness. In addition to items typically regarded as indebtedness such as mortgages, promissory notes, debt instruments, loans, and bonds, the term includes all other liabilities of the taxpayer that are treated as such for federal income tax purposes as of the date such liabilities are so treated. In determining a taxpayer's indebtedness, any secured indebtedness substantially all the security for which is personal use property is not taken into account.

## AGGREGATION

In applying section 453C, persons that are treated as a single employer under section 52 are generally treated as one taxpayer. In such case, each group member is treated as having the assets and liabilities of each other member.

The temporary regulations generally apply an entity level approach in the case of partnerships, S corporations, and trusts. In general, the entity level computation is made without regard to the applicable installment obligations, adjusted bases of assets, and liabilities of the partners or shareholders.

If, based upon the facts and circumstances, a transaction between an entity (including any corporation or partnership) and its owners is structured with a principal purpose of avoiding the application of section 453C, the temporary regulations treat these related parties as one taxpayer. Thus, allocable installment indebtedness is determined using the assets and liabilities of the entity and its owners.

Generally, when an entity and its members (or owners) are treated as one taxpayer, liabilities between the entity and its members (or owners) are disregarded for purposes of section 453C. Similarly, in the case of such persons, the ownership interest of a member in an entity is not taken into account as an asset of the member.

## PERSONAL USE PROPERTY, PROPERTY HELD FOR RENTAL INCOME, AND PROPERTY USED IN FARMING

As noted above, obligations arising from the sale of personal use property are not applicable installment obligations subject to section 453C. Similarly, indebtedness secured by personal use property is not taken into account for purposes of section 453C. In general, the term "personal use property" means any property held by an individual substantially all the use of which is by an individual and not in connection with a trade or business or any activity described in section 212. Nevertheless, the term does not include cash or cash equivalents. The temporary regulations provide that real property is not held for rental income if the primary motivation for holding the property is to realize gain from the appreciation of the property and the property generates no more than nominal rents.

As noted above, the term "applicable installment obligation" does not include any obligation arising from the disposition by a taxpayer of property used or produced in the trade or business of farming. A taxpayer for this purpose includes a farm-related taxpayer as that term is defined in section 464. This determination is based on the facts and circumstances.

## SALES OF TIMESHARES AND RESIDENTIAL LOTS

A taxpayer may elect to have section 453C not apply to certain sales. The election applies to any obligation arising from a sale in the ordinary course of the taxpayer's trade or business to an individual of (1) a timeshare right to use or ownership interest in residential real estate of not more than 6 weeks, or a right to use recreational campgrounds, and (2) an unimproved residential lot which the taxpayer (or a related party) will not improve, provided that the obligation is not guaranteed by any person other than an individual. In determining an individual's timeshare use or ownership, an interest held by the individual's spouse, children, grandchildren or parents is considered held by that individual. In addition, in determining whether a person is related to the seller, the rules of sections 267 and 707(b) apply with the modification that 10 percent is substituted for 50 percent each place it appears in those sections. Finally, a lot is not considered developed merely because it is provided with common infrastructure items such as roads or sewers.

If a taxpayer makes the election to have section 453C not apply, the taxpayer must pay interest on the portion of the tax for the taxable year that is attributable to the receipt of the deferred payment on the obligation. For this purpose, payments received in the year of sale are disregarded. The interest on the deferred payment on an obligation is computed from the date of sale to the date of payment using the applicable Federal rate in effect at the time of the sale. The regulations provide a simplified method of computing interest by allowing a taxpayer to elect to treat all payments as received in the middle of the year. The interest is subject to applicable limitations on the deductibility of interest and is reported as an addition to tax that is due as of the due date of the return (determined without regard to extensions) for the taxable year of the deferred payment.

## EFFECTIVE DATE, TRANSITIONAL RULES, AND 1987 ACT

As enacted by section 811(a) of the 1986 Act, section 453C applies to taxable years ending after December 31, 1986, with respect to dispositions of real or personal property in the ordinary course of the taxpayer's trade or business occurring after February 28, 1986, and with respect to dispositions of certain real property used in the taxpayer's trade or business or held for the production of rental income occurring after August 16, 1986. In the case of a disposition that occurs after February 28,

1986 (or August 16, 1986), but in a taxable year ending on or before January 1, 1987, the regulations provide that such disposition is treated as occurring on the first day of the taxpayer's first taxable year ending after December 31, 1986. This rule, nevertheless, does not affect the application of the general installment method rules applicable to the sale in the taxable year of the sale.

Section 811(c)(6) and (7) of the 1986 Act provides transitional rules that apply to dealer sales in the first and second taxable years ending after December 31, 1986. Under the transitional rules, the income or tax attributable to the application of section 453C to those sales is spread over a two-year or three-year period. These temporary regulations provide guidance with respect to those transitional rules.

In the case of dealer sales of real property, the temporary regulations provide that income attributable to a deemed 1987 payment on any applicable installment obligation is taken into account ratably over three taxable years beginning with the first taxable year ending after December 31, 1986. The deemed 1987 payment with respect to any installment obligation is the amount of allocable installment indebtedness for the first taxable year ending after December 31, 1986, that is treated under §1.453C-5T(a) as a payment on such obligation. Similarly, any income attributable to a deemed 1988 payment on any applicable installment obligation is taken into account ratably over two taxable years beginning with the second taxable year ending after December 31, 1986. The deemed 1988 payment with respect to any installment obligation is the amount of allocable installment indebtedness for the second taxable year ending after December 31, 1986, that is treated under §1.453C-5T(a) and (d) as a payment on such obligation.

In the case of dealer sales of personal property, the temporary regulations provide that, solely for purposes of determining the time for payment of tax and any interest with respect to such tax, the tax attributable to deemed 1987 payments is treated as imposed ratably over the three taxable years beginning with the first taxable year ending after December 31, 1986. Similarly, any tax attributable to deemed 1988 payments is treated as imposed ratably over the two taxable years beginning with the second taxable year ending after December 31, 1986.

The temporary regulations provide that §1.453C-5T(b) (relating to the treatment of subsequent payments as the receipt of tax paid amounts) and §1.453C-5T(c) (relating to the limitation on amounts treated as received) apply without regard to the section 811(c)(6) and (7) transitional rules. Thus, an amount is treated as received in a taxable year for purposes of §1.453-5T(b) and (c), even though under the transitional rules income or tax attributable to such amount is taken into account ratably over the two-year or three-year period beginning with such taxable year.

In addition, the temporary regulations provide special rules for determining estimated taxes and for recognizing income or paying tax attributable to deemed 1987 and 1988 payments when a dealer dies, terminates or otherwise ceases to engage in a trade or business, changes from C corporation to S corporation status, or terminates an S election.

As amended by section 10202 of the 1987 Act, section 453C does not apply to installment obligations arising from dealer dispositions of property within the meaning of section 453(l) (as added to the Code by section 10202 of the 1987 Act) effective for dispositions after December 31, 1987. In the case of installment obligations arising from dealer dispositions before January 1, 1988, section 453C does not apply to taxable years beginning after December 31, 1987.

In the case of installment obligations arising from nondealer dispositions within the meaning of section 453A (as amended by section 10202 of the 1987 Act), section 453C does not apply to dispositions in taxable years beginning after December 31, 1987. Nevertheless, a taxpayer may elect, according to the provisions of Notice 88–81, 1988–30 I.R.B. 28, to have section 453C not apply to taxable years ending after December 31, 1986, with respect to dispositions occurring after August 16, 1986.

## SPECIAL ANALYSES

A general notice of proposed rulemaking is not required by 5 U.S.C. 553 for temporary regulations. Accordingly, these temporary regulations do not constitute regulations subject to the Regulatory Flexibility Act (5 U.S.C. chapter 6).

The Commissioner of Internal Revenue has determined that this temporary rule is not a major rule as defined in Executive Order 12291. Accordingly, a Regulatory Impact Analysis is not required.

## DRAFTING INFORMATION

The principal authors of these temporary regulations are William L. Blagg of the Legislation and Regulations Division, Office of Chief Counsel, Internal Revenue Service and Ewan D. Purkiss, formerly of that Division. However, personnel from other offices of the Internal Revenue Service and the Treasury Department participated in developing the regulations on matters of both substance and style.

There is a need for immediate guidance with respect to the provisions contained in this Treasury decision. For this reason it is impracticable to issue this Treasury decision with notice and public procedure under section (b) of section 553 of Title 5 of the United States Code or subject to the effective date limitation of subsection (d) of that section.

# APPENDIX C
## NONMARITAL PARTNERSHIP AGREEMENT ("LIVING TOGETHER" AGREEMENT)

THIS AGREEMENT is made this    day of          , by and between JOAN J. FREEWOMAN (hereinafter called JOAN) and EMCEE BATCHELOR (hereinafter called EMCEE), both of whom are now residing at          , Connecticut.

### WITNESSETH:

I. This agreement is made with respect to the following facts:

   1. JOAN and EMCEE began living together on or about when JOAN moved into EMCEE's house at          , Connecticut, and have subsequently moved together to their present residence at          , Connecticut. JOAN and EMCEE contemplate continuing to live together in the future.

   2. On          , JOAN and EMCEE purchased the above property (hereafter referred to as the premises), for a total of $          This purchase price is being paid by (a) a $          mortgage loan, on which both parties are liable (but EMCEE has agreed to indemnify JOAN) from the seller, (b) a $          cash contribution by JOAN (already made at the closing) and (c) the balance contributed in cash by EMCEE (since EMCEE signed a note, until EMCEE obtains funds from the sale of EMCEE's house; EMCEE's cash contribution will be made later).

---

\* Adopted from Frank S. Berall, BS, JD, who is a member of the Connecticut and New York Bar Associations with modifications from the author.

3. JOAN and EMCEE desire and intend to define and clarify their intentions and expectations with respect to their financial rights and responsibilities between each other, including rights dealing with property and support, so as to remove these considerations as potential detractions from their relationship. They intend that this agreement shall supersede any rights either of them may have under applicable common law or statutes, including cases establishing rights between persons living together without a licensed, solemnized or registered statutory, common law, or other marriage.

4. Both JOAN and EMCEE presently own property standing in his or her respective name, the nature and extent of which has been fully disclosed by each to the other and said disclosures, in the form of a simple balance sheet of each party, are appended to this agreement as Exhibits A (JOAN's) and B (EMCEE's).

5. Both JOAN and EMCEE are unmarried persons and permanent residents of Connecticut.

6. EMCEE is presently employed by                at an annual salary of approximately $   . JOAN is presently employed by                at an annual salary of approximately $

7. JOAN and EMCEE desire that all property owned by either of them at this time and all property coming to them from whatever source during the time they live together shall be their respective separate property, except as otherwise provided in this agreement.

8. Although both JOAN and EMCEE understand that the laws of the State of Connecticut may be developing toward granting support payment to a party to a nonmarital relationship from the other party after the relationship terminates, both JOAN and EMCEE desire to waive any support from one another in the event of the termination of their relationship for whatever reason, except as otherwise provided in this agreement.

9. Except as otherwise provided in this agreement, JOAN and EMCEE intend to contribute mutually to the support of the household that they share, but without acquiring any interests in the property of one another by such contribution, even though the earnings of either may have been applied so as to enhance the value of the property of the other or even though the personal skills, services and efforts of either may have directly or indirectly enhanced and resulted in appreciation of the value of the property of the other.

II. NOW, THEREFORE, IN CONSIDERATION of the mutual promises contained herein, and with the intention of being legally bound hereby, JOAN and EMCEE agree as follows:

1. Effective dates and definition of separation

    This agreement shall be effective as of                and shall continue until the first to occur of: (a) the death of either party, (b) marriage to each other, or (c) their separation, as defined for purposes of this agreement as any one or more of the following events:

    (a) The removal by JOAN of all or a substantial part of her personal property from the premises, unless said removal occurs as a result of JOAN and EMCEE moving either temporarily or permanently to another residence or going on a trip together;

    (b) JOAN's failure to reside on the premises for a period of 30 consecutive days or more, unless such failure is caused by: (i) JOAN and EMCEE having temporarily or permanently moved elsewhere together or (ii) both JOAN and EMCEE or JOAN alone having gone away on a trip or (iii) JOAN has become ill or is injured and is either hospitalized or (whether or not following hospitalization) is in some form of a nursing home or extended care facility;

    (c) JOAN's establishment of a principal residence without EMCEE;

    (d) EMCEE's request that JOAN and EMCEE terminate their arrangements and that JOAN move out of the premises.

2. Present financial position

    While neither JOAN nor EMCEE represent his or her respective attached balance sheet to be a precise delineation of his or her assets and liabilities, it constitutes a reasonable approximation of such assets and liabilities. Both JOAN and EMCEE represent to the other that he or she has fully disclosed to the other his or her financial situation by the representations contained in the balance sheets, subject only to the caveat that the balance sheets were prepared informally and without reference to documents.

3. Assets and liabilities as separate property

    Except as otherwise provided in this agreement, JOAN and EMCEE agree that the property described below in this paragraph (3) shall remain the separate and solely owned property of its title holder and that all of the liabilities of each of them at the effective date of this agreement shall remain their separate liabilities and not that of the other.

    (a) All property, whether realty or personalty, owned by either party at the effective date of this agreement.

    (b) All property acquired by the other party out of the proceeds or income from property owned at the effective date of this agreement, or attributable to appreciation in value of such property, whether the enhancement is due to market conditions or to the services, skills or efforts of its owner.

(c) All property subsequently acquired by either party by gift, devise, bequest or inheritance.

(d) All the earnings and accumulations resulting from JOAN's and EMCEE's personal services, skill, efforts and work. Both JOAN and EMCEE understand that, except for this agreement, the earnings and accumulations from the personal services, skills, effort and work of the other throughout their cohabitation might be subject to legal or equitable rights of the other party, and that, by this agreement, JOAN's and EMCEE's earnings and income during their cohabitation are made the separate property of the person to whom the earnings and accumulations are attributable.

4. Living expenses

Except as provided elsewhere in this agreement JOAN and EMCEE agree that EMCEE shall pay          % and JOAN shall pay          % of their living expenses while they are living together.

5. Dispositions of a property to other party

Notwithstanding any of the provisions of this agreement, either party may, by appropriate written instrument or otherwise, transfer, give, convey, devise or bequeath any property to the other. Neither JOAN nor EMCEE intend by this agreement to limit or restrict in any way the right to receive any such transfer, gift, conveyance, devise or bequest from the other, except as herein stated in this agreement.

6. Transmutation

Except as otherwise provided herein, all property or interest therein now owned or hereafter acquired by JOAN and EMCEE (which by the terms of this agreement is classified as the separate property of one of them), can become the separate property of the other or can become JOAN and EMCEE's joint or common property only by written instrument executed by JOAN and EMCEE, whose separate property is thereby reclassified.

7. Parties interested in house

The deed recorded on the          land records shows that the parties took title to the premises as tenants-in-common and that EMCEE's interest is          % and JOAN's is          %. However, JOAN agrees that EMCEE shall have the sole and exclusive right, power and authority to sell, mortgage, and encumber the premises. Furthermore, JOAN has executed a document, recorded on the      land records and being Exhibit C to this agreement, confirming that EMCEE has said power and has given EMCEE a limited durable power of attorney to act accordingly. The latter is Exhibit D to this agreement.

8. Contribution for house expenses

     While both JOAN and EMCEE own the premises, JOAN will contribute a certain amount, as agreed upon by both of them from time to time, toward the payment of real estate taxes as well as for any capital improvements to be made to the premises. EMCEE has agreed to indemnify JOAN for any liability JOAN may have on the note and mortgage and all payments to be made on the mortgage will be made by EMCEE. However, to assure that both parties will have the benefit of Section 1034 of the Internal Revenue Code of 1986 (dealing with the rollover of gain on a sale of a principal residence), JOAN and EMCEE agree that any necessary changes to this agreement shall be made in a subsequent contract to be executed by them within 30 days after being advised by counsel that the $      JOAN has contributed to the purchase of the premises is insufficient for JOAN to be able to obtain said tax benefits or other changes are needed so that both JOAN and EMCEE will qualify under said Section.

9. Payment to JOAN upon termination

     If (i) JOAN's and EMCEE's arrangements are terminated (as described in the first sentence of paragraph (1) or (ii) if they sell the premises, EMCEE will pay JOAN either: (a) the sum of $      plus or an amount equal to the total amount of JOAN's contributions to the property prior to sale or separation, (b) such amount as is determined to be JOAN's percentage share of the fair market value of the property if it is in fact sold or (c) such amount as is determined to be JOAN's percentage share of the fair market value of the property according to an appraisal. JOAN will have the sole right to elect whether to take (a) $      plus an amount equal to the total amount of JOAN's contributions to the property prior to sale or separation, (b) the amount determined as a result of a sale of the property (if that is in fact what occurs) or (c) the amount determined by an appraisal (if there is no sale). If JOAN elects to have the premises appraised, JOAN and EMCEE will share the cost of the appraisal equally. If they can agree upon one appraiser in advance of his or her making said appraisal, they will accept his or her appraised price as the fair market value of the premises. If they cannot agree upon a single appraiser, then each of them will obtain an appraiser of his or her own choosing. If the higher appraised value is 110% or less of the lower value, they will agree to split the difference in determining the fair market value. If the higher value is more than        % of the lower value, they will then agree upon a third appraiser and will average the three appraisals in determining fair market value.

10. Additional payment to JOAN if separation occurs

The provisions in paragraph (9) with respect to the payment of JOAN's share of the value of the house will apply whether JOAN and EMCEE's arrangements terminate because (a) the house is sold and they continue to live together elsewhere or (b) as a result of a separation. However, if their arrangements terminate as a result of a separation, then, in addition to the amount to be paid to JOAN with respect to her share of the value of the house, as described in paragraph (9) above, including an amount equal to the total amount of JOAN's contributions to the property prior to sale or separation, EMCEE agrees to pay JOAN the sum of $        , adjusted for any changes in the price level based upon the increase in the Bureau of Labor Statistics' Consumer Price Index from the end of 1983 to the end of 1984 and to the end of each calendar year thereafter.

11. Disposition of real estate upon separation

Upon separation, (as defined in paragraph (1), above), EMCEE will become the sole owner of the premises, except that if EMCEE decides to sell the premises within 30 days of a separation EMCEE shall give JOAN the right of first refusal to buy the premises at a mutually agreeable price. Such agreement will be in EMCEE's sole discretion. Subject to EMCEE paying JOAN the amounts specified above in paragraph 9 and 10, JOAN shall execute any and all agreements necessary to implement this agreement.

12. New wills

JOAN and EMCEE have already executed a new will or a codicil providing that in the event that JOAN and EMCEE's arrangements end as the result of the death of one of them, each of their respective interests in the premises will be devised absolutely and outright in their entirety to the survivor of them and all of their personal effects are bequeathed to said survivor, except that if JOAN is the survivor the personal effects are bequeathed by JOAN to EMCEE's children, outright. Thus, subject to a requirement of survivorship for 60 days, upon the death of either of JOAN or EMCEE prior to any separation, the survivor of them shall be the sole owner of the property.

13. Major medical insurance

JOAN and EMCEE agree that they will discuss whether adequate major medical insurance exists on them and, if not, EMCEE will obtain additional coverage.

14. Marriage to modify agreement

This agreement shall continue in full force and effect in the event JOAN and EMCEE marry each other, with the exception of the provisions of paragraph II(15) (regarding liabilities), paragraph II(4) (regarding living expenses) and paragraph II(19) (concerning support), all of which shall be deleted from this agreement as of the date of JOAN and EMCEE's marriage.

15. Liabilities

Neither JOAN nor EMCEE agree to become liable to the other of them nor to any third party by the acting of one of them beyond the express terms of this agreement, and particularly paragraph II(4), dealing with living expenses, unless he or she specifically incurs such liability in a written instrument, including a joint credit application or an instrument of guarantee.

16. Benefit and burden

This agreement shall be binding upon and inure to the benefit of JOAN and EMCEE hereto and their respective heirs, administrators, executors, personal representatives, successors and assigns.

17. Consideration for agreement

The consideration of this agreement is the mutual promise of JOAN and EMCEE to act as companions and homemakers to each other, in addition to the other promises contained in this agreement.

18. Fiduciary duty

Both JOAN and EMCEE promise to act in good faith toward the other in the management of their joint or common property, and in living under the terms of this agreement.

19. Separation of JOAN and EMCEE; support and other consideration

Both JOAN and EMCEE waive all rights to be supported by the other or to claim or receive any lump sum, periodic payment, or other consideration of any kind after their separation or after the death of either party, except as set forth by the express terms of this agreement.

20. Use of name and purported spousal designations

While JOAN and EMCEE intend under most circumstances to hold themselves out as single people, nevertheless they agree that under certain circumstances JOAN shall have the right to use the name BATCHELOR and hold herself out as EMCEE's spouse. EMCEE shall similarly have the right to hold himself out as JOAN's spouse. However, this shall not affect the rights of JOAN and EMCEE as set forth in this agreement nor shall any applications for joint credit affect any financial arrangements set forth herein. No use of any name or holding out by either JOAN or EMCEE of a spousal status shall constitute any evidence in any court or legal proceeding of the existence of a common-law or solemnized marriage in this or any other jurisdiction. This agreement confirms a non-marital status between JOAN and EMCEE, neither this agreement nor actions under its provisions shall be used by or available to either party in any jurisdiction to establish a marital relationship, at common law or otherwise.

21. Compensation for services

    It is agreed between JOAN and EMCEE that any services which either party may provide to the other during the period of living together or at any time after a possible separation of JOAN and EMCEE or after the death of either of them will be fully compensated by the terms of this agreement.

22. Integration of all understandings in this instrument

    This instrument sets forth the entire agreement between JOAN and EMCEE with regard to the subject matter hereof. Integrated in it is a revised version of the terms of the             , letter agreement addressed to EMCEE by JOAN. All agreements, covenants, representations or warranties, express and implied, oral and written, of JOAN and EMCEE with respect to their financial relationship, past, present and future, commencing as of the date they began living together and terminating if and when they separate or when one of them dies, are contained herein with the exception of JOAN's agreement of             , not to sell, mortgage or encumber the             , property and the irrevocable power of attorney coupled with an interest, signed by JOAN on             , copies of which are appended hereto as Exhibits C and D, respectively. No other agreements, covenants, representations or warranties, express or implied, oral or written, have been made by JOAN or EMCEE to the other with respect to the subject matter of this agreement. All prior and contemporaneous conversations, negotiations, possible and alleged agreements, representations, covenants and warranties with respect to the subject matter hereof are waived, merged into this agreement and superseded hereby. This is an integrated agreement, which also incorporates by reference the terms of the two documents referred to hereinabove, which are attached Exhibits C and D.

23. Severability

    If any of the provisions of this agreement are deemed to be invalid or unenforceable, they shall be deemed severable from the remainder of this agreement and shall not cause the invalidity or unenforceability of the remainder of this agreement. If said provisions shall be deemed invalid due to scope or breadth, such provisions shall be deemed valid to the extent of the scope or breadth permitted by law.

24. Amendment

    This agreement can be amended only by a written agreement signed by both parties or by an executed oral agreement.

25. Governing law

    This agreement has been drafted and executed in the State of Connecticut and shall be governed by, continued and enforced in accordance with the laws of said state.

26. Signing of Agreement

    Prior to signing this agreement, each party consulted with an attorney of his or her choice. The terms and legal significance of this agreement and the effect which it has upon any interest which each party might accrue in the property of the other were fully explained. Each party acknowledges that he or she fully understands the agreement and its legal effect and that he or she is signing it freely and voluntarily and that neither party has any reason to believe the other did not understand fully the terms and effects of the agreement or that he or she did not freely and voluntarily execute said agreement.

27. Interpretation

    No provision in this agreement is to be interpreted for or against any party because that party or that party's attorney or other legal representative drafted the provision.

28. Costs and expenses

    Each party to this agreement shall bear his or her respective costs and expenses incurred in connection with this agreement, including, but not limited to, the negotiation, preparation and consummation thereof.

29. Attorneys' fees

    Should any party hereto retain counsel for the purpose of enforcing or preventing the breach of any provision of this agreement, including, but not limited to the instituting of any action or proceeding to enforce any provision hereof for damages by reason of any alleged breach of any provision of this agreement, for a declaration of such parties' rights or obligations hereunder or for any other judicial remedy relating hereto, then the prevailing party shall be entitled to be reimbursed by the losing party for all costs and expenses incurred thereby, including, but not limited to, reasonable attorneys' fees and costs for the services rendered to such prevailing party.

30. Captions

The underlined captions set forth at the beginning of paragraphs to this agreement are contained herein as a matter of convenience and for reference and in no way define, limit, extend or describe the scope of this agreement or any provision hereof.

31. Execution and counterparts

This agreement may be executed in two counterparts, each of which shall be an original but all of which shall constitute one and the same instrument.

_____

JOAN J. FREEWOMAN

_____

EMCEE BATCHELOR

In the State of Connecticut, County of                    , and City of
           , on this              day of                                ,
personally appeared JOAN J. FREEWOMAN, and EMCEE BATCHELOR known to me to be the persons whose names are subscribed to the within instrument and acknowledged that they executed the same for the purposes therein contained.

_____

Notary Public

APPROVED AS TO FORM:

_____

Attorney for EMCEE BATCHELOR

_____

Attorney for JOAN J. FREEWOMAN

# APPENDIX D

## ANTENUPTIAL AGREEMENT

THIS AGREEMENT made between WILL U. MARRYME of Hartford, Connecticut, ("WILL") and CONSTANCE A. TRUELOVE of West Hartford, Connecticut, ("CONSTANCE").

### WITNESSETH:

The parties, each of whom have children by a former marriage, are about to marry each other. In anticipation thereof, they desire to fix and determine by antenuptial agreement the rights and claims that will accrue to each of them in the estate and property of the other by reason of and in full discharge, settlement and satisfaction of all such rights and claims.

NOW, THEREFORE, in consideration of the premises and of the marriage, and in further consideration of the mutual promises and undertakings hereinafter set forth, the parties agree:

1. CONSTANCE shall receive and accept from WILL's estate after his death, as a creditor thereof, subject to the consideration set forth in article 3 hereof, the sum of ONE HUNDRED THOUSAND DOLLARS ($100,000) free of any and all transfer, succession, inheritance, estate and other death taxes or duties, in place and stead of, and in full and final settlement and satisfaction of, and all rights and claims which she might otherwise have had in WILL's estate and property under any statute or statutes now or hereafter in force in this or any other jurisdiction, whether by way of her right of election to take against WILL's will, her share of his estate in intestacy, dower, quasi-community property, community property, marital or quasi-marital property, distributive share, widow's allowance or otherwise.

2. Subject to the conditions specified in article 3 below, said sums shall be paid, without interest, to CONSTANCE by WILL's estate as follows:

   (a) THIRTY FIVE THOUSAND DOLLARS ($35,000) thereof within

---

Adopted from 2 Lindsey, Forms 90.01 and 90.13 and from Rabkin & Johnson 4 Current Legal Forms with Tax Analysis, Forms 10.01 and 10.02. Mathew Bender Publishers, and Frank S. Berall, BS, JD, with modifications by the author.

THIRTY (30) days after the probate of WILL's will, but in no event later than NINETY (90) days after WILL's death;

(b) THIRTY FIVE THOUSAND DOLLARS ($35,000) thereof within SIX (6) months after WILL's death; and

(c) THIRTY THOUSAND DOLLARS ($30,000) thereof within TWELVE (12) months after WILL's death.

3. It is of the essence of this agreement that CONSTANCE shall be entitled to receive, and shall receive, the total sum of ONE HUNDRED THOU-SAND DOLLARS ($100,000) if and only if (a) she survives WILL, (b) the parties were living together as man and wife at the time of WILL's death, and (c) they were living together as such continuously from the time of marriage to the date of WILL's death. If CONSTANCE does not survive WILL, or if the parties were not living together as man and wife at the time of WILL's death, CONSTANCE shall not be entitled to receive any sum whatsoever from WILL's estate; and in such event, her waiver and release of any and all rights and claims she may have had in WILL's estate, as more particularly set forth in article 4 hereof, shall be of full force and effect and shall be conclusive and binding on her.* In the event that WILL and CONSTANCE die under circumstances in which there is no sufficient evidence as to which one of them died first or the other of their deaths cannot be established by proof, it shall be conclusively presumed that WILL survived CONSTANCE notwithstanding any presumption of law to the contrary.

4. Except as provided in articles 1 through 3, WILL and CONSTANCE, each acting alone, shall have the right to dispose of during lifetime or by will all of his or her respective real and personal property, of every kind and nature, wherever situated and whenever acquired. But nothing in this agreement shall prevent either WILL or CONSTANCE from voluntarily making provisions or additional provisions for the other during lifetime or on death, but neither is relying on the other making any provisions not set forth in this agreement. WILL shall not, in the absence of a written consent by CONSTANCE transfer any property for less than full consideration in money or money's worth if such transfer would reduce his net worth for distribution upon his death to less than TWO HUNDRED THOUSAND DOLLARS ($200,000), or if at the time of such transfer or imminent thereto, his net worth is less than said amount.

5. CONSTANCE hereby waives and releases any and all rights and claims of every kind, nature and description that she may acquire as WILL's surviving spouse in his estate upon his death, specifically including (but not by way of limitation) any and all rights in testacy and any and all right of election to take against WILL's last will and testament under

---

* (*Author's Note:* This provision would in all likelihood be enforced if the parties were not living together at the time of the husband's death because of the wife's fault. But what if the husband deserted the wife, or she left him with cause? What if they lived apart briefly because of a quarrel but were reunited at the husband's death?)

Connecticut General Statutes Section 45-273a(a), any law amendatory thereof or supplementary or similar thereto, and the same or similar law of any other jurisdiction, including any claims of dower, inchoate or otherwise, and any rights to community property or quasi-community property, marital property or quasi-marital property. This agreement shall evidence WILL's right to convey any and all of his present and future real estate free from any such claim of dower and his right to have any and all of his present and future property free of any community property or quasi-community property claims under the laws of any jurisdiction.*

6. WILL hereby waives and releases any and all rights and claims of every kind, nature and description that he may acquire as CONSTANCE's surviving spouse in her estate upon her death, specifically including (but not by way of limitation) any and all rights in intestacy and any and all right of election to take against CONSTANCE's last will and testament under Connecticut General Statutes Section 45-273a(a), any law amendatory thereof or supplementary or similar thereto, and the same or similar law of any other jurisdiction, including any claims of curtesy, inchoate or otherwise, and any rights to community property or quasi-community property. This agreement shall evidence CONSTANCE's right to convey any and all of her present and future real estate free from any such claim of curtesy and her rights to have any and all of her present and future property free of any community property, quasi-community property or marital or quasi-marital property claims under the laws of any jurisdiction.*

7. Each party shall during his or her lifetime keep and retain sole ownership, control and enjoyment of all property, real and personal, now owned or hereafter acquired by him or her, free and clear of any claim by the other. Should the parties ever become domiciled in a community or marital property jurisdiction or their domiciliary jurisdiction adopts such property rules, it is their intention that neither community property, quasi-community property, marital nor quasi-marital property rules shall apply to them.*

8. The consideration for this agreement is the mutual promises herein contained and the marriage about to be solemnized. If the contemplated marriage does not take place, this agreement shall be in all respects and for all purposes null and void.

9. Each party shall, upon the other's request, take any and all steps and execute, acknowledge and deliver to the other party or his or her personal representative any and all further instruments and documents necessary or expedient to effectuate the purpose and intent of this agreement.

10. CONSTANCE and WILL BOTH acknowledge that:

    (a) They are fully acquainted with each other's business, means and resources;

---

* (*Author's Note:* These provisions are designed to deal with a change of domicile to a state with common law dower and curtesy or with community property or quasi-community property concepts or one that has adopted the Uniform Marital Property Act (UMPA) or where the state of domicile later adopts the UMPA.)

(b) WILL has informed CONSTANCE in detail that he is a person of substantial wealth with a net worth in excess of ONE MILLION DOLLARS ($1,000,000) and he has a substantial income;

(c) CONSTANCE has informed WILL in detail that she is a person of moderate means with a net worth of about ONE HUNDRED THOUSAND DOLLARS ($100,000) and she has a modest income;

(d) Each of them have answered all the questions the other has asked about income and assets; and financial statements of both parties are annexed;

(e) Each of them understands that by entering into this agreement the survivor will receive considerably less than the amount said survivor would otherwise be entitled to receive if the first of them to die died intestate or if the survivor elected to take the first decedent's last will and testament pursuant to statute;

(f) Each of them at all times, has had the benefit of the advice of separate and independent counsel of their own selection;

(g) Each of them has ascertained and carefully weighed all the facts, conditions and circumstances likely to influence their judgment herein;

(h) All matters embodied herein as well as all questions pertinent hereto have been fully and satisfactorily explained to each of them;

(i) Each of them has given due consideration to such matters and questions;

(j) Each of them clearly understands and consents to all the provisions hereof and they desire to marry each other regardless of any financial arrangements made by WILL for CONSTANCE's benefit; and

(k) Each of them is entering into this agreement freely, voluntarily and with full knowledge of all relevant financial data about each other and full understanding of the provisions of this agreement.

11. This agreement contains the entire understanding of the parties. There are no representation, warranties, promises, covenants or undertakings, oral or otherwise, other than those expressly set forth herein.

12. This agreement is binding on WILL and CONSTANCE and shall inure to the benefit of and shall be binding upon their respective heirs, executors and administrators and assigns. All questions concerning the validity, meaning and effect of this agreement shall be decided under Connecticut law.

IN WITNESS WHEREOF, the parties hereto have hereunto set their hands and seals this _____ day of _____, 19___ .

WITNESSES:

_____          _____[L.S.]
                                          WILL U. MARRYME

_____          _____[L.S.]
                                          CONSTANCE A. TRUELOVE

In the State of Connecticut, County of                    , and
City of                         , on this          day
of          , 19     , personally appeared
and                              , known to me to be the persons
whose names are subscribed to the within instrument and acknowledged
that they executed the same for the purposes therein contained.

_____

Notary Public

# APPENDIX E

## STATEMENT REGARDING ANATOMICAL GIFTS

If you wish to be an organ donor for purposes of scientific study or for transplantation purposes, you should express your desires in a "Statement Regarding Anatomical Gifts" so your wishes will be followed.

The statement presented on the following pages has been designed to be used with the advice of an attorney. It has been drafted in accordance with the provisions of the Uniform Anatomical Gifts Act. Because the laws regarding anatomical gifts may vary in each state, attorneys advising on the use of this form should be familiar with the law of the relevant jurisdiction.

The statement reprinted here is from the Real Property, Probate and Trust Section of the American Bar Association. Reprinted by permission of the American Bar Association.

# STATEMENT REGARDING ANATOMICAL GIFTS

I, _____ of _____, _____
make the following statement regarding anatomical gifts which I have checked and initialled:

## SPECIFIC GIFTS

### ENTIRE BODY

☐ I give my entire body, for purposes of anatomical study to _____.
If, for any reason, _____, does not accept this gift, I give my
body to _____, for purposes of anatomical study.

### GIFTS TO INDIVIDUALS

☐ I give my _____ to _____, if needed by him or her for purposes
(part or parts)
of transplantation or therapy.

☐ I give my _____ to _____, if needed by him or her for purposes
(part or parts)
of transplantation or therapy.

### GIFTS TO INSTITUTIONS AND PHYSICIANS

☐ I give my _____ to _____,
(part or parts)          (name of hospital, bank, storage facility, or physician)
for purposes of research, advancement of science, therapy, or transplantation.

☐ I give my _____ to _____,
(part or parts)          (name of hospital, bank, storage facility, or physician)
for purposes of research, advancement of science, therapy, or transplantation.

### PROSTHETIC DEVICES

☐ I give my _____ to _____ for critical
(type of prosthetic device)          (name of hospital)
evaluation, study, and research.

## INTENTION

☐ If any anatomical gift cannot be effectuated because of the donee's non-existence,
inability, or unwillingness to accept it, I request that one of the authorized persons
make anatomical donations in a manner consistent with my desires expressed in this
statement.

☐ I express my desire not to make anatomical gifts under any circumstances. It is my wish
that no part be used for transplantation, therapy, study, or research. I request that
my personal representative and next of kin respect my wishes.

THIS STATEMENT INCORPORATES ALL OF THE PROVISIONS ON THE REVERSE OF IT.

Signed this ____ day of _____, 19____ at _____.


_____


_____          _____
Witness                                    Witness

## PRIORITY OF DONATION

A gift of any part to an individual recipient for therapy or transplantation shall take precedence over a gift of that part to any other donee.

## INSTRUCTIONS

If I have made any written instructions regarding the burial, cremation, or other disposition of my body, I direct that any donee take possession of my body subject to those instructions, if that donee has actual knowledge of those instructions. If there is any conflict between the statements made in this document and any of those instructions, my wishes regarding anatomical gifts shall be given preference over my instructions regarding the disposition of my body.

## COUNTERPARTS

I may be signing more than one statement regarding anatomical gifts. I intend that only signed documents be effective and that no person shall give any effect to any photocopy or other reproduction of a signed document.

## DEFINITIONS

The terms "bank or storage facility," "hospital," "part," and "physician" have the same meaning which the Uniform Anatomical Gifts Act accords to them. The term "authorized persons" means the persons authorized to make donations under the Uniform Anatomical Gifts Act in the order or priority provided in that Act.

---

## WARNING

This form is designed to be used with the advice of an attorney. It has been drafted in accordance with the provisions of the Uniform Anatomical Gifts Act. Because the law regarding anatomical gifts may vary in each state, attorneys advising on use of this form should be familiar with the law of the relevant jurisdiction.

# APPENDIX F

## LIVING WILL FORM

The following information is published by Concern for Dying, an educational council, in connection with their Living Will and Appointment of a Surrogate Decision Maker (see page 288).

### HOW TO USE YOUR LIVING WILL

The Living Will should clearly state your preferences about life-sustaining treatment. You may wish to add specific statements to the Living Will in the space provided for that purpose. Such statements might concern:

- Cardiopulmonary resuscitation
- Artificial or invasive measures for providing nutrition and hydration
- Kidney dialysis
- Mechanical or artificial respiration
- Blood transfusion
- Surgery (such as amputation)
- Antibiotics

You may also wish to indicate any preferences you may have about such matters as dying at home.

### The Durable Power of Attorney for Health Care

This optional feature permits you to name a surrogate decision maker (also known as a proxy, health agent or attorney-in-fact), someone to make health care decisions on your behalf if you lose that ability. As this person should act according to your preferences and in your best interests, you should select this person with care and make certain that he or she knows what your wishes are. Some states have their own laws and forms for executing a durable power of attorney for health care decisions.

You should not name someone who is a witness to your Living Will. You may want to name an alternate agent in case the first person you select is unable or unwilling to serve. If you do name a surrogate decision maker,

285

the form must be notarized. (It is a good idea to notarize the document in any case.)

## IMPORTANT POINTS TO REMEMBER

- Sign and date your Living Will.
- Your two witnesses should not be blood relatives, your spouse, potential beneficiaries of your estate or your health care proxy.
- Discuss your Living Will with your doctors; and give them copies of your Living Will for inclusion in your medical file, so they will know whom to contact in the event something happens to you.
- Make photo copies of your Living Will and give them to anyone who may be making decisions for you if you are unable to make them yourself.
- Place the original in a safe, accessible place, so that it can be located if needed—not in a safe deposit box.
- Look over your Living Will periodically (at least every five years), initial and redate it so that it will be clear that your wishes have not changed.

## THE LIVING WILL REGISTRY

In 1983, Concern for Dying instituted the Living Will Registry, a computerized file system where you may keep an up-to-date copy of your Living Will in our New York office.

### What are the benefits of joining the Living Will Registry?

- Concern's staff will ensure that your form is filled out correctly, assign you a Registry number and maintain a copy of your Living Will.
- Concern's staff will be able to refer to *your* personal document, explain procedures and options, and provide you with the latest case law or state legislation should you, your proxy or anyone else acting on your behalf need counselling or legal guidance in implementing your Living Will.
- You will receive a permanent, credit card size plastic mini-will with your Registry number imprinted on it. The mini-will, which contains your address, Concern's address and a short version of the Living Will, indicates that you have already filled out a full-sized witnessed Living Will document.

### How do you join the Living Will Registry?

- Review your Living Will, making sure it is up to date and contains any specific provisions that you want added.
- Mail a photo copy of your original, signed and witnessed document along with a check for $25.00 to: Living Will Registry, Concern for Dying, 250 West 57th Street, Room 831, New York, New York 10107.

- The one-time Registry enrollment fee will cover the costs of processing and maintaining your Living Will and of issuing your new plastic mini-will.
- If you live in a state with Living Will legislation, send copies of any required state documents as well.
- If you have any address changes or wish to add or delete special provisions that you have included in your Living Will, please write to the Registry so that we can keep your file up to date.

Revised March 1989

(*Author's Note:* Be sure to check your own state laws as some states recognize only their own forms of living wills.)

# A LIVING WILL
## And Appointment of a Surrogate Decision Maker

## To My Family, My Physician, My Lawyer And All Others Whom It May Concern

Death is as much a reality as birth, growth, and aging—it is the one certainty of life. In anticipation of decisions that may have to be made about my own dying and as an expression of my right to refuse treatment, I _____ , (print name) being of sound mind, make this statement of my wishes and instructions concerning treatment.

By means of this document, which I intend to be legally binding, I direct my physician and other care providers, my family, and any surrogate designated by me or appointed by a court, to carry out my wishes. If I become unable, by reason of physical or mental incapacity, to make decisions about my medical care, let this document provide the guidance and authority needed to make any and all such decisions.

If I am permanently unconscious or there is no reasonable expectation of my recovery from a seriously incapacitating or lethal illness or condition, I do not wish to be kept alive by artificial means. I request that I be given all care necessary to keep me comfortable and free of pain, even if pain-relieving medications may hasten my death, and I direct that no life-sustaining treatment be provided except as I or my surrogate specifically authorize.

This request may appear to place a heavy responsibility upon you, but by making this decision according to my strong convictions, I intend to ease that burden. I am acting after careful consideration and with understanding of the consequences of your carrying out my wishes. *List optional specific provisions in the space below. (See other side)*

# Durable Power of Attorney for Health Care Decisions (Cross out if you do not wish to use this section)

To effect my wishes, I designate _____,
residing at _____ (Phone # _____),
(or if he or she shall for any reason fail to act, _____ (Phone # _____),
residing at _____) as my health care surrogate—
that is, my attorney-in-fact regarding any and all health care decisions to be made for me, including the decision to refuse life-sustaining treatment—if I am unable to make such decisions myself. This power shall remain effective during and not be affected by my subsequent illness, disability or incapacity. My surrogate shall have authority to interpret my Living Will, and shall make decisions about my health care as specified in my instructions or, when my wishes are not clear, as the surrogate believes to be in my best interests. I release and agree to hold harmless my health care surrogate from any and all claims whatsoever arising from decisions made in good faith in the exercise of this power.

I sign this document knowingly, voluntarily, and after careful deliberation, this _____ day of _____, 19_____.

_____
(signature)

Address _____

I do hereby certify that the within document was executed and acknowledged before me by the principal this _____ day of _____, 19_____.

_____
Notary Public

Witness _____

Printed Name _____

Address _____

Witness _____

Printed Name _____

Address _____

Copies of this document have been given to:

_____

(Optional) My Living Will is registered with Concern for Dying (No._____)
Distributed by Concern for Dying, 250 West 57th Street, New York, NY 10107 (212) 246-6962

Used by permission of Concern for Dying, an educational council, 250 W. 57th Street, New York, NY 10107.

# APPENDIX G

## WHERE TO WRITE
## FOR VITAL RECORDS

The following information is provided by the National Center for Health Statistics of the U.S. Department of Health and Human Services, Public Health Service; as part of its expressed purpose of mission to provide access to data and information relating to the nation's health.[1] Included here also is the Center's listing, by state and territory, of the addresses, costs, and miscellaneous information needed to obtain vital records of births, deaths, marriages, and divorces.

An official certificate of every birth, death, marriage, and divorce should be on file in the locality where the event occurred. The Federal Government does not maintain files or indexes of these records. These records are filed permanently either in a State vital statistics office or in a city, county, or other local office.

To obtain a certified copy of any of the certificates, write or go to the vital statistics office in the State or area where the event occurred. Addresses and fees are given for each event in the State or area concerned.

To ensure that you receive an accurate record for your request and that your request is filled with all due speed, please follow the steps outlined below for the information in which you are interested:

- Write to the appropriate office to have your request filled.

- Under the appropriate office, information has been included for birth and death records concerning whether the State will accept checks or money orders and to whom they should be made payable. This same information would apply when marriage and divorce records are available from the State office. However, it is impossible for us to list fees and addresses for all county offices where marriage and divorce records may be obtained.

- For all certified copies requested, make check or money order payable for the correct amount for the number of copies you wish to obtain. Cash is not recommended because the office cannot refund cash lost in transit.

[1] From *Where to Write for Vital Records*, DHHS Publication No. (PHS) 87–1142, August 1987. Hyattsville, MD: U.S. Department of Health and Human Services, Public Health Service, National Center for Health Statistics.

- All fees are subject to change. A telephone number has been included in the information for each State for use in verifying the current fee.
- Type or print all names and addresses in the letter.
- Give the following facts when writing for **birth or death records:**

1. Full name of person whose record is being requested.
2. Sex.
3. Parents' names, including maiden name of mother.
4. Month, day, and year of birth or death.
5. Place of birth or death (city or town, county, and State; and name of hospital, if known).
6. Purpose for which copy is needed.
7. Relationship to person whose record is being requested.

- Give the following facts when writing for **marriage records:**

1. Full names of bride and groom.
2. Month, day, and year of marriage.
3. Place of marriage (city or town, county, and State).
4. Purpose for which copy is needed.
5. Relationship to persons whose record is being requested.

- Give the following facts when writing for **divorce records:**

1. Full names of husband and wife.
2. Date of divorce or annulment.
3. Place of divorce or annulment.
4. Type of final decree.
5. Purpose for which copy is needed.
6. Relationship to persons whose record is being requested.

## FOREIGN OR HIGH-SEA BIRTHS AND DEATHS AND CERTIFICATES OF CITIZENSHIP

### Birth Records of Persons Born in Foreign Countries Who Are U.S. Citizens at Birth

Births of U.S. citizens in foreign countries should be reported to the nearest American consular office as soon after the birth as possible on the Consular Report of Birth (Form FS–240). This report should be prepared and filed by one of the parents. However, the physician or midwife attending the birth or any other person having knowledge of the facts can prepare the report.

Documentary evidence is required to establish citizenship. Consular offices provide complete information on what evidence is needed. The Consular Report of Birth is a sworn statement of facts of birth. When approved, it establishes in documentary form the child's acquisition of U.S. citizenship. It has the same value as proof of citizenship as the Certificate of Citizenship issued by the Immigration and Naturalization Service.

A $13.00 fee is charged for reporting the birth. The original document is filed in the Passport Services, Correspondence Branch, U.S. Department of State, Washington, DC 20524. The parents are given a certified copy of the Consular Report of Birth (Form FS–240) and a short form, Certification of Birth (Form DS–1350 or Form FS–545).

To obtain a copy of a report of the birth in a foreign country of a U.S. citizen, write to Passport Services, Correspondence Branch, U.S. Department of State, Washington, DC 20524. State the full name of the child at birth, date of birth, place of birth, and names of parents. Also include any information about the U.S. passport on which the child's name was first included. Sign the request and state the relationship to the person whose record is being requested and the reason for the request.

The fee for each copy is $4.00. Enclose a check or money order made payable to the U.S. Department of State. Fee may be subject to change.

The Department of State issues two types of copies from the Consular Report of Birth (Form FS–240):

1. A full copy of Form FS–240 as it was filed.

2. A short form, Certification of Birth (Form DS–1350), which shows only the name and sex of child and the date and place of birth.

The information on both forms is valid. The Certification of Birth may be obtained in a name subsequently acquired by adoption or legitimation after proof is submitted to establish that such an action legally took place.

## Birth Records of Alien Children Adopted by U.S. Citizens

Birth certifications for alien children adopted by U.S. citizens and lawfully admitted to the United States may be obtained from the Immigation and Naturalization Service (INS) if the birth information is on file.

Certification may be issued for children under 21 years of age who were born in a foreign country. Requests must be submitted on INS Form G–641, which can be obtained from any INS office. (Address can be found in a telephone directory.) For Certification of Birth Data (INS Form G–350), a $15.00 search fee, paid by check or money order, should accompany INS Form G–641.

Certification can be issued in the new name of an adopted or legitimate child after proof of an adoption or legitimation is submitted to INS. Because it may be issued for a child who has not yet become a U.S. citizen, this certification (Form G–350) is not proof of U.S. nationality.

## Certificate of Citizenship

U.S. citizens who were born abroad and later naturalized or who were born in a foreign country to a U.S. citizen (parent or parents) may apply for a certificate of citizenship pursuant to the provisions of Section 341 of the Immigration and Nationality Act. Application can be made for this document in the United States at the nearest office of the Immigration and Naturalization Service (INS). The INS will issue a certificate of citizenship for the person if proof of citizenship is submitted and the person is within the United States. The decision whether to apply for a certificate of citizenship is optional; its possession is not mandatory because a valid U.S. Passport or a form FS–240 has the same evidentiary status.

## Death Records of U.S. Citizens Who Die in Foreign Countries

The death of a U.S. citizen in a foreign country is normally reported to the nearest U.S. consular office. The consul prepares the official "Report of the Death of an American Citizen Abroad" (Form OF–180), and a copy of the Report of Death is filed permanently in the U.S. Department of State (see exceptions below).

To obtain a copy of a report, write to Passport Services, Correspondence Branch, U.S. Department of State, Washington, DC 20524. The fee for a copy is $4.00. Fee may be subject to change.

**Exception:** Reports of deaths of members of the Armed Forces of the United States are made only to the branch of the service to which the person was attached at the time of death—Army, Navy, Air Force, or Coast Guard. In these cases, requests for copies of records should be directed as follows:

For members of the Army, Navy, or Air Force:

Secretary of Defense
Washington, DC 20301

For members of the Coast Guard:

Commandant, P.S.
U.S. Coast Guard
Washington, DC 20226

## Records of Birth and Death Occurring on Vessels or Aircraft on the High Seas

When a birth or death occurs on the high seas, whether in an aircraft or on a vessel, the determination of where the record is filed is decided by the direction in which the vessel or aircraft was headed at the time the event occurred.

1. If the vessel or aircraft was outbound or docked or landed at a foreign port, requests for copies of the record should be made to the U.S. Department of State, Washington, DC 20520.
2. If the vessel or aircraft was inbound and the first port of entry was in the United States, write to the registration authority in the city where the vessel or aircraft docked or landed in the United States.
3. If the vessel was of U.S. registry, contact the U.S. Coast Guard facility at the port of entry.

## Records Maintained by Foreign Countries

Most, but not all, foreign countries record births and deaths. It is not feasible to list in this publication all foreign vital record offices, the charges they make for copies of records, or the information they may require to locate a record. However, most foreign countries will provide certification of births and deaths occurring within their boundaries.

U.S. citizens who need a copy of a foreign birth or death record may obtain assistance by writing to the Office of Overseas Citizens Services, U.S. Department of State, Washington, DC 20520.

Aliens residing in the United States who seek records of these events should contact their nearest consular office.

| Place of event | Cost of copy | Address | Remarks |
|---|---|---|---|
| **Alabama** | | | |
| **Birth or Death** | $5.00 | Bureau of Vital Statistics State Department of Public Health Montgomery, AL 36130 | State office has had records since January 1908. Additional copies at same time are $2.00 each. Fee for special searches is $5.00 per hour. |
| | | | Money order should be made payable to **Alabama Bureau of Vital Statistics**. To verify current fees, the telephone number is area code **205–261–5033**. |
| **Marriage** | Varies | Same as Birth or Death | State office has had records since August 1936. |
| | | See remarks | Probate Judge in county where license was issued. |
| **Divorce** | $5.00 | Same as Birth or Death | State office has had records since January 1950. |
| | Varies | See remarks | Clerk or Register of Court of Equity in county where divorce was granted. |
| **Alaska** | | | |
| **Birth or Death** | $5.00 | Department of Health and Social Services Bureau of Vital Statistics P.O. Box H–02G Juneau, AK 99811–0675 | State office has had records since January 1913. Additional copies requested at same time are $2.00 each. |
| | | | Money order should be made payable to **Bureau of Vital Records**. Personal checks are not accepted. To verify current fees, the telephone number is area code **907–465–3391**. This will be a **recorded** message. |
| **Marriage** | $5.00 | Same as Birth or Death | State office has had records since 1913. |
| **Divorce** | $5.00 | Same as Birth or Death | State office has had records since 1950. |
| | Varies | See remarks | Clerk of Superior Court in judicial district where divorce was granted. Juneau and Ketchikan (First District), Nome (Second District), Anchorage (Third District), Fairbanks (Fourth District). |

296

# American Samoa

| | | | |
|---|---|---|---|
| **Birth or Death** | $2.00 | Registrar of Vital Statistics<br>Vital Statistics Section<br>Government of American Samoa<br>Pago Pago, AS 96799 | Registrar has had records since 1900.<br><br>Money order should be made payable to **ASG Treasurer, Government of American Samoa 96799**. Personal checks are not accepted. To verify current fees, the telephone is area code **684-633-1222, extension 214.**<br><br>Personal identification required before record will be sent. |
| **Marriage** | $2.00 | Same as Birth or Death | |
| **Divorce** | $1.00 | High Court of American Samoa<br>Tutuila, AS 96799 | |

# Arizona

| | | | |
|---|---|---|---|
| **Birth (long form)**<br>**Birth (short form)**<br>**Death** | $5.00<br>$3.00<br>$3.00 | Vital Records Section<br>Arizona Department of Health Services<br>P.O. Box 3887<br>Phoenix, AZ 85030 | State office has had records since July 1909 and abstracts of records filed in counties before then.<br><br>Check or money order should be made payable to **Arizona Department of Health Services**. Personal checks are accepted. To verify current fees, the telephone number is area code **602-255-1080.** This will be a **recorded** message.<br><br>Applicants must submit a copy of picture identification or have their request notarized. |
| **Marriage** | Varies | See remarks | Clerk of Superior Court in county where license was issued. |
| **Divorce** | Varies | See remarks | Clerk of Superior Court in county where divorce was granted. |

| Place of event | Cost of copy | Address | Remarks |
|---|---|---|---|
| **Arkansas** | | | |
| **Birth** | $5.00 | Division of Vital Records | State office has had records since February 1914 and some |
| **Death** | $4.00 | Arkansas Department of Health | original Little Rock and Fort Smith records from 1881. Ad- |
| | | 4815 West Markham Street | ditional copies of death record, when requested at the |
| | | Little Rock, AR 72201 | same time, are $1.00 each. |
| | | | Check or money order should be made payable to **Arkansas Department of Health.** Personal checks are accepted. To verify current fees, the telephone number is area code **501–661–2336.** This will be a **recorded** message. |
| **Marriage** | $5.00 | Same as Birth or Death | Records since 1917. |
| | $2.00 | See remarks | Full certified copy may be obtained from County Clerk in county where license was issued. |
| **Divorce** | $5.00 | Same as Birth or Death | Coupons since 1923. |
| | Varies | See remarks | Full certified copy may be obtained from Circuit or Chancery Clerk in county where divorce was granted. |
| **California** | | | |
| **Birth** | $11.00 | Vital Statistics Section | State office has had records since July 1905. For earlier |
| **Death** | $7.00 | Department of Health Services | records, write to County Recorder in county where event |
| | | 410 N Street | occurred. |
| | | Sacramento, CA 95814 | Check or money order should be made payable to **State Registrar, Department of Health Services** or **Vital Statistics.** Personal checks are accepted. To verify current fees, the telephone number is area code **916–445–2684.** |
| **Marriage** | $11.00 | Same as Birth or Death | State office has had records since July 1905. For earlier records, write to County Recorder in county where event occurred. |

298

| Type | Cost | Address | Remarks |
|---|---|---|---|
| Divorce | $11.00 | Same as Birth or Death | Fee is for search and identification of county where certified copy can be obtained. Certified copies are not available from State Health Department. |
| Divorce | Varies | See remarks | Clerk of Superior Court in county where divorce was granted. |

## Canal Zone

| Type | Cost | Address | Remarks |
|---|---|---|---|
| Birth or Death | $2.00 | Panama Canal Commission Vital Statistics Clerk APO Miami, FL 34011 | Records available from May 1904 to September 1979. |
| Marriage | $1.00 | Same as Birth or Death | Records available from May 1904 to September 1979. |
| Divorce | $0.50 | Same as Birth or Death | Records available from May 1904 to September 1979. |

## Colorado

| Type | Cost | Address | Remarks |
|---|---|---|---|
| Birth or Death | $6.00 Regular service $10.00 Priority service | Vital Records Section Colorado Department of Health 4210 East 11th Avenue Denver, CO 80220 | State office has had death records since 1900 and birth records since 1910. State office also has birth records for some counties for years before 1910. Regular service means the record is mailed within 4 weeks. Priority service means the record is mailed within 5 days. Check or money order should be made payable to **Vital Records.** Personal checks are accepted. To verify current fees, the telephone number is area code **303-320-8474.** For a recorded message call **303-320-8333.** |
| Marriage | See remarks | Same as Birth or Death | Statewide index of records for 1900–39 and 1975 to present. Inquiries will be forwarded to appropriate office. Fee for verification is $6.00. Certified copies are not available from State Health Department. |
| | Varies | See remarks | County Clerk in county where license was issued. |

| Place of event | Cost of copy | Address | Remarks |
|---|---|---|---|
| **Divorce** | See remarks | Same as Birth or Death | Statewide index of records for 1900–39 and 1968 to present. Inquiries will be forwarded to appropriate office. Fee for verification is $6.00. Certified copies are not available from State Health Department. |
|  | Varies | See remarks | Clerk of District Court in county where divorce was granted. |
| **Connecticut** |  |  |  |
| **Birth or Death**<br>Short form | $3.00<br>$2.00 | Department of Health Services<br>Vital Records Section<br>Division of Health Statistics<br>State Department of Health<br>150 Washington Street<br>Hartford, CT 06106 | State office has had records since July 1897. For earlier records, write to Registrar of Vital Statistics in town or city where event occurred.<br><br>Check or money order should be made payable to **Department of Health Services**. Personal checks are accepted. To verify current fees, the telephone number is area code **203-566-1124.** |
| **Marriage** | $3.00 | Same as Birth or Death | Records since July 1897. |
|  | $3.00 | See remarks | Registrar of Vital Statistics in town where license was issued. |
| **Divorce** | See remarks | Same as Birth or Death | Index of records since 1947. Inquiries will be forwarded to appropriate office. Certified copies are not available from State office. |
|  | Varies | See remarks | Clerk of Superior Court in county where divorce was granted. |
| **Delaware** |  |  |  |
| **Birth or Death** | $5.00 | Office of Vital Statistics<br>Division of Public Health<br>P.O. Box 637<br>Dover, DE 19903 | State office has records for 1861–63 and since 1881 but no records for 1864–80. Additional copies of the same record requested at the same time are $3.00 each. |

300

| | Fee | Address | Remarks |
|---|---|---|---|
| | | | Check or money order should be made payable to **Office of Vital Statistics**. Personal checks are accepted. To verify current fees, the telephone number is area code **302–736–4721**. |
| **Marriage** | $5.00 | Same as Birth or Death | Records since 1847. Additional copies of the same record requested at the same time are $3.00 each. |
| **Divorce** | See remarks | Same as Birth or Death | Records since 1935. Inquiries will be forwarded to appropriate office. Fee for search and verification of essential facts of divorce is $5.00 for each 5-year period searched. Certified copies are not available from State office. |
| | $2.00 | See remarks | Prothonotary in county where divorce was granted up to 1975. For divorces granted after 1975 the parties concerned should contact Family Court in county where divorce was granted. |

# District of Columbia

| | Fee | Address | Remarks |
|---|---|---|---|
| **Birth or Death** | $5.00 | Vital Records Branch, Room 3009, 425 I Street, NW, Washington, DC 20001 | Office has had death records since 1855 and birth records since 1874 but no death records were filed during the Civil War. |
| | | | Check or money order should be made payable to **D.C. Treasurer**. Personal checks are accepted. To verify current fees, the telephone number is area code **202–727–5316**. This will be a **recorded** message. |
| **Marriage** | $5.00 | Same as Birth or Death | |
| | $5.00 | Marriage Bureau, 515 5th Street, NW, Washington, DC 20001 | Records since January 1982. |

| Place of event | Cost of copy | Address | Remarks |
|---|---|---|---|
| **Divorce** | $2.00 | Clerk, Superior Court for the District of Columbia, Family Division 500 Indiana Avenue, NW Washington, DC 20001 | Records since September 16, 1956. |
| | Varies | Clerk, U.S. District Court for the District of Columbia Washington, DC 20001 | Records before September 16, 1956. |

## Florida

| Place of event | Cost of copy | Address | Remarks |
|---|---|---|---|
| **Birth** **Death** | $6.50 $2.50 | Department of Health and Rehabilitative Services Office of Vital Statistics P.O. Box 210 Jacksonville, FL 32231–0042 | State office has some birth records dating back to April 1865 and some death records dating back to August 1877. The majority of records date from January 1917. (If the exact date is unknown, the fee is $6.50 (births) or $2.50 (deaths) for the first year searched and $1.00 for each additional year up to a maximum of $25.00. Fee includes one certification of record if found or certified statement stating record not on file.) Additional copies are $2.00 each when requested at the same time.

Check or money order should be made payable to **Office of Vital Statistics**. Personal checks are accepted. To verify current fees, the telephone number is area code **904–359–6900**. This will be a **recorded** message. |
| **Marriage** | $2.50 | Same as Birth or Death | Records since June 6, 1927. (If the exact date is unknown, the fee is $2.50 for the first year searched and $1.00 for each additional year up to a maximum of $25.00. Fee includes one copy of record if found or certified statement stating record not on file.) Additional copies are $2.00 each when requested at the same time. |

**Divorce** — $2.50 — Same as Birth or Death

Records since June 6, 1927. (If the exact date is unknown, the fee is $2.50 for the first year searched and $1.00 for each additional year up to a maximum of $25.00. Fee includes one copy of record if found or certified statement stating record not on file.) Additional copies are $2.00 each when requested at the same time.

## Georgia

**Birth or Death** — $3.00 — Georgia Department of Human Resources
Vital Records Unit
Room 217–H
47 Trinity Avenue, SW
Atlanta, GA 30334

State office has had records since January 1919. For earlier records in Atlanta or Savannah, write to County Health Department in county where event occurred. Additional copies of same record ordered at same time are $1.00 each except birth cards, which are $2.00 each.

Money order should be made payable to **Vital Records, GA. DHR.** Personal checks are not accepted. To verify current fees, the telephone number is area code **404–656–4900.** This is a **recorded** message.

**Marriage** — $3.00 — Same as Birth or Death

Centralized State records since June 9, 1952. Certified copies are issued at State office. Inquiries before June 9, 1952, will be forwarded to appropriate Probate Judge in county where license was issued.

**Divorce** — Varies — See remarks

Probate Judge in county where license was issued.

Centralized State records since June 9, 1952. Certified copies are not issued at State office. Inquiries will be forwarded to appropriate Clerk of Superior Court in county where divorce was granted.

— $3.00 — See remarks

Clerk of Superior Court in county where divorce was granted.

303

| Place of event | Cost of copy | Address | Remarks |
|---|---|---|---|
| **Guam** | | | |
| **Birth or Death** | $2.00 | Office of Vital Statistics<br>Department of Public Health and Social Services<br>Government of Guam<br>P.O. Box 2816<br>Agana, GU, M.I. 96910 | Office has had records since October 16, 1901.<br><br>Money order should be made payable to **Treasurer of Guam**. Personal checks are not accepted. To verify current fees, the telephone number is area code **671–734–3050**. |
| **Marriage** | $2.00 | Same as Birth or Death | |
| **Divorce** | Varies | Clerk, Superior Court of Guam<br>Agana, GU, M.I. 96910 | |
| **Hawaii** | | | |
| **Birth or Death** | $2.00 | Research and Statistics Office<br>State Department of Health<br>P.O. Box 3378<br>Honolulu, HI 96801 | State office has had records since 1853.<br><br>Check or money order should be made payable to **State Department of Health**. Personal checks are accepted for the correct amount only. To verify current fees, the telephone number is area code **808–548–5819**. This is a **recorded** message. |
| **Marriage** | $2.00 | Same as Birth or Death | |
| **Divorce** | $2.00 | Same as Birth or Death | Records since July 1951. |
| | Varies | See remarks | Circuit Court in county where divorce was granted. |
| **Idaho** | | | |
| **Birth or Death** | $6.00 | Bureau of Vital Statistics, Standards, and Local Health Services<br>State Department of Health and Welfare<br>Statehouse | State office has had records since 1911. For records from 1907 to 1911, write to County Recorder in county where event occurred. |

304

Check or money order should be made payable to **Idaho Vital Statistics**. Personal checks are accepted. To verify current fees, the telephone number is area code **208–334–5988**. This is a **recorded** message.

**Marriage** — $6.00 — Same as Birth or Death

Records since 1947. Earlier records are with County Recorder in county where license was issued.

Varies — See remarks

County Recorder in county where license was issued.

**Divorce** — $6.00 — Same as Birth or Death

Records since January 1947. Earlier records are with County Recorder in county where divorce was granted.

Varies — See remarks

County Records in county where divorce was granted.

## Illinois

**Birth or Death** — $15.00 certified copy $10.00 certification — Division of Vital Records
State Department of Health
605 West Jefferson Street
Springfield, IL 62702

State office has had records since January 1916. For earlier records and for copies of State records since January 1916, write to County Clerk in county where event occurred. (The fee for a search of the files is $5.00. If the record is found, one certification is issued at no additional charge. Additional certifications of the same record ordered at the same time are $2.00 each. The fee for a full certified copy is $10.00. Additional certified copies of the same record ordered at the same time are $2.00 each.)

Money order or certified check should be made payable to **Illinois Department of Public Health**. To verify current fees, the telephone number is area code **217–782–6553**.

**Marriage** — See remarks $5.00 — Same as Birth or Death

Records since January 1962. All items may be verified (fee $5.00). Inquiries will be forwarded to appropriate office. Certified copies are not available from State office.

See remarks

County Clerk in county where license was issued.

| Place of event | Cost of copy | Address | Remarks |
|---|---|---|---|
| **Divorce** | See remarks | Same as Birth or Death | Records since January 1962. Some items may be verified (fee $5.00). Certified copies are not available from State office. |
| | Varies | See remarks | Clerk of Circuit Court county where divorce was granted. |
| ## Indiana | | | |
| **Birth** | $6.00 | Division of Vital Records | State office has had birth records since October 1907 and |
| **Death** | $4.00 | State Board of Health<br>1330 West Michigan Street<br>P.O. Box 1964<br>Indianapolis, IN 46206–1964 | death records since 1900. Additional copies of same record ordered at same time are $1.00 each. For earlier records, write to Health Officer in city or county where event occurred. |
| | | | Check or money order should be made payable to **Indiana State Board of Health**. Personal checks are accepted. To verify current fees, the telephone number is area code **317–633–0274.** |
| **Marriage** | See remarks | Same as Birth or Death | Marriage Index since 1958. Certified copies are not available from State Health Department. |
| | Varies | See remarks | Clerk of Circuit Court or Clerk of Superior Court in county where license was issued. |
| **Divorce** | Varies | See remarks | County Clerk in county where divorce was granted. |
| ## Iowa | | | |
| **Birth or Death** | $6.00 | Iowa Department of Public Health<br>Vital Records Section<br>Lucas Office Building<br>Des Moines, IA 50319 | State office has had records since July 1880.<br>Check or money order should be made payable to **Iowa Department of Public Health**. To verify current fees, the telephone number is area code **515–281–5871.** This will be a **recorded** message. |

| | | | |
|---|---|---|---|
| **Marriage** | Same as Birth or Death | $6.00 | State office has had records since July 1880. |
| **Divorce** | Same as Birth or Death | See remarks | Brief statistical record only since 1906. Inquiries will be forwarded to appropriate office. Certified copies are not available from State Health Department. |
| | See remarks | $6.00 | Clerk of District Court in county where divorce was granted. |

## Kansas

| | | | |
|---|---|---|---|
| **Birth or Death** | Office of Vital Statistics<br>Kansas State Department of Health and Environment<br>900 Jackson Street<br>Topeka, KS 66612–1290 | $6.00 | State office has had records since July 1911. For earlier records, write to County Clerk in county where event occurred. Additional copies of same record ordered at same time are $3.00 each.<br><br>Check or money order should be made payable to **State Registrar of Vital Statistics**. Personal checks are accepted. To verify current fees, the telephone number is area code **913–296–1400**. |
| **Marriage** | Same as Birth or Death | $6.00 | State office has had records since May 1913. |
| | See remarks | Varies | District Judge in county where license was issued. |
| **Divorce** | Same as Birth or Death | $6.00 | State office has had records since July 1951. |
| | See remarks | Varies | Clerk of District Court in county where divorce was granted. |

## Kentucky

| | | | |
|---|---|---|---|
| **Birth**<br>**Death** | Office of Vital Statistics<br>Department for Health Services<br>275 East Main Street<br>Frankfort, KY 40621 | $5.00<br>$4.00 | State office has had records since January 1911 and some records for the cities of Louisville, Lexington, Covington, and Newport before then.<br><br>Check or money order should be made payable to **Kentucky State Treasurer**. Personal checks are accepted. To verify current fees, the telephone number is area code **502–564–4212**. |

| Place of event | Cost of copy | Address | Remarks |
|---|---|---|---|
| **Marriage** | $4.00 | Same as Birth or Death | Records since June 1958. |
| | Varies | See remarks | Clerk of County Court in county where license was issued. |
| **Divorce** | $4.00 | Same as Birth or Death | Records since June 1958. |
| | Varies | See remarks | Clerk of Circuit Court in county where decree was issued. |
| **Louisiana** | | | |
| **Birth (long form)** | $8.00 | Division of Vital Records | State office has had records since July 1914. Birth records |
| **Birth (short form)** | $5.00 | Office of Health Services and | for City of New Orleans are available from 1790, and death |
| **Death** | $5.00 | Environmental Quality | records from 1803. |
| | | P.O. Box 60630 | Check or money order should be made payable to **Vital** |
| | | New Orleans, LA 70160 | **Records**. Personal checks are accepted. To verify current |
| | | | fees, the telephone number is area code **504-568-5175**. |
| **Marriage** | | | |
| Orleans Parish | $5.00 | Same as Birth or Death | Certified copies are issued by Clerk of Court in parish |
| Other Parishes | Varies | See remarks | where license was issued. |
| **Divorce** | Varies | See remarks | Clerk of Court in parish where divorce was granted. For Orleans Parish, copies may be obtained from State office for $2.00. |
| **Maine** | | | |
| **Birth or Death** | $5.00 | Office of Vital Records | State office has had records since 1892. For earlier records, |
| | | Human Services Building | write to the municipality where the event occurred. Addi- |
| | | Station 11 | tional copies of same record ordered at same time are |
| | | State House | $2.00 each. |
| | | Augusta, ME 04333 | |

308

| Event | Cost | Address | Remarks |
|---|---|---|---|
| **Marriage** | $5.00 | Same as Birth or Death | Check or money order should be made payable to **Treasurer, State of Maine**. Personal checks are accepted. To verify current fees, the telephone number is area code **207-289-3181**. Additional copies of same record ordered at same time are $2.00 each. |
|  | $2.00 | See remarks | Town Clerk in town where license was issued. |
| **Divorce** | $2.00 | Same as Birth or Death | Records since January 1892. |
|  | $5.00 | See remarks | Clerk of District Court in judicial division where divorce was granted. |

## Maryland

| Event | Cost | Address | Remarks |
|---|---|---|---|
| **Birth or Death** | $3.00 | Division of Vital Records<br>State Department of Health and Mental Hygiene<br>State Office Building<br>P.O. Box 13146<br>201 West Preston Street<br>Baltimore, MD 21203 | State office has had records since August 1898. Records for City of Baltimore are available from January 1875. Check or money order should be made payable to **Department of Health and Mental Hygiene**. Personal checks are accepted. To verify current fees, the telephone number is area code **301-225-5988**. This will be a **recorded** message. |
| **Marriage** | $3.00 | Same as Birth or Death | Records since June 1951. |
|  | Varies | See remarks | Clerk of Circuit Court in county where license was issued or Clerk of Court of Common Pleas of Baltimore City (for licenses issued in City of Baltimore). |
| **Divorce** | $3.00 | Same as Birth or Death | Records since January 1961. Certified copies are not available from State office. Some items may be verified. Inquiries will be forwarded to appropriate office. |
|  | Varies | See remarks | Clerk of Circuit Court in county where divorce was granted. |

| Place of event | Cost of copy | Address | Remarks |
|---|---|---|---|

## Massachusetts

| Place of event | Cost of copy | Address | Remarks |
|---|---|---|---|
| **Birth or Death** | $3.00 | Registry of Vital Records and Statistics 150 Tremont Street, Room B-3 Boston, MA 02111 | State office has had records since 1896. For earlier records, write to the State Archives, State House, Boston, MA. Check or money order should be made payable to **Commonwealth of Massachusetts**. Personal checks are accepted. To verify current fees, the telephone number is area code **617-727-0110**. |
| **Marriage** | $3.00 | Same as Birth or Death | Records since 1891. |
| **Divorce** | See remarks | Same as Birth or Death | Index only since 1952. Inquirer will be directed where to send request. Certified copies are not available from State office. |
| | $3.00 | See remarks | Registrar of Probate Court in county where divorce was granted. |

## Michigan

| Place of event | Cost of copy | Address | Remarks |
|---|---|---|---|
| **Birth or Death** | $10.00 | Office of the State Registrar and Center for Health Statistics Michigan Department of Public Health 3500 North Logan Street Lansing, MI 48909 | State office has had records since 1867. Copies of records since 1867 may also be obtained from County Clerk in county where event occurred. Fees vary from county to county. Detroit records may be obtained from the City of Detroit Health Department for births occurring since 1893 and for deaths since 1897. Check or money order should be made payable to **State of Michigan**. Personal checks are accepted. To verify current fees, the telephone number is area code **517-335-8655**. This will be a **recorded** message. |
| **Marriage** | $10.00 | Same as Birth or Death | Records since April 1867. |
| | Varies | See remarks | County Clerk in county where license was issued. |

| Event | Fee | Address | Remarks |
|---|---|---|---|
| **Divorce** | $10.00 | Same as Birth or Death | Records since 1897. |
| | Varies | See remarks | County Clerk in county where divorce was granted. |

## Minnesota

| Event | Fee | Address | Remarks |
|---|---|---|---|
| **Birth** | $11.00 | Minnesota Department of Health Section of Vital Statistics 717 Delaware Street, SE P.O. Box 9441 Minneapolis, MN 55440 | State office has had records since January 1908. Copies of earlier records may be obtained from Court Administrator in county where event occurred or from the St. Paul City Health Department if the event occurred in St. Paul. Additional copies of the birth record when ordered at the same time are $5.00 each. Additional copies of the death record when ordered at the same time are $2.00 each. |
| **Death** | $8.00 | | Check or money order should be made payable to **Treasurer, State of Minnesota.** Personal checks are accepted. To verify current fees, the telephone number is area code **612–623–5121.** This will be a **recorded** message. |
| **Marriage** | See remarks | Same as Birth or Death | Statewide index since January 1958. Inquiries will be forwarded to appropriate office. Certified copies are not available from State Department of Health. |
| | $8.00 | See remarks | Court Administrator in county where license was issued. Additional copies of the marriage record when ordered at the same time are $2.00 each. |
| **Divorce** | See remarks | Same as Birth or Death | Index since January 1970. Certified copies are not available from State office. |
| | $8.00 | See remarks | Court Administrator in county where divorce was granted. |

| Place of event | Cost of copy | Address | Remarks |
|---|---|---|---|

## Mississippi

| Place of event | Cost of copy | Address | Remarks |
|---|---|---|---|
| Birth | $10.00 | Vital Records | State office has had records since 1912. Full copies of birth certificates obtained within 1 year after the event are $5.00. Additional copies of same record ordered at same time are $1.00 each. |
| Birth (short form) | $5.00 | State Board of Health | |
| Death | $5.00 | P.O. Box 1700 | |
| | | Jackson, MS 39215–1700 | |
| | | | For out-of-State requests only bank or postal money orders are accepted and should be made payable to **Mississippi State Department of Health**. Personal checks are accepted for in-State requests only. To verify current fees, the telephone number is area code **601–354–6606**. A recorded message may be reached on area code **601–354–6600**. |
| Marriage | $5.00 | Same as Birth or Death | Statistical records only from January 1926 to July 1, 1938, and since January 1942. |
| | $3.00 | See remarks | Circuit Clerk in county where license was issued. |
| Divorce | See remarks $0.50 per page plus $1.00 for certification | Same as Birth or Death | Records since January 1926. Certified copies are not available from State office. Inquiries will be forwarded to appropriate office. |
| | Varies | See remarks | Chancery Clerk in county where divorce was granted. |

## Missouri

| Place of event | Cost of copy | Address | Remarks |
|---|---|---|---|
| Birth or Death | $4.00 | Department of Health Bureau of Vital Records P.O. Box 570 Jefferson City, MO 65102 | State office has had records since January 1910. If event occurred in St. Louis (City), St. Louis County, or Kansas City before 1910, write to the City or County Health Department. Copies of these records are $3.00 each in St. Louis City and County. In Kansas City, $6.00 for first copy and $3.00 |

## Missouri (continued)

**Marriage** — No fee — Same as Birth or Death — Check or money order should be made payable to **Missouri Department of Health.** Personal checks are accepted. To verify current fees on **Birth** records, the telephone number is area code **314–751–6387**; for **Death** records, area code **314–751–6376.**

Indexes since July 1948. Correspondent will be referred to appropriate Recorder of Deeds in county where license was issued.

**Marriage** — Varies — See remarks — Recorder of Deeds in county where license was issued.

**Divorce** — See remarks — Same as Birth or Death — Indexes since July 1948. Certified copies are not available from State Health Department. Inquiries will be forwarded to appropriate office.

**Divorce** — Varies — See remarks — Clerk of Circuit Court in county where divorce was granted.

# Montana

**Birth or Death** — $5.00 — Bureau of Records and Statistics State Department of Health and Environmental Sciences Helena, MT 59620 — State office has had records since late 1907.

Check or money order should be made payable to **Montana Department of Health and Environmental Sciences.** Personal checks are accepted. To verify current fees, the telephone number is area code **406–444–2614.**

**Marriage** — See remarks — Same as Birth or Death — Records since July 1943. Some items may be verified. Inquiries will be forwarded to appropriate office. Apply to county where license was issued if known. Certified copies are not available from State office.

**Marriage** — Varies — See remarks — Clerk of District Court in county where license was issued.

| Place of event | Cost of copy | Address | Remarks |
|---|---|---|---|
| **Divorce** | See remarks | Same as Birth or Death | Records since July 1943. Some items may be verified. Inquiries will be forwarded to appropriate office. Apply to court where divorce was granted if known. Certified copies are not available from State office. |
| | Varies | See remarks | Clerk of District Court in county where divorce was granted. |
| **Nebraska** | | | |
| **Birth**<br>**Death** | $6.00<br>$5.00 | Bureau of Vital Statistics<br>State Department of Health<br>301 Centennial Mall South<br>P.O. Box 95007<br>Lincoln, NE 68509–5007 | State office has had records since late 1904. If birth occurred before then, write the State office for information.<br><br>Check or money order should be made payable to **Bureau of Vital Statistics**. Personal checks are accepted. To verify current fees, the telephone number is area code **402–471–2871**. |
| **Marriage** | $5.00 | Same as Birth or Death | Records since January 1909. |
| | Varies | See remarks | County Court in county where license was issued. |
| **Divorce** | $5.00 | Same as Birth or Death | Records since January 1909. |
| | Varies | See remarks | Clerk of District Court in county where divorce was granted. |
| **Nevada** | | | |
| **Birth or Death** | $6.00 | Division of Health—Vital Statistics<br>Capitol Complex<br>Carson City, NV 89710 | State office has had records since July 1904. For earlier records, write to County Recorder in county where event occurred. Additional copies of death records ordered at the same time are $4.00 for second and third copies, $3.00 each for the next three copies, and $2.00 each for any additional copies.<br><br>Check or money order should be made payable to **Section of Vital Statistics**. Personal checks are accepted. To verify current fees, the telephone number is area code **702–885–** |

| | Cost | Address | Remarks |
|---|---|---|---|
| **Marriage** | See remarks | Same as Birth or Death | Indexes since January 1968. Certified copies are not available from State Health Department. Inquiries will be forwarded to appropriate office. |
| | Varies | See remarks | County Recorder in county where license was issued. |
| **Divorce** | See remarks | Same as Birth or Death | Indexes since January 1968. Certified copies are not available from State Health Department. Inquiries will be forwarded to appropriate office. |
| | Varies | See remarks | County Clerk in county where divorce was granted. |

## New Hampshire

| | Cost | Address | Remarks |
|---|---|---|---|
| **Birth or Death** | $3.00 | Bureau of Vital Records<br>Health and Human Services Building<br>6 Hazen Drive<br>Concord, NH 03301 | State office has had records since 1640. Copies of records may be obtained from State office or from City or Town Clerk in place where event occurred.<br><br>Check or money order should be made payable to **Treasurer, State of New Hampshire**. Personal checks are accepted. To verify current fees, the telephone number is area code **603–271–4654**. |
| **Marriage** | $3.00 | Same as Birth or Death | Records since 1640. |
| | Varies | See remarks | Town Clerk in town where license was issued. |
| **Divorce** | $3.00 | Same as Birth or Death | Records since 1808. |
| | Varies | See remarks | Clerk of Superior Court where divorce was granted. |

| Place of event | Cost of copy | Address | Remarks |
|---|---|---|---|
| **New Jersey** | | | |
| **Birth or Death** | $4.00 | State Department of Health<br>Bureau of Vital Statistics<br>CN 360<br>Trenton, NJ 08625 | State office has had records since June 1878. Additional copies of same record ordered at same time are $2.00 each. If the exact date is unknown, the fee is an additional $1.00. |
| | | Archives and History Bureau<br>State Library Division<br>State Department of Education<br>Trenton, NJ 08625 | For records from May 1848 to May 1878.<br><br>Check or money order should be made payable to **New Jersey State Registrar** or **New Jersey State Department of Health**. Personal checks are accepted. To verify current fees, the telephone number is area code **609-292-4087**. |
| **Marriage** | $4.00 | Same as Birth or Death | If the exact date is unknown, the fee is an additional $1.00 per year searched. |
| | $2.00 | Archives and History Bureau<br>State Library Division<br>State Department of Education<br>Trenton, NJ 08625 | For records from May 1848 to May 1878. |
| **Divorce** | $2.00 | Superior Court<br>Chancery Division<br>State House Annex<br>Room 320<br>CN 971<br>Trenton, NJ 08625 | The fee is for the first four pages. Additional pages cost $0.50 each. |
| **New Mexico** | | | |
| **Birth or Death** | $10.00 | Vital Statistics Bureau<br>New Mexico Health Services Division<br>P.O. Box 968<br>Santa Fe, NM 87504-0968 | State office has had records since 1920, and delayed records since 1880. |

316

Check or money order should be made payable to **Vital Statistics Bureau**. Personal checks are accepted. To verify current fees, the telephone number is area code **505–827–2338**. This will be a **recorded** message.

| | | | |
|---|---|---|---|
| **Marriage** | Varies | See remarks | County Clerk in county where license was issued. |
| **Divorce** | Varies | See remarks | Clerk of Superior Court where divorce was granted. |

## New York (except New York City)

| | | | |
|---|---|---|---|
| **Birth or Death** | $5.00 | Bureau of Vital Records<br>State Department of Health<br>Empire State Plaza<br>Tower Building<br>Albany, NY 12237 | State office has had records since 1880. For records before 1914 in Albany, Buffalo, and Yonkers, or before 1880 in any other city, write to Registrar of Vital Statistics in city where event occurred. For the rest of the State, except New York City, write to State office.<br><br>Check or money order should be made payable to **New York State Department of Health**. Personal checks are accepted. To verify current fees, the telephone number is area code **518–474–3075**. This will be a **recorded** message. |
| **Marriage** | $5.00<br>$5.00 | Same as Birth or Death<br>See remarks | Records from 1880 to present.<br><br>For records from 1880–1907 and licenses issued in the cities of Albany, Buffalo, or Yonkers, apply to—Albany: City Clerk, City Hall, Albany, NY 12207: Buffalo: City Clerk, City Hall, Buffalo, NY 14202; Yonkers: Registrar of Vital Statistics, Health Center Building, Yonkers, NY 10701. |
| **Divorce** | $5.00<br>Varies | Same as Birth or Death<br>See remarks | Records since January 1963.<br>County Clerk in county where divorce was granted. |

# New York City

| Place of event | Cost of copy | Address | Remarks |
|---|---|---|---|
| **Birth or Death** | $5.00 | Bureau of Vital Records<br>Department of Health of New York City<br>125 Worth Street<br>New York, NY 10013 | Office has had birth records since 1898 and death records since 1920. For Old City of New York (Manhattan and part of the Bronx) birth records for 1865–97 and death records for 1865–1919 write to Archives Division, Department of Records and Information Services, 31 Chambers Street, New York, NY 10007.<br><br>Money order should be made payable to **New York City Department of Health**. To verify current fees, the telephone number is area code **212–619–4530**. This will be a **recorded** message. |
| **Marriage** | $10.00 | See remarks | Records from 1847 to 1865. Archives Division, Department of Records and Information Services, 31 Chambers Street, New York, NY 10007, except Brooklyn records for this period which are filed with County Clerk's Office, Kings County, Supreme Court Building, Brooklyn, NY 11201. Additional copies of same record ordered at same time are $5.00 each. |
| | $10.00 | See remarks | Records from 1866 to 1907. City Clerk's Office in borough where marriage was performed. |
| | $10.00 | See remarks | Records from 1908 to May 12, 1943. New York City residents write to City Clerk's Office in the borough of bride's residence; nonresidents write to City Clerk's Office in borough where license was obtained. |
| | $10.00 | See remarks | Records since May 13, 1943. City Clerk's Office in borough where license was issued. |
| Bronx Borough | $10.00 | City Clerk's Office<br>1780 Grand Concourse<br>Bronx, NY 10457 | |

| | | | |
|---|---|---|---|
| Brooklyn Borough | $10.00 | City Clerk's Office Municipal Building Brooklyn, NY 11201 | |
| Manhattan Borough | $10.00 | City Clerk's Office Municipal Building New York, NY 10007 | |
| Queens Borough | $10.00 | City Clerk's Office 120–55 Queens Boulevard Kew Gardens, NY 11424 | |
| Staten Island Borough (no longer called Richmond) | $10.00 | City Clerk's Office Staten Island Borough Hall Staten Island, NY 10301 | |
| Divorce | | | See New York State |

## North Carolina

| | | | |
|---|---|---|---|
| Birth or Death | $5.00 | Department of Human Resources Division of Health Services Vital Records Branch P.O. Box 2091 Raleigh, NC 27602 | State office has had birth records since October 1913 and death records since January 1, 1930. Death records from 1913 through 1929 are available from Archives and Records Section, State Records Center, 215 North Blount Street, Raleigh, NC 27602. |
| | | | Check or money order should be made payable to **Vital Records Branch**. Personal checks are accepted. To verify current fees, the telephone number is area code **919–733–3526**. |
| Marriage | $5.00 | Same as Birth or Death | Records since January 1962. |
| | $3.00 | See remarks | Registrar of Deeds in county where marriage was performed. |

| Place of event | Cost of copy | Address | Remarks |
|---|---|---|---|
| Divorce | $5.00 | Same as Birth or Death | Records since January 1958. |
| | Varies | See remarks | Clerk of Superior Court where divorce was granted. |

## North Dakota

| Place of event | Cost of copy | Address | Remarks |
|---|---|---|---|
| Birth | $7.00 | Division of Vital Records | State office has had some records since July 1893. Years from 1894 to 1920 are incomplete. Additional copies of birth records are $4.00 each; death records are $2.00 each. |
| Death | $5.00 | State Department of Health | |
| | | Office of Statistical Services | |
| | | Bismarck, ND 58505 | Money order should be made payable to **North Dakota State Department of Health**. To verify current fees, the telephone number is area code **701–224–2360**. |
| Marriage | $5.00 | Same as Birth or Death | Records since July 1925. Requests for earlier records will be forwarded to appropriate office. Additional copies are $2.00 each. |
| | Varies | See remarks | County Judge in county where license was issued. |
| Divorce | See remarks | Same as Birth or Death | Index of records since July 1949. Some items may be verified. Certified copies are not available from State Health Department. Inquiries will be forwarded to appropriate office. |
| | Varies | See remarks | Clerk of District Court in county where divorce was granted. |

## Ohio

| Place of event | Cost of copy | Address | Remarks |
|---|---|---|---|
| Birth or Death | $7.00 | Division of Vital Statistics | State office has had records since December 20, 1908. For earlier records, write to Probate Court in county where event occurred. |
| | | Ohio Department of Health | |
| | | G–20 Ohio Department Building | |
| | | 65 South Front Street | |
| | | Columbus, OH 43266–0333 | Check or money order should be made payable to **State Treasurer**. Personal checks are accepted. To verify current fees, the telephone number is area code **614–466–2531**. |

| Type | Cost | Address | Remarks |
|---|---|---|---|
| **Marriage** | See remarks | Same as Birth or Death | Records since September 1949. All items may be verified. Certified copies are not available from State Health Department. Inquiries will be referred to appropriate office. Probate Judge in county where license was issued. |
| **Divorce** | See remarks | Same as Birth or Death | Records since September 1949. All items may be verified. Certified copies are not available from State Health Department. Inquiries will be forwarded to appropriate office. Clerk of Court of Common Pleas in county where divorce was granted. |

## Oklahoma

| Type | Cost | Address | Remarks |
|---|---|---|---|
| **Birth or Death** | $5.00 | Vital Records Section<br>State Department of Health<br>Northeast 10th Street and Stonewall<br>P.O. Box 53551<br>Oklahoma City, OK 73152 | State office has had records since October 1908. Check or money order should be made payable to **Oklahoma State Department of Health**. Personal checks are accepted. To verify current fees, the telephone number is area code **405–271–4040**. |
| **Marriage** | Varies | See remarks | Clerk of Court in county where license was issued. |
| **Divorce** | Varies | See remarks | Clerk of Court in county where divorce was granted. |

## Oregon

| Type | Cost | Address | Remarks |
|---|---|---|---|
| **Birth or Death** | $8.00 | Oregon State Health Division<br>Vital Statistics Section<br>P.O. Box 116<br>Portland, OR 97207 | State office has had records since January 1903. Some earlier records for the City of Portland since approximately 1880 are available from the Oregon State Archives, 1005 Broadway, NE, Salem, OR 97310. |

| Place of event | Cost of copy | Address | Remarks |
|---|---|---|---|
| **Heirloom Birth** | $25.00 | Same as Birth or Death | Presentation style calligraphy certificate suitable for framing. |
| | | | Check or money order should be made payable to **Oregon State Health Division**. To verify current fees, the telephone number is area code **503–229–5710**. This will be a **recorded** message. |
| **Marriage** | $8.00 | Same as Birth or Death | Records since January 1906. |
| | Varies | See remarks | County Clerk in county where license was issued. County Clerks also have some records before 1906. |
| **Divorce** | $8.00 | Same as Birth or Death | Records since 1925. |
| | Varies | See remarks | County Clerk in county where divorce was granted. County Clerks also have some records before 1925. |
| **Pennsylvania** | | | |
| **Birth** | $4.00 | Division of Vital Records | State office has had records since January 1906. |
| Wallet card | $5.00 | State Department of Health | |
| **Death** | $3.00 | Central Building | For earlier records, write to Register of Wills, Orphans Court, in county seat where event occurred. **Persons born in Pittsburgh from 1870 to 1905 or in Allegheny City, now part of Pittsburgh, from 1882 to 1905** should write to Office of Biostatistics, Pittsburgh Health Department, City-County Building, Pittsburgh, PA 15219. For events occurring in City of Philadelphia from 1860 to 1915, write to Vital Statistics, Philadelphia Department of Public Health. City Hall Annex, Philadelphia, PA 19107. |
| | | 101 South Mercer Street | |
| | | P.O. Box 1528 | |
| | | New Castle, PA 16103 | |
| | | | Check or money order should be made payable to **Vital Records**. Personal checks are accepted. To verify current fees, the telephone number is area code **412–656–3100**. |

| Type | Cost | Address | Remarks |
|---|---|---|---|
| **Marriage** | See remarks | Same as Birth or Death | Records since January 1906. Certified copies are not available from State Health Department. Inquiries will be forwarded to appropriate office. |
|  | Varies | See remarks | Marriage License Clerks, County Court House, in county where license was issued. |
| **Divorce** | Varies | Same as Birth or Death | Records since January 1946. Certified copies are not available from State Health Department. Inquiries will be forwarded to appropriate office. |
|  | Varies | See remarks | Prothonotary, Court House, in country seat where divorce was granted. |

## Puerto Rico

| Type | Cost | Address | Remarks |
|---|---|---|---|
| **Birth or Death** | $2.00 | Division of Demographic Registry and Vital Statistics, Department of Health, San Juan, PR 00908 | Central office has had records since July 22, 1931. Copies of earlier records may be obtained by writing to local Registrar (Registrador Demografico) in municipality where event occurred or by writing to central office for information. Money order should be made payable to **Secretary of the Treasury**. Personal checks are not accepted. To verify current fees, the telephone number is area code **809–728–4300**. |
| **Marriage** | $2.00 | Same as Birth or Death |  |
| **Divorce** | $2.00 | Same as Birth or Death | Superior Court where divorce was granted. |

| Place of event | Cost of copy | Address | Remarks |
| --- | --- | --- | --- |
| **Rhode Island** | | | |
| **Birth or Death** | $5.00 | Division of Vital Statistics State Health Department Room 101, Cannon Building 75 Davis Street Providence, RI 02908 | State office has had records since 1853. For earlier records, write to Town Clerk in town where event occurred. Additional copies of the same record ordered at the same time are $3.00 each. Money order should be made payable to **General Treasurer, State of Rhode Island.** To verify current fees, the telephone number is area code **401–277–2811.** This will be a **recorded** message. |
| **Marriage** | $5.00 | Same as Birth or Death | Records since January 1853. Additional copies of the same record ordered at the same time are $3.00 each. |
| **Divorce** | $1.00 | Clerk of Family Court 1 Dorrance Plaza Providence, RI 02903 | |
| **South Carolina** | | | |
| **Birth or Death** | $5.00 | Office of Vital Records and Public Health Statistics S.C. Department of Health and Environmental Control 2600 Bull Street Columbia, SC 29201 | State office has had records since January 1915. City of Charleston births from 1877 and deaths from 1821 are on file at Charleston County Health Department. Ledger entries of Florence City births and deaths from 1895 to 1914 are on file at Florence County Health Department. Ledger entries of Newberry City births and deaths from the late 1800's are on file at Newberry County Health Department. These are the only early records obtainable. Check or money order should be made payable to **Office of Vital Records.** Personal checks are accepted. To verify current fees, the telephone number is area code **803–734–4830.** |

| | | | |
|---|---|---|---|
| **Marriage** | $5.00 | Same as Birth or Death | Records since July 1950. |
| | Varies | See remarks | Records since July 1911. Probate Judge in county where license was issued. |
| **Divorce** | $5.00 | Same as Birth or Death | Records since July 1962. |
| | Varies | See remarks | Records since April 1949. Clerk of county where petition was filed. |

## South Dakota

| | | | |
|---|---|---|---|
| **Birth or Death** | $5.00 | State Department of Health Center for Health Policy and Statistics Vital Records 523 E. Capitol Pierre, SD 57501 | State office has had records since July 1905 and access to other records for some events that occurred before then. Money order should be made payable to **South Dakota Department of Health**. To verify current fees, the telephone number is area code **605–773–3355**. |
| **Marriage** | $5.00 | Same as Birth or Death | Records since July 1905. |
| | $5.00 | See remarks | County Treasurer in county where license was issued. |
| **Divorce** | $5.00 | Same as Birth or Death | Records since July 1905. |
| | Varies | See remarks | Clerk of Court in county where divorce was granted. |

| Place of event | Cost of copy | Address | Remarks |
|---|---|---|---|
| **Tennessee** | | | |
| Birth (long form) | $6.00 | Tennessee Vital Records | State office has had birth records for entire State since |
| Birth (short form) | $4.00 | Department of Health and Environment | January 1914, for Nashville since June 1881, for Knoxville |
| Death | $4.00 | Cordell Hull Building | since July 1881, and for Chattanooga since January 1882. |
| | | Nashville, TN 37219–5402 | State office has had death records for entire State since |
| | | | January 1914, for Nashville since July 1874, for Knoxville |
| | | | since July 1887, and for Chattanooga since March 6, 1872. |
| | | | Birth and death enumeration records by school district are |
| | | | available for July 1908 through June 1912. For Memphis |
| | | | birth records from April 1874 through December 1887 and |
| | | | November 1898 to January 1, 1914, and for Memphis death |
| | | | records from May 1848 to January 1, 1914, write to |
| | | | Memphis-Shelby County Health Department, Division of |
| | | | Vital Records, Memphis, TN 38105. |
| | | | |
| | | | Check or money order should be made payable to **Tennessee Vital Records**. Personal checks are accepted. To verify current fees, the telephone number is area code **615–741–1763**. In Tennessee call **1–800–423–1901**. |
| | | | |
| Marriage | $4.00 | Same as Birth or Death | Records since July 1945. |
| | Varies | See remarks | County Clerk in county where license was issued. |
| | | | |
| Divorce | $4.00 | Same as Birth or Death | Records since July 1945. |
| | Varies | See remarks | Clerk of Court in county where divorce was granted. |
| | | | |
| **Texas** | | | |
| Birth or Death | $5.00 | Bureau of Vital Statistics | State office has had records since 1903. Additional copies |
| | | Texas Department of Health | of same record ordered at same time are $2.00 each. |
| | | 1100 West 49th Street | Check or money order should be made payable to **Texas** |
| | | Austin, TX 78756–3191 | |

**Department of Health.** Personal checks are accepted. To verify current fees, the telephone number is area code **512-458-7380.**

| Marriage | See remarks | Same as Birth or Death | Records since January 1966. Certified copies are not available from State office. Fee for search and verification of essential facts of marriage is $2.00. |
| | Varies | See remarks | County Clerk in county where license was issued. |
| Divorce | See remarks | Same as Birth or Death | Records since January 1968. Certified copies are not available from State office. Fee for search and verification of essential facts of divorce is $2.00. |
| | Varies | See remarks | Clerk of District Court in county where divorce was granted. |

# Trust Territory of the Pacific Islands

**Birth or Death**

| Commonwealth of Northern Mariana Islands | $2.50 | Commonwealth Courts Commonwealth Governments Saipan, CM 96950 | Courts have had records since November 12, 1952. Beginning in 1950, a few records have been filed with the Hawaii Bureau of Vital Statistics. If not sure of the area in which the event occurred, write to the Director of Health Services, Trust Territory of the Pacific Islands, Saipan, Northern Mariana Islands 96950 to have the inquiry referred to the correct area. |
| Republic of the Marshall Islands | $0.25 plus $0.10 per 100 words | Chief Clerk of Supreme Courts Republic of the Marshall Islands Majuro, Marshall Islands 96960 | |
| Republic of Palau | $0.25 plus $0.10 per 100 words | Chief Clerk of Supreme Courts Republic of Palau Koror, Palau, W.C.I. 96940 | Money order should be made payable to **Clerk of Courts** in area where inquiries are made. Personal checks are **not** accepted. |

327

| Place of event | Cost of copy | Address | Remarks |
|---|---|---|---|
| Federated States of Micronesia | $0.25 plus $0.10 per 100 words | Clerk of Courts State of Truk, FSM Moen, Truk, E.C.I. 96942 | |
| | | Clerk of Courts State of Ponape, FSM Kolonia, Ponape, E.C.I. 96941 | |
| | | Clerk of Courts State of Kosrae, FSM Lelu, Losrae, E.C.I. 96944 | |
| | | Clerk of Courts State of Yap, FSM Colonia, Yap, W.C.I. 96943 | |
| **Marriage** | Varies | See remarks | Clerk of Court in district where marriage was performed. |
| **Divorce** | Varies | See remarks | Clerk of Court in district where divorce was granted. |
| **Utah** **Birth** **Death** | $10.00 $7.00 | Bureau of Vital Records Utah Department of Health 288 North 1460 West P.O. Box 16700 Salt Lake City, UT 84116–0700 | State office has had records since 1905. If event occurred from 1890 to 1904 in Salt Lake City or Ogden, write to City Board of Health. For records elsewhere in the State from 1898 to 1904, write to County Clerk in county where event occurred. Additional copies, when requested at the same time, are $3.00 each. Check or money order should be made payable to **Utah Department of Health**. Personal checks are accepted. To verify current fees, the telephone number is area code **801–538–6105**. |
| **Marriage** | $7.00 | Same as Birth or Death | State office has had records since 1978. Only short form certified copies are available. |
| | Varies | See remarks | County Clerk in county where license ... issued |

328

| Type | Fee | Address | Remarks |
|---|---|---|---|
| Divorce | $7.00 | Same as Birth or Death | State office has had records since 1978. Only short form certified copies are available. |
| | Varies | See remarks | County Clerk in county where divorce was granted. |

## Vermont

| Type | Fee | Address | Remarks |
|---|---|---|---|
| Birth or Death | $5.00 | Vermont Department of Health Vital Records Section Box 70 60 Main Street Burlington, VT 05402 | State has had records since 1955. Check or money order should be made payable to **Vermont Department of Health**. Personal checks are accepted. To verify current fees, the telephone number is area code **802-863-7275.** |
| Birth, Death, or Marriage | $5.00 | Division of Public Records 6 Baldwin Street Montpelier, VT 05602 | Records prior to 1955. |
| | $5.00 | See remarks | Town or City Clerk of town where birth or death occurred. |
| Marriage | $5.00 | Same as Birth or Death | State has had records since 1955. |
| | $5.00 | See remarks | Town Clerk in town where license was issued. |
| Divorce | $5.00 | Same as Birth or Death | State has had records since 1968. |
| | $5.00 | See remarks | Town Clerk in town where divorce was granted. |

## Virginia

| Place of event | Cost of copy | Address | Remarks |
|---|---|---|---|
| **Birth or Death** | $5.00 | Division of Vital Records<br>State Health Department<br>P.O. Box 1000<br>Richmond, VA 23208–1000 | State office has had records from January 1853 to December 1896 and since June 14, 1912. For records between those dates, write to the Health Department in the city where event occurred. |
| | | | Check or money order should be made payable to **State Health Department**. Personal checks are accepted. To verify current fees, the telephone number is area code **804–786–6228**. |
| **Marriage** | $5.00 | Same as Birth or Death | Records since January 1853. |
| | Varies | See remarks | Clerk of Court in county or city where license was issued. |
| **Divorce** | $5.00 | Same as Birth or Death | Records since January 1918. |
| | Varies | See remarks | Clerk of Court in county or city where divorce was granted. |

## Virgin Islands

| Place of event | Cost of copy | Address | Remarks |
|---|---|---|---|
| **Birth or Death**<br>St. Croix | $5.00 | Registrar of Vital Statistics<br>Charles Harwood Memorial Hospital<br>St. Croix, VI 00820 | Registrar has had birth and death records on file since 1840. |
| St. Thomas and<br>St. John | $5.00 | Registrar of Vital Statistics<br>Charlotte Amalie<br>St. Thomas, VI 00802 | Registrar has had birth records on file since July 1906 and death records since January 1906. |
| | | | Money order for birth and death records should be made payable to **Bureau of Vital Statistics**. Personal checks are not accepted. |
| **Marriage** | See<br>remarks | Bureau of Vital Records and Statistical Services<br>Virgin Islands Department of Health<br>Charlotte Amalie | Certified copies are not available. Inquiries will be forwarded to appropriate office. |

| | | | |
|---|---|---|---|
| St. Croix | $2.00 | Chief Deputy Clerk<br>Territorial Court of the Virgin Islands<br>P.O. Box 929<br>Christiansted<br>St. Croix, VI 00820 | |
| St. Thomas and<br>St. John | $2.00 | Clerk of the Territorial Court of the<br>Virgin Islands<br>P.O. Box 70<br>Charlotte Amalie<br>St. Croix, VI 00801 | |
| **Divorce** | See<br>remarks | Same as Marriage | Certified copies are not available. Inquiries will be forwarded to appropriate office. |
| St. Croix | $5.00 | Same as Marriage | Money order for marriage and divorce records should be made payable to **Territorial Court of the Virgin Islands**. Personal checks are not accepted. |
| St. Thomas and<br>St. John | $5.00 | Same as Marriage | |

# Washington

| | | | |
|---|---|---|---|
| **Birth or Death** | $6.00 | Vital Records<br>P.O. Box 9709, ET-11<br>Olympia, WA 98504-9709 | State office has had records since July 1907. For King, Pierce, and Spokane counties copies may also be obtained from county health departments. County Auditor of county of birth has registered births prior to July 1907. |
| | | | Money order should be made payable to **Vital Records**. To verify current fees, the telephone number is area code **206-753-5396**. Recorded messages for out of State, call **1-800-551-0562**; in State, call **1-800-331-0680**. |
| **Marriage** | $6.00 | Same as Birth or Death | State office has had records since January 1968. |
| | $2.00 | See remarks | County Auditor in county where license was issued. |

331

| Place of event | Cost of copy | Address | Remarks |
|---|---|---|---|
| **Divorce** | $6.00 | Same as Birth or Death | State office has had records since January 1968. |
| | Varies | See remarks | County Clerk in county where divorce was granted. |
| **West Virginia** | | | |
| **Birth or Death** | $5.00 | Division of Vital Statistics State Department of Health State Office Building No. 3 Charleston, WV 25305 | State office has had records since January 1917. For earlier records, write to Clerk of County Court in county where event occurred. |
| | | | Check or money order should be made payable to **Division of Vital Statistics**. Personal checks are accepted. To verify current fees, the telephone number is area code **304–348–2931**. |
| **Marriage** | $5.00 | Same as Birth or Death | Records since 1921. Certified copies available from 1964. |
| | Varies | See remarks | County Clerk in county where license was issued. |
| **Divorce** | See remarks | Same as Birth or Death | Index since 1968. Some items may be verified (fee $5.00). Certified copies are not available from State office. |
| | Varies | See remarks | Clerk of Circuit Court, Chancery Side, in county where divorce was granted. |
| **Wisconsin** | | | |
| **Birth** | $7.00 | Bureau of Health Statistics Wisconsin Division of Health P.O. Box 309 Madison, WI 53701 | State office has scattered records earlier than 1857. Records before October 1, 1907, are very incomplete. Additional copies of the same record ordered at the same time are $2.00 each. |
| **Death** | $5.00 | | Check or money order should be made payable to **Center for Health Statistics**. Personal checks are accepted. To verify current fees, the telephone number is area code **608–266–1371**. |

| | | | |
|---|---|---|---|
| **Marriage** | $5.00 | Same as Birth or Death | Records since April 1836. Records before October 1, 1907, are incomplete. Additional copies of the same record ordered at the same time are $2.00 each. |
| **Divorce** | $5.00 | Same as Birth or Death | Records since October 1907. Additional copies of the same record ordered at the same time are $2.00 each. |

## Wyoming

| | | | |
|---|---|---|---|
| **Birth** | $5.00 | Vital Records Services | State office has had records since July 1909. |
| **Death** | $3.00 | Division of Health and Medical Services Hathaway Building Cheyenne, WY 82002 | Money order should be made payable to **Vital Records Services**. To verify current fees, the telephone number is area code **307-777-7591**. |
| **Marriage** | $5.00 | Same as Birth or Death | Records since May 1941. |
| | Varies | See remarks | County Clerk in county where license was issued. |
| **Divorce** | $5.00 | Same as Birth or Death | Records since May 1941. |
| | Varies | See remarks | Clerk of District Court where divorce took place. |

333

This listing of addresses, costs, and miscellaneous information needed to obtain vital records is taken from *Where to Write for Vital Records*, DHHS Publication No. (PHS) 87–1142, August 1987. Hyattsville, MD: U.S. Department of Health and Human Services, Public Health Service, National Center for Health Statistics.

# Index